William Richard Hughes

A Week's Tramp in Dickens-Land

William Richard Hughes

A Week's Tramp in Dickens-Land

ISBN/EAN: 9783337217822

Printed in Europe, USA, Canada, Australia, Japan

Cover: Foto ©Thomas Meinert / pixelio.de

More available books at **www.hansebooks.com**

A WEEK'S TRAMP

IN

DICKENS-LAND

The Marshes, Cooling

A WEEK'S TRAMP

IN

DICKENS-LAND

TOGETHER WITH

Personal Reminiscences of the 'Inimitable Boz'

THEREIN COLLECTED.

BY

WILLIAM R. HUGHES, F.L.S.

WITH MORE THAN A HUNDRED ILLUSTRATIONS BY F. G. KITTON AND OTHER ARTISTS.

LONDON: CHAPMAN & HALL, LIMITED.

1891.

TO

MY WIFE AND DAUGHTERS,

EMILY AND EDITH,

I DEDICATE

THIS RECORD OF "A WEEK'S TRAMP,"

TO REMIND THEM OF

THE MANY PLEASANT READINGS FROM DICKENS

WE HAVE ENJOYED TOGETHER

AT HOME.

PREFACE.

* * * * * *

"'I should like to show you a series of eight articles, Sir, that have appeared in the Eatanswill Gazette. I think I may venture to say that you would not be long in establishing your opinions on a firm and solid basis, Sir.'

"'I dare say I should turn very blue long before I got to the end of them,' responded Bob.

"Mr. Pott looked dubiously at Bob Sawyer for some seconds, and turning to Mr. Pickwick said:—

"'You have seen the literary articles which have appeared at intervals in the Eatanswill Gazette in the course of the last three months, and which have excited such general—I may say such universal—attention and admiration?'

"'Why,' replied Mr. Pickwick, slightly embarrassed by the question, 'the fact is, I have been so much engaged in other ways, that I really have not had an opportunity of perusing them.'

"'You should do so, Sir,' said Pott with a severe countenance.

"'I will,' said Mr. Pickwick.

"'They appeared in the form of a copious review of a work on Chinese metaphysics, Sir,' said Pott.

"'Oh,' observed Mr. Pickwick—'from your pen I hope?'

"'From the pen of my critic, Sir,' rejoined Pott with dignity.

"'An abstruse subject I should conceive,' said Mr. Pickwick.

"'Very, Sir,' responded Pott, looking intensely sage. 'He *crammed* for it, to use a technical but expressive term; he read up for the subject, at my desire, in the *Encyclopædia Britannica*.'

"'Indeed!' said Mr. Pickwick; 'I was not aware that that valuable work contained any information respecting Chinese metaphysics.'

"'He read, Sir,' rejoined Mr. Pott, laying his hand on Mr. Pickwick's knee, and looking round with a smile of intellectual superiority, 'he read for metaphysics under the letter M, and for China under the letter C; and combined his information, Sir!'

"Mr. Pott's features assumed so much additional grandeur at the recollection of the power and research displayed in the learned effusions in question, that some minutes elapsed before Mr. Pickwick felt emboldened to renew the conversation."

* * * * * *

The above perennial extract from the immortal *Pickwick Papers* suggests to some extent the nature of the contents of this Volume. It is the record of a pilgrimage made by two enthusiastic Dickensians during the late summer of 1888, together with "combined information,"—not indeed "crammed" from the ninth edition just completed of the valuable work above referred to, but gathered mostly from original sources,—respecting the places visited, the characters alluded to in some of the novels, personal reminiscences of their Author, appropriate passages from his works (for which acknowledgments are due to Messrs. Chapman and Hall), and some little mention of the thoughts developed by the associations of "Dickens-Land."

Although the pilgrimage only extended to a week, and every spot referred to (save one) was actually visited during that time, it is but right to state that on three subsequent occasions the author has gone over the greater part of the same ground—once in the early winter, when the blue clematis and the aster had given place to the yellow jasmine and the chrysanthemum; once in the early spring, when those had been succeeded by the almond-blossom and the crocus; and again in the following year, when the beautiful county of Kent was rehabilitated in summer clothing, thus enabling him to verify observations, to correct possible errors arising from first impressions, and to gain new experiences.

As our head-quarters were at Rochester, and most of the city and other parts were taken at odd times, it has not been found practicable to preserve in consecutive chapters a perfect sequence of the records of each day's tramp, although they appear in fairly chronological order throughout the work. "A preliminary tramp in London" will possibly be dull to those familiar with the great Metropolis, but it may be useful to foreign tramps in "Dickens-Land."

Availing myself of the privilege adopted by most travellers at home and abroad, I have made occasional references to the weather. This is perhaps excusable when it is remembered that the year 1888 was a very remarkable one in that respect, so much so indeed, that the writer of a leading article in *The Times* of January 18th, 1889, in commenting on Mr. G. J. Symons' report of the British rainfall of the previous year, remarked that "seldom within living memory had there been a twelve-month with more unpleasantness in it and less of genial sunshine." We were specially favoured, however, in getting more "sunshine" than "unpleasantness," thus adding to the enjoyment of our never-to-be-forgotten tramp.

Upwards of three years have elapsed since this book was commenced, and the limited holiday leisure of a hard-working official life has necessarily prevented its completion for such a lengthened period, that it has come to be pleasantly referred to by my many Dickensian friends as the "Dictionary," in allusion to the important work of that nature contemplated by Dr. Strong, respecting which (says David Copperfield) "Adams, our head-boy, who had a turn for mathematics, had made a calculation, I was informed, of the time this Dictionary would take in completing, on the Doctor's plan, and at the Doctor's rate of going. He considered that it might be done in one thousand six hundred and forty-nine years, counting from the Doctor's last, or sixty-second, birthday."

My hearty and sincere acknowledgments are due to the publishers, Messrs. Chapman and Hall, not only for the very handsome manner in which they have allowed my book to be got up as regards print, paper, and execution (to follow the model of their Victoria Edition of *Pickwick* is indeed an honour to me), but especially for their great liberality in the matter of the Illustrations, which number more than a hundred. These were selected in conference by Mr. Fred Chapman, Mr. Kitton, and myself, and include about fifty original drawings by Mr. Kitton, from sketches specially made by him for this work. Of the remainder, six are from Forster's *Life of Dickens*, fifteen from Langton's *Childhood and Youth of Charles Dickens*, seven from *Charles Dickens by Pen and Pencil*, ten from the Jubilee Edition of *Pickwick*, and five from Rimmer's *About England with Dickens.* A few interesting fac-similes of handwriting, etc., have also been introduced. Surely such an eclectic series of Dickens Illustrations has never before been presented in one volume.

To Messrs. Chapman and Hall, Mr. Robert Langton, F.R.H.S., Messrs. Frank T. Sabin and John F. Dexter, Messrs. Macmillan and Co., and Messrs. Chatto and Windus (the proprietors of the above-mentioned works), the author's acknowledgments are also due, and are hereby tendered. Mr. Stephen T. Aveling has kindly supplied an illustration of Restoration House as it appeared in Dickens's time, and Mr. William Ball, J.P., generously commissioned a local artist to make a sketch of the Marshes, which forms the frontispiece to the book, and gives a good idea of the "long stretches of flat lands" on the Kent and Essex coasts.

To those friends whom we then met for the first time, and from whom we subsequently received help, the author's most cordial acknowledgments are due, and are also tendered, for kind information and assistance. They are a goodly number, and include Mr. A. A. Arnold, Mr. Stephen T. Aveling, Mr. William Ball, J.P., Mr. James Baird, Mr. Charles Bird, F.G.S., Major and Mrs. Budden, Mr. W. J. Budden, Mr. R. L. Cobb, Mr. J. Couchman, The Misses Drage, Mrs. Easedown, Mr. Franklin Homan, Mr. James Hulkes, J.P., and Mrs. Hulkes, Mr. Apsley Kennette, Mrs. Latter, Mr. J. Lawrence, Mr. C. D. Levy, Mr. B. Lillie, Mr. J. E. Littlewood, Mr. J. N. Malleson, Rev. J. J. Marsham, M.A., Mrs. Masters, Mr. Miles, Mr. W. Millen, Mr. Geo. Payne, F.S.A., Mr. William Pearce, Mr. George Robinson, Mr. T. B. Rosseter, F.R.M.S., Dr. Sheppard, Mr. Henry Smetham, Dr. Steele, M.R.C.S., Mr. William Syms, Mrs. Taylor, Miss Taylor, Mr. W. S. Trood, Major Trousdell, Rev. Robert Whiston, M.A., Mr. W. T. Wildish, Mr. Humphrey Wood, Mr. C. K. Worsfold, and Mrs. Henry Wright. The late Mr. Roach Smith, F.S.A., took much interest in my work and gave valuable assistance. Mr. Luke Fildes, R.A., and Mrs. Lynn Linton generously contributed very interesting information. The Right Honourable the Earl of Darnley, Mr. Henry Fielding Dickens, Mr. W. P. Frith, R.A., and Lady Head, also kindly answered enquiries.

Miss Hogarth has at my request very kindly consented to the publication of the original letters of the Novelist—about a dozen—now printed for the first time.

My sincere thanks are due to Mr. E. W. Badger, F.R.H.S., the friend of many years, for valuable help.

To my old friend and fellow-tramp, Mr. F. G. Kitton, with whose memory this delightful excursion will ever be pleasantly connected, my warmest thanks are due for reading proofs and for much kind help in many ways. "He wos werry good to me, he wos." As Pip wrote to another "Jo," "woT LARX" we did have.

Last, but not least, my cordial thanks are due to Mr. Charles Dickens for much kind information and valuable criticism.

So long as readers continue to be, so long will our great English trilogy of cognate authors, Shakespeare, Scott, and Dickens, continue to be read. Indeed as regards Dickens, a writer in *Blackwood*, June, 1871 (and *Blackwood* was not always a sympathetic critic), said:—"We may apply to him, without doubt, the surest test to which the maker can be subject: were all his books swept by some intellectual catastrophe out of the world, there would still exist in the world some score at least of people, with all whose ways and sayings we are more intimately acquainted than with those of our brothers and sisters, who would owe to him their being. While we live Sam Weller and Dick Swiveller, Mr. Pecksniff and Mrs. Gamp, the Micawbers and the Squeerses, can never die. . . . They are more real than we are ourselves, and will outlive and outlast us, as they have outlived their creator. This is the one proof of genius which no critic, not the most carping or dissatisfied, can gainsay."

So long also, the author ventures to think, will pilgrimages continue to be made to the shrines of Stratford-on-Avon, Abbotsford, and Gad's Hill Place, and to their vicinities. The modest aim of this Volume is, that it may add a humble unit in helping to keep *his* memory green, and that it may be a useful and acceptable companion to pilgrims, not only of our own country, but also from that still "Greater Britain," where "All the Year round" the name of Charles Dickens is almost a dearer "Household Word" than it is with us.

WILLIAM R. HUGHES.

WOOD HOUSE, HANDSWORTH WOOD,
near BIRMINGHAM.
30th September, 1891.

CONTENTS.

LIST OF ILLUSTRATIONS

A WEEK'S TRAMP

IN

DICKENS-LAND.

CHAPTER I.

INTRODUCTORY.

"So wishing you well in the way you go, we now conclude with the observation, that perhaps you'll go it."—*Our Mutual Friend.*

AMONG the many interesting books that have been published relating to Charles Dickens since his death, more than twenty years ago (it seems but yesterday to some of his admirers), there are at least half a dozen that describe the "country" peopled by the deathless characters created by his genius.

Probably the pioneer in this class of literature was that comprehensive work, *Dickens's London, or London in the Works of Charles Dickens*, by my friend, that thorough Dickensian, Mr. T. Edgar Pemberton, 1876; this was followed by a very readable volume, *In Kent with Charles Dickens*, by Thomas Frost, 1880; then came a dainty tome from Boston, U.S.A., entitled, *A Pickwickian Pilgrimage*, by John R. G.

Hassard, 1881. Afterwards appeared *The Childhood and Youth of Charles Dickens*, by Robert Langton, 1883, beautifully illustrated by the late William Hull of Manchester, the author, and others—a work developed from the *brochure* by the same author, *Charles Dickens and Rochester*, 1880, which has passed through five editions. Next to Forster's *Life of Dickens*, Mr. Robert Langton's larger work undoubtedly ranks—especially from the richness of the illustrations—as a very valuable original contribution to the biography of the great novelist. Another handsome volume, containing the illustrations to a series of papers in *Scribner's Monthly*—written by B. E. Martin—entitled *About England with Dickens*, came from the pen of Mr. Alfred Rimmer, 1883, and included additional illustrations drawn by the author, C. A. Vanderhoof, and others. Yet another little *brochure* recently appeared, called *London Rambles en zigzag with Charles Dickens*, by Robert Allbut, 1886. Lastly, there was published in the Christmas Number of *Scribner's Magazine*, 1887, an article, "In Dickens-Land," by Edward Percy Whipple, in which this veteran and appreciative critic of the eminent English writer's works points out that, "In addition to the practical life that men and women lead. constantly vexed as it is by obstructive facts, there is an interior life which they *imagine*, in which facts smoothly give way to sentiments, ideas, and aspirations. Dickens has, in short, discovered and colonized one of the waste districts of 'Imagination,' which we may call 'Dickens-Land,' or 'Dickens-Ville,' . . . better known than such geographical countries as Canada and Australia, . . . and confirming us in the belief of the *reality* of a population which has no *actual* existence."

It must not be assumed that the above list exhausts the literature on the subject of "Dickens-Land," many references to which are made in such high-class works as Augustus J. C. Hare's *Walks in London*, and Lawrence Hutton's *Literary Landmarks of London.*

Since the above was written, a very interesting and prettily illustrated article has appeared in the *English Illustrated Magazine* for October, 1888, entitled "Charles Dickens and Southwark," by Mr. J. Ashby-Sterry, who is second to none as an enthusiastic admirer and loyal student of Dickens. There is also a paper in *Longman's Magazine* for the same month, by the delightful essayist A. K. H. B., called "That Longest Day," in which there are several allusions to Dickens and "Dickens-Land." It, however, lacks the freshness of his earlier writings. Surely he must have lost his old love for Dickens, or things must have gone wrong at the Ecclesiastical Conference which took place at Gravesend on "That Longest Day." Altogether it is pitched in a minor key.

None of these contributions (with the exception of Mr. Langton's book), interesting as they are, and indispensable to the collector, attempt in any way to give personal reminiscences of Charles Dickens from friends or others, nor do they in any way help to throw light on his everyday life at home, beyond what was known before.

The circumstances narrated in this work do not concern the imaginary "Dickens-Land" of Mr. Whipple, but refer to the actual country in which the imaginary characters played their parts, and to that still more interesting actual country in which Dickens lived long and loved most—the county of Kent.

On Friday, 24th August, 1888, two friends met in London—one of them, the writer of these lines, a Dickens collector of some years' experience; the other, Mr. F. G. Kitton, author of that sumptuous work, *Charles Dickens by Pen and Pencil;* both ardent admirers of "the inimitable 'Boz,'" and lovers of nature and art.

We were a sort of self-constituted roving commission, to carry into effect a long-projected intention to make a week's tramp in "Dickens-Land," for purposes of health and recreation; to visit Gad's Hill, Rochester, Chatham, and neighbouring classical ground; to go over and verify some of the most important localities rendered famous in the novels; to identify, if possible, doubtful spots; and to glean, under whatever circumstances naturally developed in the progress of our tramp, additions in any form to the many interesting memorials already published, and still ever growing, relating to the renowned novelist. The idea of recording our reminiscences was not a primary consideration. It grew out of our experiences, generating a desire for others to become acquainted with the results of our enjoyable peregrinations; and the labour therein involved has been somewhat of the kind described by Lewis Morris:—

> "For this of old is sure,
> That change of toil is toil's sufficient cure."

We mixed with representatives of the classes of domestics, labourers, artizans, traders, professional men, and scientists. Many of those whom we met were advanced in years,—several were octogenarians,—and there is no doubt that we have been the means of placing on record here and there an interesting item from the past generation (mostly told in the exact words of the narrators) that might otherwise have perished. This is a special feature of this work, which makes it different from all the preceding. In every instance we were received with very great kindness, courtesy, and attention. The replies to our questions were frank and generous, and in several cases permission was accorded us to make copies of original documents not hitherto made public.

Considering that almost every inch of ground connected with Dickens has been so thoroughly explored, we were, on the whole, quite satisfied with our excursion: "the results were equal to the appliances."

By a coincidence, the month which we selected (August) was Dickens's favourite month, if we may judge from the opening sentences of the sixteenth chapter of *Pickwick*:—

> "There is no month in the whole year, in which nature wears a more beautiful appearance than in the month of August. Spring has many beauties, and May is a fresh and blooming month, but the charms of this time of year are enhanced by their contrast with the winter season. August has no such advantage. It comes when we remember nothing but clear skies, green fields, and sweet-smelling flowers—when the recollection of snow, and ice, and bleak winds, has faded from our minds as completely as they have disappeared from the earth,—and yet what a pleasant time it is. Orchards and cornfields ring with the hum of labour; trees bend beneath the thick clusters of rich fruit which bow their branches to the ground; and the corn, piled in graceful sheaves, or waving in every light breath that sweeps above it, as if it wooed the sickle, tinges the landscape with a golden hue. A mellow softness appears to hang over the whole earth; the influence of the season seems to extend itself to the very wagon, whose slow motion across the well-reaped field, is perceptible only to the eye, but strikes with no harsh sound upon the ear."

By another coincidence, the day which we selected to commence our tramp was Friday—the day upon which most of the important incidents of Dickens's life happened, as appears from frequent references in Forster's *Life* to the subject.

Provided with a selection of books inseparably connected with the subject of our tour, including, of course, copies of *Pickwick*, *Great Expectations*, *Edwin Drood*, *The Uncommercial Traveller*, Bevan's *Tourist's Guide to Kent*, one or two local Handbooks, one of Bacon's useful cycling maps, with a sketch map of the geology of the district (which greatly helped us to understand many of its picturesque effects, and was kindly furnished by Professor Lapworth, LL.D., F.R.S., of the Mason College, Birmingham), and with a pocket aneroid barometer, which every traveller should possess himself with if he wishes to make convenient arrangements as regards weather, we make a preliminary tramp in London.

CHAPTER II.

A PRELIMINARY TRAMP IN LONDON.

"We Britons had at that time particularly settled that it was treasonable to doubt our having and our being the best of everything: otherwise, while I was scared by the immensity of London, I think I might have had some faint doubts whether it was not rather ugly, crooked, narrow, and dirty."—*Great Expectations.*

SOME sixty or seventy years must have elapsed since Dickens (through the mouthpiece of Pip, as above) recorded his first impressions of London; and although he lived in it many years, and in after life he loved to study its people in every stratum of society and every phase of their existence, it seems doubtful, apart from these studies, whether he ever really liked London itself, for in the *Uncommercial Traveller*, on "The Boiled Beef of New England," in describing London as it existed subsequently, he contrasts it unfavourably in some respects, not only with such continental cities as Paris, Bordeaux, Frankfort, Milan, Geneva, and Rome, but also with such British cities as Edinburgh, Aberdeen, Exeter, and Liverpool, with such American cities as New York, Boston, and Philadelphia, and with "a bright little town like Bury St. Edmunds." Nevertheless, it is indubitable that his writings, beyond those of any other author, have done wonders to popularize our knowledge of London,—more particularly the London of the latter half of the last and the first half of the present century,—and that those writings have given it a hold on our affections which it might not otherwise have acquired. In almost all his works we are introduced to a fresh spot in the Metropolis, perhaps previously known to us, but to which the fidelity of his descriptions and the reality of the characters peopling it, certainly give a historical value never before understood or appreciated. In *The Life of Charles Dickens*, written by his devoted friend, John Forster, may be found a corroboration of this view:—

"There seemed," says this biographer, "to be not much to add to our knowledge of London until his books came upon us, but each in this respect outstripped the other in its marvels. In *Nickleby*, the old city reappears under every aspect; and whether warmth and light are playing over what is good and cheerful in it, or the veil is uplifted from its darker scenes, it is at all times our privilege to see and feel it as it absolutely is. Its interior hidden life becomes familiar as its commonest outward forms, and we discover that we hardly knew anything of the places we supposed that we knew the best."

What Scott did for Edinburgh and the Trossachs, Dickens did for London and the county of Kent. His fascination for the London streets has been dwelt on by many an author. Mr. Frank T. Marzials says in his interesting *Life of Charles Dickens*:—

"London remained the walking-ground of his heart. As he liked best to walk in London, so he liked best to walk at night. The darkness of the great city had a strange fascination for him. He never grew tired of it."

Mr. Sala records that he had been encountered "in the oddest places and in the most inclement weather: in Ratcliff Highway, on Haverstock Hill, on Camberwell Green, in Gray's Inn Lane, in the Wandsworth Road, at Hammersmith Broadway, in Norton Folgate, and at Kensal New Town. A hansom whirled you by the 'Bell and Horns' at Brompton, and there was Charles Dickens striding as with seven-leagued boots, seemingly in the direction of North End, Fulham. The Metropolitan Railway disgorged you at Lisson Grove, and you met Charles Dickens plodding sturdily towards the 'Yorkshire Stingo.' He was to be met rapidly skirting the grim brick wall of the prison in Coldbath Fields, or trudging along the Seven Sisters' Road at Holloway, or bearing under a steady press of sail through Highgate Archway, or pursuing the even tenor of his way up the Vauxhall Bridge Road."

That his feelings were intensely sympathetic with all classes of humanity there is amply evidenced in the following lines, written so far back as 1841, which Master Humphrey, "from his clock side in the chimney corner," speaks in the last page before the opening of *Barnaby Rudge*:—

"Heart of London, there is a moral in thy every stroke! as I look on at thy indomitable working, which neither death, nor press of life, nor grief, nor gladness out of doors will influence one jot, I seem to hear a voice within thee which sinks into my heart, bidding me, as I elbow my way among the crowd, have some thought for the meanest wretch that passes, and, being a man, to turn away with scorn and pride from none that bear the human shape."

On a sultry day, such as this of Friday, the 24th August, 1888, with the thermometer at nearly 80 degrees in the shade, one needs some enthusiasm to undertake a tramp for a few hours over the hot and dusty streets of London, that we may glance at a few of the memorable spots that we have visited over and over again before. This preliminary tramp is therefore necessarily limited to visiting the houses where Dickens lived, from the year 1836 until he finally left it in 1860, on disposing of Tavistock House, and took up his residence at

Gad's Hill Place. In our way we shall take a few of the places rendered famous in the novels, but it would require a "knowledge of London" as "extensive and peculiar" as that of Mr. Weller, and would occupy a week at least, to exhaust the interest of all these associations.

Our temporary quarters are at our favourite "Morley's," in

Trafalgar Square, one of those old-fashioned, comfortable hotels of the last generation, where the guest is still known as "Mr. H.," and not as "Number 497." And what is very relevant to our present purpose, Morley's revives associations of the hotels, or "Inns," as they were more generally called in Charles Dickens's early days. Strolling from Morley's eastward along the Strand, to which busy thoroughfare there are numerous references in the works of Dickens, we pass on our left the Golden Cross Hotel, a great coaching-house half a century ago, from whence the Pickwickians and Mr. Jingle started, on the 13th of May, 1827, by the "Commodore" coach for Rochester. "The low archway," against which Mr. Jingle thus prudently cautioned the passengers,—"Heads! Heads! Take care of your heads!" with the addition of a very tragic reference to the head of a family, was removed in 1851, and the hotel has the same appearance now that it presented after that alteration. The house was a favourite with David Copperfield, who stayed there with his friend Steerforth on his arrival "outside the Canterbury coach;" and it was in one of the public rooms here, approached by "a side entrance to the stable-yard," that the affecting interview took place with his humble friend Mr. Peggotty, as touchingly recorded in the fortieth chapter of *David Copperfield.* The two famous "pudding shops" in the Strand, so minutely described in connection with David's early days, have of course long been removed:—

"One was in a court close to St. Martin's Church—at the back of the Church,—which is now removed altogether. The pudding at that shop was made of currants, and was rather a special pudding, but was dear, two pennyworth not being larger than a pennyworth of more ordinary pudding. A good shop for the latter was in the

Strand,—somewhere in that part which has been rebuilt since. It was a stout pale pudding, heavy and flabby, and with great flat raisins in it, stuck in whole at wide distances apart. It came up hot at about my time every day, and many a day did I dine off it."

Nearly opposite the Golden Cross Hotel is Craven Street,

Young Dickens at the Blacking Warehouse.

where (says Mr. Allbut), at No. 39, Mr. Brownlow in *Oliver Twist* resided after removing from Pentonville, and where the villain Monks was confronted, and made a full confession of his guilt.

"Ruminating on the strange mutability of human affairs," after the manner of Mr. Pickwick, we call to mind, on the same side of the way, Hungerford Stairs, Market, and Bridge, all well remembered in the days of our youth, but now swept away to make room for the commodious railway terminus at Charing Cross. Here poor David Copperfield "served as a labouring hind," and acquired his grim experience with poverty in Murdstone and Grinby's (*alias* Lamert's) Blacking Warehouse. Hungerford Suspension Bridge many years ago was removed to Clifton, and we never pass by it on the Great Western line without recalling recollections of poor David's sorrows.

Next in order comes Buckingham Street, at the end house of which, on the east side (No. 15), lived Mrs. Crupp, who let apartments to David Copperfield in happier days. Here he had his "first dissipation," and entertained Steerforth and his two friends, Mrs. Crupp imposing on him frightfully as regards the dinner; "the handy young man" and the "young gal" being equally troublesome as regards the waiting. The description of "my set of chambers" in *David Copperfield* seems to point to the possibility of Dickens having resided here, but there is no evidence to prove it. At Osborn's Hotel, now the Adelphi, in John Street, Mr. Wardle and his daughter Emily stayed on their visit to London, after Mr. Pickwick was released from the Fleet Prison.

Durham Street, a little further to the right, leads to the "dark arches," which had attractions for David Copperfield, who "was fond of wandering about the Adelphi, because it was a mysterious place with those dark arches." He says:— "I see myself emerging one evening from out of these arches, on a little public-house, close to the river, with a space before it, where some coal-heavers were dancing." Nearly opposite is the Adelphi Theatre, notable as having been the stage whereon most of the dramas founded on Dickens's works were first produced, from *Nicholas Nickleby* in 1838, in which Mrs. Keeley, John Webster, and O. Smith took part, down to 1867, when *No Thoroughfare* was performed, "the only story," says Mr. Forster, "Dickens himself ever helped to dramatize," and which was rendered with such fine effect by Fechter, Benjamin Webster, Mrs. Alfred Mellon, and other important actors. He certainly assisted in Madame Celeste's production of *A Tale of Two Cities*, even if he had no actual part in the writing of the piece.

Mr. Allbut thinks that the residence of Miss La Creevy, the good-natured miniature painter (whose prototype was Miss Barrow, Dickens's aunt on his mother's side) in *Nicholas Nickleby*, was probably at No. 111, Strand. It was "a private door about half-way down that crowded thoroughfare."

We proceed onwards, passing Wellington Street North, where at No. 16, the office of the famous *Household Words* formerly stood; *All the Year Round*, its successor, conducted by Mr. Charles Dickens, the novelist's eldest son, now being at No. 26 in the same street.

A little further on, on the same side of the way, and almost facing Somerset House, at No. 332, was the office of the once celebrated *Morning Chronicle*, on the staff of which Dickens in early life worked as a reporter. The *Chronicle* was a great power in its day, when Mr. John Black ("Dear old Black!" Dickens calls him, "my first hearty out-and-out appreciator, . . . with never-forgotten compliments . . . coming in the broadest of Scotch from the broadest of hearts I ever knew,") was editor, and Mr. J. Campbell, afterwards Lord Chief-Justice Campbell, its chief literary critic. The *Chronicle* died in 1862.

The west corner of Arundel Street (No. 186, Strand, where

now stand the extensive premises of Messrs. W. H. Smith and Son) was formerly the office of Messrs. Chapman and Hall, the publishers of almost all the original works of Charles Dickens. After 1850 the firm removed to 193, Piccadilly, their present house being at 11, Henrietta Street, Covent Garden. They own the copyright, and publish all Dickens's works; and they estimate that two million copies of *Pickwick*[1] have been sold in England alone, exclusive of the almost innumerable popular editions, from one penny upwards, published by other firms, the copyright of this work having expired. The penny edition was sold by hundreds of thousands in the streets of London some years ago.

This statement will probably be surprising to the remarkable class of readers thus described by that staunch admirer of Dickens, Mr. Andrew Lang, in "Phiz," one of his charming *Lost Leaders*. He says:—

"It is a singular and gloomy feature in the character of young ladies and gentlemen of a particular type, that they have ceased to care for Dickens, as they have ceased to care for Scott. They say they cannot read Dickens. When Mr. Pickwick's adventures are presented to the modern maid, she behaves like the Cambridge freshman. 'Euclide viso, cohorruit et evasit.' When he was shown Euclid he evinced dismay, and sneaked off. Even so do most young people act when they are expected to read *Nicholas Nickleby* and *Martin Chuzzlewit*. They call these master-

[1] In *The History of Pickwick*, a handsome octavo volume of nearly 400 pages, just published (1891), Mr. Percy Fitzgerald, the author, who is one of the few surviving friends of Charles Dickens, mentions the interesting fact that there are 360 characters, 70 episodes, and 22 inns, described in this wonderful book, written when the author was only twenty-four.

pieces 'too gutterly gutter'; they cannot sympathize with this honest humour and conscious pathos. Consequently the innumerable references to Sam Weller, and Mrs. Gamp, and Mr. Pecksniff, and Mr. Winkle, which fill our ephemeral literature, are written for these persons in an unknown tongue. The number of people who could take a good pass in Mr. Calverley's *Pickwick* Examination Paper is said to be

Fountain Court, Temple.

diminishing. Pathetic questions are sometimes put. Are we not too much cultivated? Can this fastidiousness be anything but a casual passing phase of taste? Are all people over thirty who cling to their Dickens and their Scott old fogies? Are we wrong in preferring them to *Bootles' Baby*, and *The Quick or the Dead*, and the novels of M. Paul Bourget?"

But this by the way. Turning down Essex Street, we visit the Temple, celebrated in several of Dickens's novels—*Barnaby Rudge*, *A Tale of Two Cities*, *Great Expectations*, and *Our Mutual Friend*,—but in none more graphically than in *Martin Chuzzlewit*, in which is described the fountain in Fountain Court, where Ruth Pinch goes to meet her lover, "coming briskly up, with the best little laugh upon her face that ever played in opposition to the fountain; and beat it all to nothing." And when John Westlock came at last, "merrily the fountain leaped and danced, and merrily the smiling dimples twinkled and expanded more and more, until they broke into a laugh against the basin's rim, and vanished." As we saw the fountain on the bright August morning of our tramp, the few shrubs, flowers, and ferns planted round it gave it quite a rural effect, and we wished long life to the solitary specimen of eucalyptus, whose glaucous-green leaves and tender shoots seemed ill-fitted to bear the nipping frosts of our variable climate.

Coming out of the Temple by Middle Temple Lane, we pass on our left Child's Bank, the "Tellson's Bank" of *A Tale of Two Cities*, "which was an old-fashioned place even in the year 1780," but was replaced in 1878 by the handsome building suitable to its imposing neighbours, the Law Courts. Temple Bar, which adjoined the Old Bank, and was one of the relics of Dickens's London, has passed away, having since been re-erected on "Theobalds," near Waltham Cross.

"A walk down Fleet Street"—one of Dr. Johnson's enjoyments—leads us to Whitefriars Street, on the east side of which, at No. 67, is the office of *The Daily News*, edited by Dickens from 21 Jany. to 9 Feby., 1846, and for which he wrote the original prospectus, and subsequently, in a series of letters descriptive of his Italian travel, his delightful *Pictures from Italy*. St. Dunstan's Church in Fleet Street is supposed to have been that immortalized in *The Chimes*.

It was in this street many years before (in the year 1833, when he was only twenty-one), as recorded in Forster's *Life*, that Dickens describes himself as dropping his first literary sketch, *Mrs. Joseph Porter over the Way*, "stealthily one evening at twilight, with fear and trembling, into a dark letter-box in a dark office up a dark court in Fleet Street; and he has told his agitation when it appeared in all the glory of print:—'On which occasion I walked down to Westminster Hall, and turned into it for half an hour, because my eyes were so dimmed with joy and pride, that they could not bear the street, and were not fit to be seen there.'" The "dark court" referred to was no doubt Johnson's Court, as the printers of the *Monthly Magazine*, Messrs. Baylis and Leighton, had their offices here. This contribution appeared in the January number 1834 of this magazine, published by Messrs. Cochrane and Macrone of 11 Waterloo Place.

Turning up Chancery Lane, also celebrated in many of Charles Dickens's novels, we leave on our left Bell Yard, where lodged the ruined suitor in Chancery, poor Gridley, "the man from Shropshire" in *Bleak House*, but the yard has, through part of it being required for the New Law Courts and other modern improvements, almost lost its identity.

On our right is Old Serjeant's Inn, which leads into Clifford's Inn, where the conference took place between John Rokesmith and Mr. Boffin, when the former, to the latter's amazement, said:—"If you would try me as your Secretary." The place is thus referred to in the eighth chapter of *Our Mutual Friend*:—

"Not very well knowing how to get rid of this applicant, and feeling the more embarrassed because his manner and appearance claimed a delicacy in which the worthy Mr. Boffin feared he himself might be deficient, that gentleman glanced into the mouldy little plantation or cat preserve, of Clifford's Inn, as it was that day, in search of a suggestion. Sparrows were there, dry-rot and wet-rot were there, but it was not otherwise a suggestive spot."

Symond's Inn, described as "a little, pale, wall-eyed, woe-begone inn, like a large dust-bin of two compartments and a sifter,"—where Mr. Vholes had his chambers, and where Ada Clare came to live after her marriage, there tending lovingly the blighted life of the suitor in Jarndyce and Jarndyce, poor Richard Carstone,—exists no more. It formerly stood on the site of Nos. 25, 26, and 27, now handsome suites of offices.

Lincoln's Inn, a little higher up on the opposite side of the way, claims our attention, in the Hall of which was formerly the Lord High Chancellor's Court, wherein the wire-drawn Chancery suit of Jarndyce and Jarndyce in *Bleak House* dragged its course wearily along. The offices of Messrs. Kenge and Carboy, of Old Square, Solicitors in the famous suit, were visited by Esther Summerson, who says:—"We passed into sudden quietude, under an old gallery, and drove on through a silent square, until we came to an old nook in a corner, where there was an entrance up a steep broad flight of stairs like an entrance to a church." Mr. Serjeant Snubbin, Mr. Pickwick's counsel in the notorious cause of Bardell *v.* Pickwick, also had his chambers in this square. We then enter Lincoln's Inn Fields, and pay a visit to No. 58, on the furthest or west side near Portsmouth Street. This ancient mansion was the residence of Dickens's friend and biographer, John Forster, before he went to live at Palace

Gate. It is minutely described in the tenth chapter of *Bleak House* as the residence of Mr. Tulkinghorn, "a large house, formerly a house of state, . . . let off in sets of chambers now; and in those shrunken fragments of its greatness lawyers lie like maggots in nuts." The "foreshortened allegory in the person of one impossible Roman upside down," who afterwards points to the "new meaning" (*i. e.* the murder of Mr. Tulkinghorn) has, it is to be regretted, since been white-washed. On the 30th November, 1844, here Dickens read *The Chimes* to a few intimate friends, an event immortalized by Maclise's pencil, and, as appreciative of the feelings of the audience, Forster alludes "to the grave attention of Carlyle, the eager interest of Stanfield and Maclise, the keen look of poor Laman Blanchard, Fox's rapt solemnity, Jerrold's sky-ward gaze, and the tears of Harness and Dyce."

That celebrated tavern called the "Magpie and Stump," referred to in the twenty-first chapter of *Pickwick*,—where that hero spent an interesting evening on the invitation of Lowten (Mr. Perker's clerk), and heard "the old man's tale about the queer client,"—is supposed to have been "The old George the IVth" in Clare Market, close by. Retracing our steps through Bishop's Court (where lived Krook the marine-store dealer, and in whose house lodged poor Miss Flite and Captain Hawdon, *alias* Nemo) into Chancery Lane, we arrive at the point from whence we diverged, and turn into Cursitor Street. Like other places adjacent, this street has been subjected to "improvements," and it is scarcely possible to trace "Coavinses," so well known to Mr. Harold Skimpole, or indeed the place of business and residence of Mr. Snagsby, the good-natured law stationer, and his jealous "little woman." It will be remembered that it was here the Reverend Mr.

Staple Inn, Holborn.

Chadband more than once "improved a tough subject":—"toe your advantage, toe your profit, toe your, gain, toe your welfare, toe your enrichment,"—and refreshed his own. Thackeray was partial to this neighbourhood, and Rawdon Crawley had some painful experiences in Cursitor Street.

Bearing round by Southampton Buildings, we reach Staple Inn,—behind the most ancient part of Holborn,—originally a hostelry of the merchants of the Wool-staple, who were removed to Westminster by Richard II. in 1378. At No. 10 in the first court, opposite the pleasant little garden and picturesque hall, resided the "angular" but kindly Mr. Grewgious, attended by his "gloomy" clerk, Mr. Bazzard, and on the front of the house over the door still remains the tablet with the mysterious initials:—

P.
J. T.
1747.

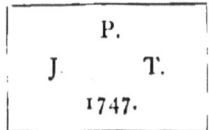

but our enquiries fail to discover their meaning. Dickens humorously suggests "Perhaps John Thomas," "Perhaps Joe Tyler," and under hilarious circumstances, "Pretty Jolly too," and "Possibly jabbered thus!" They are understood to be the initials of the treasurer of the Inn at the date above-mentioned. It is interesting to state that the Inn has been most appropriately restored by the enterprising Prudential Assurance Company, who have recently purchased it; and on the seat in the centre of the second Court (facing Holborn), under the plane trees which adorn it, were resting a few wayfarers, who seemed to enjoy this thoughtful provision made by the present owners. We can picture in one of the rooms on the first floor of P. J. T.'s house (very memorable to the writer of these lines, some brief part of his early life having been passed there), the conference described in the twentieth

chapter of *Edwin Drood*, between Mr. Grewgious and his charming ward,—so aptly pourtrayed by Mr. Luke Fildes in his beautiful drawing, "Mr. Grewgious experiences a new sensation,"—as well as all the other scenes which took place here.

Turning into Holborn through the Archway of Staple Inn, and stopping for a minute to admire the fine effect of the recently restored fourteenth-century old-timbered houses of the Inn which face that thoroughfare, a few steps lower down take us to Barnard's Inn, where Pip in *Great Expectations* lodged with his friend Herbert Pocket when he came to London. Dickens calls it, "the dingiest collection of shabby buildings ever squeezed together in a rank corner as a club for tom-cats." Simple-minded Joe Gargery, who visited Pip here, persisted for a time in calling it an "hotel," and after his visit thus recorded his impressions of the place:—

"The present may be a werry good inn, and I believe its character do stand i; but I wouldn't keep a pig in it myself—not in the case that I wished him to fatten wholesome and to eat with a meller flavour on him."

A few plane trees—the glory of all squares and open spaces in London, where they thrive so luxuriantly—give a rural appearance to this crowded place, while the sparrows tenanting them enjoy the sunbeams passing through the scanty branches.

Our next halting-place, Furnival's Inn, is one of profound interest to all pious pilgrims in "Dickens-Land," for there the genius of the young author was first recognized, not only by the novel-reading world, but also by his contemporaries in literature. Thackeray generously spoke of him as "the young man who came and took his place calmly at the head of the whole tribe, and who has kept it."

Furnival's Inn in Holborn, which stands midway between Barnard's Inn and Staple Inn on the opposite side of the way, is famous as having been the residence of Charles Dickens in his bachelor days, when a reporter for the *Morning Chronicle.*

He removed here from his father's lodgings at No. 18, Bentinck Street, and had chambers, first the "three pair back" (rather gloomy rooms) of No. 13 from Christmas 1834 until Christmas 1835, when he removed to the "three pair floor south" (bright

little rooms) of No. 15, the house on the right-hand side of the square having Ionic ornamentations, which he occupied from 1835 until his removal to No. 48, Doughty Street, in March 1837. The brass-bound iron rail still remains, and the sixty stone steps which lead from the ground-floor to the top of each house are no doubt the same over which the eager feet of the youthful "Boz" often trod. He was married from Furnival's Inn on 2nd April, 1836, to Catherine, eldest daughter of Mr. George Hogarth, his old colleague on the *Morning Chronicle*, the wedding taking place at St. Luke's Church, Chelsea, and doubtless lived here in his early matrimonial days much in the same way probably as Tommy Traddles did, as described in *David Copperfield*. Here the *Sketches by Boz* were written, and most of the numbers of the immortal *Pickwick Papers*, as also the lesser works: *Sunday under Three Heads*, *The Strange Gentleman*, and *The Village Coquettes*. The quietude of this retired spot in the midst of a busy thoroughfare, and its accessibility to the *Chronicle* offices in the Strand, must have been very attractive to the young author. His eldest son, the present Mr. Charles Dickens, was born here on the 6th January, 1837.

It was in Furnival's Inn, probably in the year 1836, that Thackeray paid a visit to Dickens, and thus described the meeting:—

"I can remember, when Mr. Dickens was a very young man, and had commenced delighting the world with some charming humorous works in covers which were coloured light green and came out once a month, that this young man wanted an artist to illustrate his writings; and I remember walking up to his chambers in Furnival's Inn, with two or three drawings in my hand, which, strange to say, he did not find suitable."

How wonderfully interesting these "two or three drawings" would be now if they could be discovered! Of the score or so of "Extra Illustrations" to *Pickwick* which have appeared, surely these (if they were such) which Dickens "did not find suitable," combining as they did the genius of

Dickens and Thackeray, whatever their merits or defects may have been, would be most highly prized.

John Westlock, in *Martin Chuzzlewit*, had apartments in Furnival's Inn, and was there visited by Tom Pinch. Wood's Hotel occupies a large portion of the square, and is mentioned in *The Mystery of Edwin Drood* as having been the Inn where Mr. Grewgious took rooms for his charming ward Rosa Bud, from whence he ordered for her refreshment, soon after her arrival at Staple Inn to escape Jasper's importunities, "a nice jumble of all meals," to which it is to be feared she did not do justice, and where "at the hotel door he afterwards confided her to the Unlimited head chamber-maid."

The Society of Arts have considerately put up on the house No. 15 one of their neat terra-cotta memorial tablets with the following inscription :—

CHARLES
DICKENS,
Novelist,
Lived here.
B. 1812,
D. 1870.

We proceed along Holborn, and go up Kingsgate Street, where "Poll Sweedlepipe, Barber and Bird Fancier," lived, "next door but one to the celebrated mutton-pie shop, and directly opposite the original cats'-meat warehouse." The immortal Sairey Gamp lodged on the first floor, where doubtless she helped herself from the "chimley-piece" whenever she felt "dispoged." Here also the quarrel took place between that old lady and her friend Betsey Prig anent that mythical personage, "Mrs. Harris." We pass through Red Lion Square and up Bedford Row, and after proceeding along Theobald's Road for a short distance, turn up John Street, which leads into Doughty Street, where, at No. 48,

No. 48, Doughty Street, Mecklenburgh Square.
Dickens's Residence 1837-9.

Charles Dickens lived from 1837 to 1839. The house, situated on the east side of the street, has twelve rooms, is single-fronted, three-storied, and not unlike No. 2, Ordnance Terrace, Chatham. A tiny little room on the ground-floor, with a bolt inside in addition to the usual fastening, is pointed out as having been the novelist's study. It has an outlook into a garden, but of late years this has been much reduced in size. A bill in the front window announces "Apartments to let," and they look very comfortable. Doughty Street, now a somewhat noisy thoroughfare, must have been in Charles Dickens's time a quiet, retired spot. A large pair of iron gates reach across the street, guarded by a gate-keeper in livery. "It was," says Mr. Marzials in his *Life of Dickens*, "while living at Doughty Street that he seems, in great measure, to have formed those habits of work and relaxation which every artist fashions so as to suit his own special needs and idiosyncrasies. His favourite time for work was the morning between the hours of breakfast and lunch; . . he was essentially a day worker and not a night worker. . . . And for relaxation and sedative when he had thoroughly worn himself with mental toil, he would have recourse to the hardest bodily exercise. . . . At first riding seems to have contented him, . . . but soon walking took the place of riding, and he became an indefatigable pedestrian. He would think nothing of a walk of twenty or thirty miles, and that not merely in the vigorous hey-day of youth, but afterwards to the very last. . . ."

It was at Doughty Street that he experienced a bereavement which darkened his life for many years, and to which Forster thus alludes:—

"His wife's next younger sister Mary, who lived with them, and by sweetness of nature even more than by graces of person had made herself the ideal of his life, died with a terrible suddenness that for a time completely bore him down. His grief and suffering were intense, and affected him . . . through many after years." *Pickwick* was temporarily suspended, and he sought change of scene at Hampstead. Forster visited him there, and to him he opened his heart. He says:—"I left him as much his friend, and as entirely in his confidence, as if I had known him for years."

Tavistock House, Tavistock Square.
Dickens's Residence 1851-60.

Some time afterwards, we find him inviting Forster "to join him at 11 A.M. in a fifteen-mile ride out and ditto in, lunch on the road, with a six o'clock dinner in Doughty Street."

Charles Dickens's residence in Doughty Street was but of

short duration—from 1837 to 1840 only; but there he completed *Pickwick*, and wrote *Oliver Twist*, *Memoirs of Grimaldi*, *Sketches of Young Gentlemen*, *Sketches of Young Couples*, and *The Life and Adventures of Nicholas Nickleby*. His eldest daughter Mary was born here.

In proper sequence we ought to proceed to Dickens's third London residence, No. 1, Devonshire Terrace, but it will be more convenient to take his fourth residence on our way. We therefore retrace our steps into Theobald's Road, pass through Red Lion and Bloomsbury Squares, and along Great Russell Street as far as the British Museum, where Dickens is still remembered as "a reader" (merely remarking that it of course contains a splendid collection of the original impressions of the novelist's works, and "Dickensiana," as is evidenced by the comprehensive Bibliography furnished by Mr. John P. Anderson, one of the librarians, to Mr. Marzials' *Life of Dickens*), which we leave on our left, and turn up Montague Street, go along Upper Montague Street, Woburn Square, Gordon Square, and reach Tavistock Square, at the upper end of which, on the east side, Gordon Place leads us into a retired spot cut off as it were from communication with the rest of this quiet neighbourhood. Three houses adjoin each other—handsome commodious houses, having stone porticos at entrance—and in the first of these, Tavistock House, Dickens lived from 1851 until 1860, with intervals at Gad's Hill Place. This beautiful house, which has eighteen rooms in it, is now the Jews' College. The drawing-room on the first floor still contains a dais at one end, and it is said that at a recent public meeting held here, three hundred and fifty people were accommodated in it, which serves to show what ample quarters Dickens had to entertain his friends.

Hans Christian Andersen, who visited Dickens here in 1857, thus describes this fine mansion :—

"In Tavistock Square stands Tavistock House. This and the strip of garden in front are shut out from the thoroughfare by an iron railing. A large garden with a grass-plat and high trees stretches behind the house, and gives it a countrified look, in the midst of this coal and gas steaming London. In the passage from street to garden hung pictures and engravings. Here stood a marble bust of Dickens, so like him, so youthful and handsome; and over a bedroom door were inserted the bas-reliefs of Night and Day, after Thorwaldsen. On the first floor was a rich library, with a fireplace and a writing-table, looking out on the garden; and here it was that in winter Dickens and his friends acted plays to the satisfaction of all parties. The kitchen was underground, and at the top of the house were the bedrooms."

It appears that Andersen was wrong about the plays being acted in the "rich library," as I am informed by Mr. Charles Dickens that "the stage was in the school-room at the back of the ground-floor, with a platform built outside the window for scenic purposes."

With reference to the private theatricals (or "plays," as Andersen calls them, including *The Frozen Deep*, by Wilkie Collins, in which Dickens, the author, Mark Lemon, and others performed, and for which in the matter of the scenery "the priceless help of Stanfield had again been secured"), on a temporary difficulty arising as to the arrangements, Dickens applied to Mr. Cooke of Astley's, "who drove up in an open phaeton drawn by two white ponies with black spots all over them (evidently stencilled), who came in at the gate with a little jolt and a rattle exactly as they come into the ring when they draw anything, and went round and round the centre bed (lilacs and evergreens) of the front court, apparently looking for the clown. A multitude of boys, who felt them to be no common ponies, rushed up in a breathless state—twined themselves like ivy about the railings, and were only deterred from storming the enclosure by the Inimitable's eye." Mr. Cooke was not, however, able to render any assistance.

Mrs. Arthur Ryland of The Linthurst, near Bromsgrove, Worcestershire, who was present at Tavistock House on the occasion of the performance of *The Frozen Deep*, informs me that when Dickens returned to the drawing-room after the play was over, the constrained expression of face which he had assumed in presenting the character of Richard Wardour remained for some time afterwards, so strongly did he seem to realize the presentment. The other plays performed were *Tom Thumb*, 1854, and *The Lighthouse* and *Fortunus*, 1855.

The following copy of a play-bill—in my collection—of one of these performances is certainly worth preserving in a permanent form, for the double reason that it is extremely rare, and contains one of Dickens's few poetical contributions, *The Song of the Wreck*, which was written specially for the occasion.

The smallest Theatre in the World!

TAVISTOCK HOUSE.

Lessee and Manager - - - MR. CRUMMLES.

On Tuesday evening, June 19th, 1855, will be presented, at exactly eight o'clock,

An entirely New and Original

Domestic Melo-drama, in Two Acts, by Mr. Wilkie Collins, now first performed, called

THE LIGHTHOUSE.

The Scenery painted by Mr. Stanfield, R.A.

Aaron Gurnock, the head Light-keeper	MR. CRUMMLES.
Martin Gurnock, his son; the second Light-keeper ...	MR. WILKIE COLLINS.
Jacob Dale, the third Light-keeper	MR. MARK LEMON.
Samuel Furley, a Pilot ...	MR. AUGUSTUS EGG, A.R.A.
The Relief of Light-keepers, by	MR. CHARLES DICKENS, JUNIOR, MR. EDWARD HOGARTH, MR. ALFRED AINGER, and MR. WILLIAM WEBSTER.
The Shipwrecked Lady	MISS HOGARTH.
Phœbe	MISS DICKENS,

Who will sing a new Ballad, the music by Mr. Linley, the words by Mr. Crummles, entitled

THE SONG OF THE WRECK.

I.

"The wind blew high, the waters raved,
A Ship drove on the land,
A hundred human creatures saved,
Kneeled down upon the sand.
Three-score were drowned, three-score were thrown
Upon the black rocks wild;
And thus among them left alone,
They found one helpless child.

II.

A Seaman rough, to shipwreck bred,
Stood out from all the rest,
And gently laid the lonely head
Upon his honest breast.
And trav'ling o'er the Desert wide,
It was a solemn joy,
To see them, ever side by side,
The sailor and the boy.

III.

In famine, sickness, hunger, thirst,
  The two were still but one,
Until the strong man drooped the first,
  And felt his labours done.
Then to a trusty friend he spake :
  'Across this Desert wide,
O take the poor boy for my sake!'
  And kissed the child, and died.

IV.

Toiling along in weary plight,
  Through heavy jungle-mire,
These two came later every night
  To warm them at the fire,
Until the Captain said one day:
  'O seaman good and kind,
To save thyself now come away
  And leave the boy behind!'

V.

The child was slumb'ring near the blaze :
  'O Captain let him rest
Until it sinks, when GOD's own ways
  Shall teach us what is best!'
They watched the whiten'd ashey heap,
  They touched the child in vain,
They did not leave him there asleep,
  He never woke again."

Half an hour for Refreshment.

To conclude with
'he Guild Amateur Company's Farce, in one act, by Mr. Crummles and Mr. Mark Lemon;

MR. NIGHTINGALE'S DIARY.

Mr. Nightingale	MR. FRANK STONE, A.R.A.
Mr. Gabblewig, of the Middle Temple	MR. CRUMMLES.
Charley Bit, a Boots	
Mr. Poulter, a Pedestrian and cold water drinker	
Captain Blower, an invalid ...	
A Respectable Female ...	
A Deaf Sexton	
Tip, Mr. Gabblewig's Tiger ...	MR. AUGUSTUS EGG, A.R.A.
Christopher, a Charity Boy ...	
Slap, Professionally Mr. Flormiville, a country actor	MR. MARK LEMON.
Mr. Tickle, Inventor of the Celebrated Compounds	
A Virtuous Young Person in the confidence of Maria	
Lithers, Landlord of the Water-lily	MR. WILKIE COLLINS.
Rosina, Mr. Nightingale's niece ...	MISS KATE DICKENS.
Susan her Maid	MISS HOGARTH.

Composer and Director of the music, MR. FRANCESCO BERGER, who will preside at the pianoforte.

Costume makers, MESSRS. NATHAN of Titchbourne Street, Haymarket.

Perruquier, MR. WILSON, of the Strand.

Machinery and Properties by MR. IRELAND, of the Theatre Royal, Adelphi.

Doors open at half-past seven. Carriages may be ordered at a quarter past eleven.

It was from Tavistock House that Dickens received this startling message from a confidential servant:—

"The gas-fitter says, sir, that he can't alter the fitting of your gas in your bedroom without taking up almost the ol[illegible] of your bedroom floor, and pulling your room to pieces. He says of course you can have it done if you wish, and he'll do it for you and make a good job of it, but he would have to destroy your room first, and go entirely under the jistes."

The same female, in allusion to Dickens's wardrobe, also said, "Well, sir, your clothes is all shabby, and your boots is all burst."

Among the important works of Charles Dickens which were

No. 141, Bayham Street, Camden Town,
where the Dickens Family lived in 1823.

wholly or partly written at Tavistock House are:—*Bleak House*, *A Child's History of England*, *Hard Times*, *Little Dorrit*, *A Tale of Two Cities*, *The Uncommercial Traveller*, and *Great Expectations*. *All the Year Round* was also determined upon while he lived here, and the first number was dated 30th April, 1859.

Tavistock House is the nearest point to Camden Town, interesting as being the place where, in 1823, at No. 16 (now No. 141) Bayham Street, the Dickens family resided for a short time[2] on leaving Chatham. There is an exquisite sketch of the humble little house by Mr. Kitton in his *Charles Dickens by Pen and Pencil*, and it is spoken of as being "in one of the then poorest parts of the London suburbs." We therefore proceed along Gordon Square, and reach Gower Street. At No. 147, Gower Street, formerly No. 4, Gower Street North, on the west side, was once the elder Mr. Dickens's establishment. The house, now occupied by Mr. Müller, an artificial human eye-maker ("human eyes warious," says Mr. Venus), has six rooms, with kitchens in basement. The rooms are rather small, each front room having two windows, which in the case of the first floor reach from floor to ceiling. It seems to be a comfortable house, but has no garden. There is an old-fashioned brass knocker on the front door, probably the original one, and there is a dancing academy next door. (Query, Mr. Turveydrop's?) The family of the novelist, which had removed from Bayham Street, were at this time (1823) in such indifferent circumstances that poor Mrs. Dickens had to

[2] Forster (I. 14) infers that the family removed to London in 1821, but Mr. Langton considers (*Childhood and Youth of Charles Dickens*, 1883, pp. 62-3), from the fact of the birth of Dickens's brother Alfred having been registered at Chatham on 3rd April, 1822, and from the further fact of there being no record of Mr. John Dickens's recall throughout this year to Somerset House, that the family did not remove to London until the winter of 1822-3, and I agree with Mr. Langton. Mr. Kitton in *Charles Dickens by Pen and Pencil*, 1890, also recognizes this period as the date of the removal of the Dickens family to London.

exert herself in adding to the finances by trying to teach, and a school was opened for young children at this house, which was decorated with a brass-plate on the door, lettered MRS. DICKENS'S ESTABLISHMENT, a faint description of which occurs in the fourth chapter of *Our Mutual Friend*, and of its abrupt removal "for the interests of all parties." These facts, and also that of young Charles Dickens's own efforts to obtain pupils for his mother, are alluded to in a letter written by Dickens to Forster in later life:—

"I left, at a great many other doors, a great many circulars calling attention to the merits of the establishment. Yet nobody ever came to school, nor do I ever recollect that anybody ever proposed to come, or that the least preparation was made to receive anybody. But I know that we got on very badly with the butcher and baker; that very often we had not too much for dinner; and that at last my father was arrested."

This period, subsequently most graphically described in *David Copperfield* as the "blacking bottle period," was the darkest in young Charles's existence; but happier times and brighter prospects soon came to drown the recollections of that bitter experience.

Walking up Euston Road from Gower Street, we see St. Pancras Church (not the old church of "Saint Pancridge" in the Fields, by the bye, situated in the St. Pancras Road, where Mr. Jerry Cruncher and two friends went "fishing" on a memorable night, as recorded in *A Tale of Two Cities*, when their proceedings, and especially those of his "honoured parent," were watched by young Jerry), and proceed westward along the Marylebone Road, called the New Road in Dickens's time, past Park Crescent, Regent's Park, and do not stop until we

No. 1, Devonshire Terrace, Regent's Park.—*Dickens's Residence* 1839-50.

reach No. 1, Devonshire Terrace. This commodious double-fronted house, in which Dickens resided from 1839 to 1850, is entered at the side, and the front looks into the Marylebone Road. Maclise's beautiful sketch of the house (made in 1840), as given in Forster's *Life*, shows the windows of the lower and first floor rooms as largely bowed, while over the top flat of one of the former is a protective iron-work covering, thus allowing the children to come out of their nursery on the third floor freely to enjoy the air and watch the passers-by. In the sketch Maclise has characteristically put in a shuttle-cock just over the wall, as though the little ones were playing in the garden. Forster calls it "a handsome house with a garden of considerable size, shut out from the New Road by a brick wall, facing the York Gate into Regent's Park;" and Dickens himself admitted it to be "a house of great promise (and great premium), undeniable situation, and excessive splendour." That he loved it well is shown by the passage in a letter which he addressed to Forster, "in full view of Genoa's perfect bay," when about to commence *The Chimes* (1844); he says:—"Never did I stagger so upon a threshold before. I seem as if I had plucked myself out of my proper soil when I left Devonshire Terrace, and could take root no more until I return to it. . . . Did I tell you how many fountains we have here? No matter. If they played nectar, they wouldn't please me half so well as the West Middlesex water-works at Devonshire Terrace."

Mr. Jonathan Clark, who resides here, kindly shows us over the house, which contains thirteen rooms. The polished mahogany doors in the hall, and the chaste Italian marble mantel-pieces in the principal rooms, are said to have been put up by the novelist. On the ground floor, the smaller room to the eastward of the house, with window facing north and looking into the pleasant garden where the plane trees and turf are beautifully green, is pointed out as having been his study.

Mr. Benjamin Lillie, of 70, High Street, Marylebone, plumber and painter, remembers Mr. Dickens coming to Devonshire Terrace. He did a good deal of work for him while he lived there, and afterwards, when he removed to Tavistock House, including the fitting up of the library shelves and the curious counterfeit book-backs, made to conceal the backs of the doors. He also removed the furniture to Tavistock House, and subsequently to Gad's Hill Place. He spoke of the interest which Mr. Dickens used to take in the work generally, and said he would stand for hours with his back to the fire looking at the workmen. In the summer time he used to lie on the lawn with his pocket-handkerchief over his face, and when thoughts occurred to him, he would go into his study, and after making notes, would resume his position on the lawn. On the next page we give an illustration of the courteous and precise manner—not without a touch of humour—in which he issued his orders.

Here it was that Dickens's favourite ravens were kept, in a stable on the south side of the garden, one of which died in 1841, it was supposed from the effects of paint, or owing to "a malicious butcher," who had been heard to say that he "would do for him." His death is described by Dickens in a long passage which thus concludes:—

> "On the clock striking twelve he appeared slightly agitated, but he soon recovered, walked twice or thrice along the coach-house, stopped to bark, staggered, exclaimed, '*Holloa, old girl!*' (his favourite expression), and died."

In an interesting letter addressed to Mr. Angus Fletcher, recently in the possession of Mr. Arthur Hailstone of

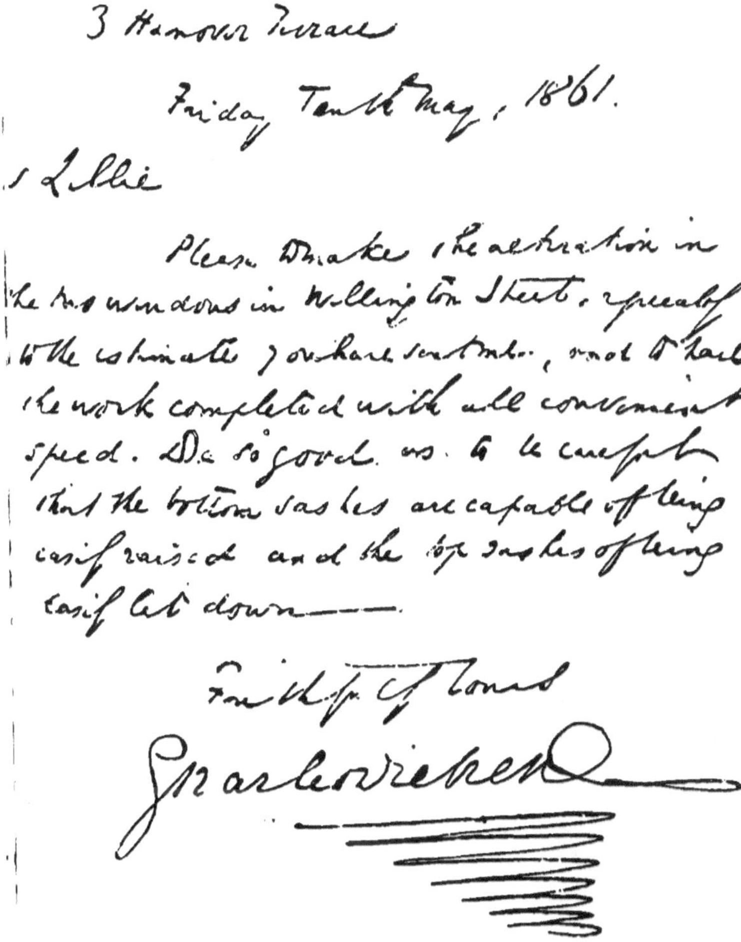
3 Hanover Terrace

Friday Tenth May, 1861.

Lillie

Please to make the alteration in the two windows in Wellington Street, agreeably to the estimate you have sent me, and to have the work completed with all convenient speed. Be so good as to be careful that the bottom sashes are capable of being easily raised and the top sashes of being easily let down ——

Faithfully Yours

Charles Dickens

Manchester, Dickens further describes the event:—"Suspectful of a butcher who had been heard to threaten, I had the body opened. There were no traces of poison, and it appeared he died of influenza. He has left considerable property, chiefly in cheese and halfpence, buried in different parts of the garden. The new raven (I have a new one, but he is comparatively of weak intellect) administered to his effects, and turns up something every day. The last piece of *bijouterie* was a hammer of considerable size, supposed to have been stolen from a vindictive carpenter, who had been heard to speak darkly of vengeance down the mews."

Maclise on hearing the news sent to Forster a letter, and a pen-and-ink sketch, being the famous "Apotheosis." The second raven died in 1845, probably from "having indulged the same illicit taste for putty and paint, which had been fatal to his predecessor." Dickens says:—

> "Voracity killed him, as it did Scott's; he died unexpectedly by the kitchen fire. He kept his eye to the last upon the meat as it roasted, and suddenly turned over on his back with a sepulchral cry of '*Cuckoo!*'"

These ravens were of course the two "great originals" of which Grip in *Barnaby Rudge* was the "compound." There was a third raven at Gad's Hill, but he "gave no evidence of ever cultivating his mind." The novelist's remarkable partiality for ravens called forth at the time the preposterous rumour that "Dickens had gone raving (raven) mad."

Here Longfellow visited Dickens in 1841, and thus referred to his visit:—"I write this from Dickens's study, the focus from which so many luminous things have radiated. The raven croaks in the garden, and the ceaseless roar of London fills my ears."

Dickens lived longer at Devonshire Terrace than he did at any other of his London homes, and a great deal of his best work was done here, including *Master Humphrey's Clock* (I. *The Old Curiosity Shop*, II. *Barnaby Rudge*), *American Notes*, *Martin Chuzzlewit*, *A Christmas Carol*, *The*

Apotheosis of "Grip" the Raven. Drawn by D. Maclise, R.A.

Cricket on the Hearth, *Dombey and Son*, *The Haunted Man*, and *David Copperfield*. *The Battle of Life* was written at Geneva in 1846. All these were published from his twenty-eighth to his thirty-eighth year; and *Household Words*, his famous weekly popular serial of varied high-class literature, was determined upon here, the first number being issued on 30th March, 1850.

From Devonshire Terrace we pass along High Street, and turn into Devonshire Street, which leads into Harley Street, minutely described in *Little Dorrit* as the street wherein resided the great financier and "master-spirit" Mr. Merdle, who entertained "Bar, Bishop, and the Barnacle family" at the "Patriotic conference" recorded in the same work, in his noble mansion there, and he subsequently perishes "in the warm baths, in the neighbouring street"—as one may say—in the luxuriant style in which he had always lived.

Harley Street leads us into Oxford Street, and a pleasant ride outside an omnibus—which, as everybody knows, is the best way of seeing London—takes us to Hyde Park Place, a row of tall stately houses facing Hyde Park. Here at No. 5, (formerly Mr. Milner Gibson's town residence) Charles Dickens temporarily resided during the winter months of 1869, and occasionally until May 1870, during his readings at St. James's Hall, and while he was engaged on *Edwin Drood*, part of which was written here; this being illustrative of Dickens's power of concentrating his thoughts even near the rattle of a public thoroughfare. In a letter addressed to Mr. James T. Fields from this house, under date of 14th January, 1870, he says:—"We live here (opposite the Marble Arch) in a charming house until the 1st of June, and then return to Gad's. . . . I have a large room here with three fine windows over-looking the park—unsurpassable for airiness and cheerfulness."

A similar public conveyance takes us back to Morley's by way of Regent Street, about the middle of which, on the west side, is New Burlington Street, containing, at No. 8, the well-known publishing office of Messrs. Richard Bentley and Son, whose once celebrated magazine, *Bentley's Miscellany*, Dickens edited for a period of two years and two months, terminating, 1838, on his resignation of the editorship to Mr. W. Harrison Ainsworth; and we also pass lower down, at the bottom of Waterloo Place, that most select of clubs, "The Athenæum," at the corner of Pall Mall, of which Dickens was elected a member in 1838, and from which, on the 20th May, 1870, he wrote his last letter to his son, Mr. Alfred Tennyson Dickens, in Australia; and a tenderly loving letter it is, indicating the harmonious relations between father and son. It expresses the hope that the two (Alfred and "Plorn") "may become proprietors," and "aspire to the first positions in the colony without casting off the old connection," and thus concludes:—"From Mr. Bear I had the best accounts of you. I told him that they did not surprise me, for I had unbounded faith in you. For which take my love and blessing." Sad to say, a note to this (the last in the series of published letters) states:—"This letter did not reach Australia until after these two sons of Charles Dickens had heard, by telegraph, the news of their father's death."[3]

[3] Mr. Edward Bulwer Lytton Dickens, a son of the great Novelist, is a member of the New South Wales Parliament, having been elected in March 1889. "He stood as a Protectionist for the representation of Wilcannia, an extensive pastoral district in the western portion of the colony. His father, it will be remembered, was an ardent Free Trader, and could not be prevailed upon to enter the British Parliament on any terms, and occasionally said some severe things of our Legislative Assembly. His two sons, Alfred Tennyson and Edward Bulwer Lytton, emigrated to Australia some years ago, and became successful pastoralists."—*Yorkshire Daily Post*, March 1889. A subsequent account states that Mr. Edward Bulwer Lytton Dickens is about to retire, having been, he remarks, "out of pocket, out of brains, out of health, and out of temper,

At Morley's we refresh ourselves with Mr. Sam Weller's idea of a nice little dinner, consisting of "pair of fowls and a weal cutlet; French beans, taturs, tart and tidiness;" and then depart for Victoria Station, to take train by the London, Chatham and Dover Railway to Rochester.

The weather forecast issued by that most valuable institution, the Meteorological Office (established since Mr. Pickwick's days, in which doubtless as a scientist and traveller he would have taken great interest), was verified to the letter, and we had "thunder locally." On our way down Parliament Street, we pass Inigo Jones's once splendid Whitehall—now looking very insignificant as compared with its grand neighbours the Government Offices opposite—remembering Mr. Jingle's joke about Whitehall, which seems tc have been Dickens's first thought of "King Charles's head" —"Looking at Whitehall, Sir—fine place—little window—somebody else's head off there, eh, Sir?—he didn't keep a sharp look out enough either—eh, Sir, eh?"

We also pass "The Red Lion," No. 48, Parliament Street "at the corner of the very short street leading into Cannon Row," where David Copperfield ordered a glass of the very best ale—"The Genuine Stunning with a good head to it —at twopence half-penny the glass, but the landlord hesitate to draw it, and gave him a glass of some which he suspecte was *not* the "genuine stunning"; and the landlady comin into the bar returned his money, and gave him a "kiss th: was half-admiring and half-compassionate, but all woman' and good [he says], I'm sure."

---

by the pursuit of political glory."—*Pall Mall Gazette*, March 1891. I a since informed that Alfred is not a pastoralist, but in business, and tt Edward has not retired up to date.

The Horse-Guards' clock is the last noteworthy object, and reminds us that Mark Tapley noticed the time there, on the occasion of his last meeting with Mary Graham in St. James's Park, before starting for America. It also reminds us of Mr. Micawber's maxim, "Procrastination is the thief of time—collar him;"—a few minutes afterwards we are comfortably seated in the train, and can defy the storm, which overtakes us

"My magnificent order at the Public House" (*vide* "*David Copperfield*").

precisely in the manner described in *The Old Curiosity Shop*:—

"It had been gradually getting overcast, and now the sky was lark and lowering, save where the glory of the departing sun piled p masses of gold and burning fire, decaying embers of which leamed here and there through the black veil, and shone redly own upon the earth. The wind began to moan in hollow murmurs, s the sun went down, carrying glad day elsewhere; and a train of dull clouds coming up against it menaced thunder and lightning. Large drops of rain soon began to fall, and, as the storm clouds came sailing onward, others supplied the void they left behind, and spread over all the sky. Then was heard the low rumbling of distant thunder, then the lightning quivered, and then the darkness of an hour seemed to have gathered in an instant."

We pass Dulwich,—where Mr. Snodgrass and Emily Wardle were married,—a fact that recalls kindly recollections of Mr. Pickwick and his retirement there, as recorded in the closing pages of the *Pickwick Papers*, where he is described as "employing his leisure hours in arranging the memoranda which he afterwards presented to the secretary of the once famous club, or in hearing Sam Weller read aloud, with such remarks as suggested themselves to his mind, which never failed to afford Mr. Pickwick great amusement." He is subsequently described as "somewhat infirm now, but he retains all his former juvenility of spirit, and may still be frequently seen contemplating the pictures in the Dulwich Gallery, or enjoying a walk about the pleasant neighbourhood on a fine day."

Although it is but a short distance—under thirty miles—to Rochester, the journey seems tedious, as the "iron-horse" does not keep pace with the pleasurable feelings of eager expectation afloat in our minds on this our first visit to "Dickens-Land"; it is therefore with joyful steps that we leave the train, and, the storm having passed away, find ourselves in the cool of the summer evening on the platform of Strood and Rochester Bridge Station.

CHAPTER III.

ROCHESTER CITY.

"The silent High Street of Rochester is full of gables, with old beams and timbers carved into strange faces. It is oddly garnished with a queer old clock that projects over the pavement out of a grave red brick building, as if Time carried on business there, and hung out his sign."—*The Seven Poor Travellers.*

"The town was glad with morning light."—*The Old Curiosity Shop.*

MUDFOG, Our Town, Dullborough, the Market Town, and Cloisterham were the varied names that Charles Dickens bestowed upon the "ancient city" of Rochester. Every reader of his works knows how well he loved it in early youth, and how he returned to it with increased affection during the years of his ripened wisdom. Among the first pages of the first chapter of Forster's *Life* we find references to it:—"That childhood exaggerates what it sees, too, has he not tenderly told? How he thought that the Rochester High-street must be at least as wide as Regent Street which he afterwards discovered to be little better than a lane; how the public clock in it, supposed to be the finest clock in the world, turned out to be as moon-faced and weak a clock as a man's eyes ever saw; and how in its Town Hall, which had appeared to him once so glorious a structure that he had set it up in his mind as the model from which the genie of the Lamp built the palace for Aladdin, he had painfully to recognize a mere mean little heap of bricks, like a chapel gone demented. Yet, not so painfully either when second thoughts wisely came. 'Ah! who was I, [he says] that I should quarrel with the town for being changed to me, when I myself had come back, so changed, to it? All my early readings and early imaginations dated from this place, and I took them away so full of innocent construction and guileless belief, and I brought them back so worn and torn, so much the wiser and so much the worse!'"

It would occupy too much space in this narrative to adequately give even a brief historical sketch of the City of Rochester, which is twenty-nine miles from London, situated on the river Medway, and stands on the chalk on the margin of the London basin; but we think lovers of Dickens will not object to a recapitulation of a few of the most noteworthy circumstances which have happened here, and which are not touched upon in the chapters relating to the Castle and Cathedral.

According to the eminent local antiquary, Mr. Roach Smith, F.S.A., the name of the city has been thus evolved:—"The ceastre or chester is a Saxon affix to the Romano-British (DU)RO. The first two letters being dropped in sound, it became Duro or Dro, and then ROchester, and it was the Roman station Durobrovis." The ancient Britons called it "Dur-brif," and the Saxons "Hrofe-ceastre"—Horf's castle, of which appellation some people think Rochester is a corruption.

Rochester is a place of great antiquity, and so far back as A.D. 600 it seems to have been a walled city. Remains o the mediæval Wall exist in very perfect condition, at the back of the Eagle Inn in High Street, and in other parts of the city. In 676 Rochester was plundered by Ethelred, King of Mercia; and in 884 the Danes sailed up the Medway and besieged it, but were effectually repulsed by King Alfred. About 930, when three Mints were established there by Athelstan, it had grown to be one of the principal ports of the kingdom. William the Conqueror gave the town to his half-brother Odo, Bishop of Bayeux. Fires in 1130 and 1137 nearly destroyed it.

Not a few royal and distinguished personages have visited Rochester on various occasions, among others Henry VIII., who came there in 1522, accompanied by the Emperor Charles V. Queen Elizabeth came in 1573, when she stayed five days, and attended the Cathedral service on Sunday. She came again in 1583, with the Duke of Anjou, and showed him her "mighty ships of war lying at Chatham." King James I. also visited the city in 1604 and 1606. On the latter occasion His Majesty, who was accompanied by Christian IV., King of Denmark, attended the Cathedral, and afterwards inspected the Navy. Charles II. paid it a visit just before the restoration in 1660, and again subsequently. It is believed that on both occasions he stayed at Restoration House (the "Satis House" of *Great Expectations*) hereafter referred to. Mr. Richard Head presented His Majesty with a silver ewer and basin on the occasion of the restoration. James II. came down to the quiet old city December 19th, 1688, and sojourned with Sir Richard Head for a week at his house (now No. 46 High Street), from whence he ignominously escaped to France by a smack moored off Sheerness. Mr. Stephen T. Aveling mentioned to us that "it is curious that Charles the Second 'came to his own' in Rochester, and that James the Second 'skedaddled' from the same city."[1] Her Majesty when Princess Victoria stayed at the Bull Inn in 1836 for a night with her mother, the Duchess of Kent, on their way from Dover to London. It was a very tempestuous night, some of the balustrades of Rochester Bridge having been blown into the river, and the Royal Princess was advised not to attempt to cross the bridge.

"On the last day of June 1667 (says Mr. W. Brenchley Rye in his pleasant *Visits to Rochester*), Mr. Samuel Pepys, after examining the defences at Chatham shortly after the disastrous expedition by the Dutch up the Medway, walked into Rochester Cathedral, but he had no mind to stay to the service, . . . 'afterwards strolled into the fields, a fine walk, and there saw Sir F. Clarke's house (Restoration House), which is a pretty seat, and into the Cherry Garden, and here met with a young, plain, silly shopkeeper and his wife, a pretty young woman, and I did kiss her!'" David Garrick was living at Rochester in 1737, for the purpose of receiving instruction in mathematics, etc., from Mr. Colson. In 1742, Hogarth visited the city, in that celebrated peregrination with his four friends, and played hop-scotch in the court-yard of the Guildhall. Dr. Johnson came here in 1783, and "returned to London by water in a common boat, landing at Billingsgate."

The city formerly possessed many ancient charters and

[1] Mr. Aveling subsequently informed me that the vessel in which the king took his departure continued to be used in the Royal Navy for many years as a lighter—its name being altered to the "Royal Escape." Afterwards it was used as a watch-vessel in the Coastguard service at Chatham, and was eventually broken up at Sheerness Dockyard so recently as 1876.

privileges granted to the citizens, but these were superseded by the Municipal Corporations Act of 1835.

The Guildhall, " marked by a gilt ship aloft,"—" where the mayor and corporation assemble together in solemn council for the public weal,"—is "a substantial and very suitable structure of brick, supported by stone columns in the Doric order," and was erected in 1687. It has several fine portraits by Sir Godfrey Kneller and other eminent painters, including those of King William III., Queen Anne, Sir Cloudesley Shovell, Richard Watts, M.P., and others. The Corporation also possess many interesting and valuable city regalia, namely, a large silver-gilt mace (1661), silver loving-cup (1719), silver oar and silver-gilt ornaments (typical of the Admiralty jurisdiction of the Corporation) (1748), two small maces of silver (1767), sword (1871—the Mayor being Constable of the Castle), and chain and badges of gold and enamel (1875), the last-mentioned commemorating many historical incidents connected with the city.

Emerging from the railway station of the London, Chatham and Dover Company at Strood, a drive of a few minutes (over the bridge) brings us to the first object of our pilgrimage, the "Bull Inn,"—we beg pardon, the "Royal Victoria and Bull Hotel,"—in High Street, Rochester, which was visited by Mr. Pickwick, Mr. Tupman, Mr. Snodgrass, Mr. Winkle, and their newly-made friend, Mr. Jingle, on the 13th May, 1827. Our cabman is so satisfied with his fare (" only a bob's worth "), that he does not, as one of his predecessors did, on a very remarkable occasion, "fling the money on the pavement, and request in figurative terms to be allowed the pleasure of fighting us for the amount," which circumstance we take to be an improving sign of the times.

Changed in name, but not in condition, it seems scarcely possible that we stand under the gateway of the charming old inn that we have known from our boyhood, when first we read our *Pickwick*, what time the two green leaves of *Martin Chuzzlewit* were putting forth monthly, and when the name of Charles Dickens, although familiar, had not become the "household word" to us, and to the world, that it is now.

We look round for evidence—"Good house, nice beds"—"(vide *Pickwick*)" appear on the two sign-boards fixed on either side of the entrance-gate. Only then are we quite sure our driver has not made a mistake and taken us to "Wright's next door," which every reader of *Pickwick* knows, on the authority of Mr. Jingle, "was dear—very dear --half a crown in the bill if you look at the waiter—charge you more if you dine out at a friend's than they would if you dined in the coffee-room—rum fellows—very."

Haunches of venison, saddles of mutton, ribs of beef, York hams, fowls and ducks, hang over our heads in the capacious covered gateway; cold viands are seen in a glass cupboard opposite, and silently promise that some good fare, like that which regaled Mr. Pickwick and his friends, is still to be found at the Bull. In the distance is seen the large old-fashioned coach-yard, surrounded by odd buildings, which on market days (Tuesdays) is crowded with all sorts of vehicles ancient and modern. On our right is the kitchen, "brilliant with glowing coals and rows of shining copper lying well open to view."

By the kindness of Mr. Richard Prall, the town-clerk, beds have been secured for us, and the landlord meets us at the door with a hearty welcome. We are conducted to our rooms on the second floor looking front, on reaching which a strange feeling takes possession of us. Surely we have been here before? Not a bit of it! But the bedrooms are nevertheless familiar to us; we see it all in a minute—the writer's apartment is Mr. Tupman's, and his friend's is Mr. Winkle's!

"Winkle's bedroom is inside mine," said Mr. Tupman, after that delightful dinner of "soles, broiled fowl, and mushrooms," in the private sitting-room at the Bull, when all the other Pickwickians had, "after the cosy couple of hours succeeding dinner, more or less succumbed to the somniferous influence which the wine had exerted over them," and he and Mr. Jingle alone remained wakeful, and were discussing the idea of attending the forthcoming ball in the evening.

It is an unexpected and pleasant coincidence that we are located in these two rooms, and altogether a good omen for our tramp generally. They are numbered 13 and 19, and the reason why the numbers are not consecutive is because 19 (Mr. Winkle's room) is also approached by a back staircase. Mr. Pickwick's room, as befitted his years and his dignity as G.C.M.P.C., is a larger room, and is number 17. They are all comfortable chambers, with "nice beds."

The principal staircase of the Bull, which is almost wid enough to drive a carriage and four up it, remains exactl as it was in Mr. Pickwick's days, as described by Dickens an delineated by Seymour. We could almost fancy we witnesse the memorable scene depicted in the illustration, where th irascible Dr. Slammer confronts the imperturbable Jingl The staircase has on its walls a large number of pictures an engravings, some curious and valuable, a few of which are of purely local interest. A series of oil paintings represent the costumes of all nations. There is a copy of "The Empty Chair," from the drawing of Mr. Luke Fildes, R.A., and also one of the scarce proof lithographs of "Dickens as Captain Bobadil," after the painting by C. R. Leslie, R.A.

Mr. Lawrence informed us that some years ago "The Owl Club" held its meetings at the Bull—a social club, reminding us strongly of one of the early papers in *Bentley's Miscellany*, illustrated by George Cruikshank, entitled the "Harmonious Owls," which has recently been reprinted in the collection called *Old Miscellany Days*, in which paper, by the bye, are several names from Dickens.

In one of the cheerful private sitting-rooms, of which there are many, we find a portrait of Dickens that is new to us. Never have we seen one that so vividly reproduced the novelist as one of us saw him, and heard him read, in the Town Hall at Birmingham, on the 10th of May, 1866. It is a vignette photograph by Watkins, coloured by Mr. J. Hopper, a local artist, representing the face of the novelist in full, wearing afternoon dress—black coat, and white shirt-front, with gold studs—the attitude being perfectly natural and unconstrained, and a pleasant calm upon the otherwise firm features. The high forehead is surmounted by the well-remembered single curl of brown hair, the sole survival of those profuse locks which grace Maclise's beautiful portrait. The bright blue eyes, with the light reflected on the pupils like diamonds, seem to follow one in every direction. The lines, of course, are marked, but not too strongly; and the faint hectic flush which was apparent in later years—notably when we saw him again in Birmingham in 1869—shows signs of development.

The beard hides the neck, and the white collar is conspicuous. Altogether it is one of the most successful portraits we remember to have seen. As witness of its popularity locally, we may mention that we saw copies of it at Major Budden's at Gad's Hill, at the Mitre Hotel, Chatham, and at the Leather Bottle Inn, Cobham. We are also informed that Mr. Henry Irving gave a good sum for a copy, in the spring of last year. Mr. Lawrence, our host, by good fortune, happening to possess a duplicate, kindly allows us the opportunity of purchasing it ("portable property" as Mr. Wemmick remarks), as an addition to our Dickens collection which it adorns. "Beautiful!" "Splendid!" "Dickens to the life!" are the comments of friends to whom we show it, who personally knew, or remembered, the original.

Here is the ball-room, entered from the first-floor landing of the principal staircase, and the card-room adjoining, precisely as it was in Mr. Pickwick's days:—

> "It was a long room with crimson-covered benches, and wax candles in glass chandeliers. The musicians were confined in an elevated den, and quadrilles were being systematically got through by two or three sets of dancers. Two card-tables were made up in the adjoining card-room, and two pair of old ladies, and a corresponding number of old gentlemen, were executing whist therein."

A very little stretch of the imagination carries us back sixty years, and, *presto!* the ball-room stands before us, with the wax candles lighted, and the room filled with the *élite* of Chatham and Rochester society, who, acting on the principle of "that general benevolence which was one of the leading features of the Pickwickian theory," had given their support to that "ball for the benefit of a charity," then being held there, and which was attended by Mr. Tracy Tupman, in his new dress-coat with the P. C. button and bust of Mr. Pickwick in the centre, and by Mr. Jingle, in the borrowed garments of the same nature belonging to Mr. Winkle.

"P. C.," said the stranger.—"Queer set out—old fellow's likeness and 'P. C.'—What does 'P. C.' stand for? 'Peculiar Coat,' eh?" Imagine the "rising indignation" and impatience

of Mr. Tupman, as with "great importance" he explains the mystic device!

Everybody remembers how, declining the usual introduction, the two entered the ball-room *incog.*, as "Gentlemen from London—distinguished foreigners—anything;" how Mr. Jingle said in reply to Mr. Tupman's remark, "Wait a minute—fun presently—nobs not come yet—queer place—Dock-yard people of upper rank don't know Dock-yard people of lower rank—Dock-yard people of lower rank don't know small gentry—small gentry don't know tradespeople—Commissioner don't know anybody."

The "man at the door,"—the local M.C.,—announces the arrivals.

"Sir Thomas Clubber, Lady Clubber, and the Miss Clubbers!" "Commissioner—head of the yard—great man—remarkably great man," whispers the stranger in Mr. Tupman's ear.

"Colonel Bulder, Mrs. Colonel Bulder, and Miss Bulder," are announced. "Head of the garrison," says Mr. Jingle. "They exchanged snuff-boxes [how old-fashioned it appears to us who don't take snuff], and looked very much like a pair of Alexander Selkirks—Monarchs of all they surveyed."

More arrivals are announced, and dancing begins in earnest; but the most interesting one to us is Dr. Slammer—"a little fat man, with a ring of upright black hair round his head, and an extensive bald plain on the top of it—Dr. Slammer, surgeon to the 97th, who is agreeable to everybody, especially to the Widow Budger.—'Lots of money—old girl—pompous doctor—not a bad idea—good fun,' says the stranger. 'I'll dance with her—cut out the doctor—here goes.'" Then comes the flirtation, the dancing, the negus and biscuits, the coquetting, the leading of Mrs. Budger to her carriage. The volcano bursts with terrific energy. . . .

"'You—you're a shuffler, sir,' gasps the furious doctor, 'a poltroon—a coward—a liar—a—a—will nothing induce you to give me your card, sir?'" and in the morning comes the challenge to the duel. It all passes before our delighted mental vision, as we picture the circumstances recorded in the beloved *Pickwick* of our youth upwards.

Here also is the bar, just opposite the coffee-room, where the "Tickets for the Ball" were purchased by Mr. Tupman for himself and Mr. Jingle at "half a guinea each" (Mr. Jingle having won the toss), and where Dr. Slammer's friend subsequently made inquiry for "the owner of the coat, who arrived here, with three gentlemen, yesterday afternoon." We find it to be a very cosy and comfortable bar-room too, wherein we subsequently enjoy many a social pipe and pleasant chat with its friendly frequenters, reminding us of the old tavern-life as described in Dr. Johnson's days.

The coffee-room of the Bull, in which we take our supper, remains unaltered since the days of the Pickwickians. It is on the left-hand side as we enter the hotel from the covered gateway—not very large, but warm and comfortable, with three windows looking into the High Street. Many scenes in the novels have taken place in this memorable apartment—in fact, it is quite historical, from a Dickensian point of view.

Here it was that the challenge to the duel from Dr. Slammer to Mr. Winkle was delivered; and, when Mr. Winkle appeared, in response to the call of the boots, that "a gentleman in the coffee-room" wanted to see him, and would not detain him a moment, but would take no denial, "an old woman and a couple of waiters were cleaning the coffee-room, and an officer in undress uniform was looking out of the window." Here also the Pickwickians assembled on that eventful morning when the party set out, three in a chaise and one on horseback, for Dingley Dell, and encountered such dire mishaps. "Mr. Pickwick had made his preliminary arrangements, and was looking over the coffee-room blinds at the passengers in the High Street, when the waiter entered, and announced that the chaise was ready—an announcement which the vehicle itself confirmed, by forthwith appearing before the coffee-room blinds aforesaid." Subsequently, as they prepare to start, "'Wo-o!' cried Mr. Pickwick, as the tall quadruped evinced a decided inclination to back into the coffee-room window."

It is highly probable that the descriptions of "the little town of Great Winglebury," and "the Winglebury Arms," in "The Great Winglebury Duel" of the *Sketches by Boz*, one of the earliest works of the novelist, refer to the city of Rochester and the Bull Inn, for they fit in very well in many respects, although it *is* stated therein that "the little town of Great Winglebury is exactly forty-two miles and three-quarters from Hyde Park Corner."

The Blue Boar mentioned in *Great Expectations*—one of the most original, touching, and dramatic of Dickens's novels—is indubitably the Bull Hotel. Although there is an inn in High Street, Rochester, called the Blue Boar, its description does not at all correspond with the text. We find several instances like this, where, probably for purposes of concealment, the real identity of places and persons is masked.

Our first introduction to the Blue Boar is on the occasion of Pip's being bound apprentice to Joe Gargery, the premium for whom was paid out of the twenty-five guineas given to Pip by Miss Havisham. Pip's sister "became so excited by the twenty-five guineas, that nothing would serve but we must have a dinner out of that windfall at the Blue Boar, and that Pumblechook must go over in his chaise cart, and bring the Hubbles and Mr. Wopsle." The dinner is duly disposed of, and although poor Pip was frequently enjoined to "enjoy himself," he certainly failed to do so on this occasion. "Among the festivities indulged in rather late in the evening," says Pip, "Mr. Wopsle gave us *Collins's Ode*, and 'threw his blood-stain'd sword in thunder down,' with such effect, that a waiter came in and said 'The Commercials underneath sent up their compliments, and it wasn't the Tumblers' Arms!'" From which we gather that the said dinner took place in a private sitting-room (No. 3) over the commercial room, on the opposite side of the gateway to the coffee-room.

It will be remembered that on Pip's attaining "the second tage of his expectations," Pumblechook had grown very bsequious and fawning to him—pressed him to take reeshment, as who should say, "But, my dear young friend, ou must be hungry, you must be exhausted. Be seated. Here is a chicken had round from the Boar, here is a tongue ad round from the Boar, here's one or two little things had ound from the Boar that I hope you may not despise. But do I,' said Mr. Pumblechook, getting up again the noment after he had sat down, 'see afore me him as I ever orted with in his times of happy infancy? And may I—*ay* I—?' This 'May I?' meant might he shake hands? consented, and he was fervent, and then sat down again."

Returning to the coffee-room, we discover it was the entical apartment in which the unexpected and very peculiar eeting took place between Pip and "the spider," Bentley rummle, "the sulky and red-looking young man, of a heavy der of architecture," both "Finches of the Grove," and als for the hand of Estella. Each stands shoulder to oulder against the fire-place, and, but for Pip's forbearance, explosion must have taken place.

Through the same coffee-room windows, poor Pip looks

under the reverses of his great expectations in consequence of the discovery and subsequent death of his patron. The "servile Pumblechook," who appears here uninvited, again changes his manner and conduct, becoming ostentatiously compassionate and forgiving, as he had been meanly servile in the time of Pip's new prosperity, thus:—"'Young man, I am sorry to see you brought low, but what else could be expected! what else could be expected! . . . This is him . . . as I have rode in my shay-cart; this is him as I have seen brought up by hand; this is him untoe the sister of which I was uncle by marriage, as her name was Georgiana M'ria from her own mother, let him deny it if he can.' . ."

Dickens takes leave of the Blue Boar, in the last chapter of the work, in these words:—

"The tidings of my high fortunes having had a heavy fall, had go down to my native place and its neighbourhood, before I got there I found the Blue Boar in possession of the intelligence, and I foun that it made a great change in the Boar's demeanour. Whereas th Boar had cultivated my good opinion with warm assiduity when was coming into property, the Boar was exceedingly cool on th subject now that I was going out of property.

"It was evening when I arrived, much fatigued by the journey had so often made so easily. The Boar could not put me into m usual bedroom, which was engaged,—probably by some one who ha expectations,—and could only assign me a very indifferent chamb among the pigeons and post-chaises up the yard. But, I had sound a sleep in that lodging as in the most superior accommodati the Boar could have given me, and the quality of my dreams w about the same as in the best bedroom."

The visitors' book in the coffee-room, at the Bull— never shall call it "The Royal Victoria and Bull Hotel" abounds with complimentary remarks on the hospitable tre ment received by its guests; and there are several poetical effusions, inspired by the classic nature of "Dickens-Land." One of these, under date of the 18th September, 1887, is worth recording:—

"The man who knows his Dickens as he should,
Enjoys a double pleasure in this place;
He loves to walk its ancient streets, and trace
The scenes where Dickens' characters have stood.
He reads *The Mystery of Edwin Drood*
In Jasper's Gatehouse, and, with Tope as guide,
Explores the old cathedral, Durdles' pride;
Descends into the Crypt, and even would
Ascend the Tower by moonlight, thence to see
Fair Cloisterham reposing at his feet;
And passing out, he almost hopes to meet
Crisparkle and the white-haired Datchery.
The gifted writer 'sleeps among our best
And noblest' in our Minster of the West;
Yet still he lives in this, his favourite scene,
Which for all time shall keep his memory green."

We follow Mr. Pickwick's example as regards early rising, nd, taking a turn before breakfast, find ourselves on Rochester ridge. Nature has not much changed since the memorable isit of that "truly great man," who in the original announce- ient of *The Pickwick Papers* is stated with his companions have "fearlessly crossed the turbid Medway in an open oat;" but the march of civilization has effaced the old idge, and lo! three bridges stand in the place thereof. The eautiful stone structure (temp. Edward III.) which Mr. ickwick leant over, having become unsuitable, was blown up by the Royal Engineers in 1856, and a handsome iron bridge erected in its place. The débris was removed by Mr. J. H. Ball, the contractor, who presented Dickens with one of the balustrades, others having been utilized to form the coping of the embankment of the esplanade under the castle walls. The iron bridge was built by Messrs. Fox and Henderson, the foundations being laid in 1850. The machinery constituting "the swing-bridge or open ship canal (fifty feet

wide) at the Strood end is very beautiful; the entire weigl to be moved is two hundred tons, yet the bridge is readil swung by two men at a capstan." So says one of the Guic Books, but as a matter of fact we find that it is not now usec The other two bridges (useful, but certainly not ornamentε belong to the respective railway companies which ha systems through Rochester, and absolutely shut out eve prospect below stream. What *would* Mr. Pickwick say, if I spirit ever visited the ancient city? Nevertheless, we realize for the first time, with all its freshness and beauty (although perhaps a little marred by the smoke of the lime-kilns, and by the "Medway coal trade," in which it will be remembered Mr. Micawber was temporarily interested, and which "he came down to see"), the charm of the prospect which Dickens describes, and which Mr. Pickwick saw, in the opening of the fifth chapter of the immortal *Posthumous Papers*:—

"Bright and pleasant was the sky, balmy the air, and beautiful the appearance of every object around, as Mr. Pickwick leant over the balustrades of Rochester Bridge, contemplating nature, and waiting for breakfast. The scene was indeed one, which might well have charmed a far less reflective mind, than that to which it was presented.

"On the left of the spectator lay the ruined wall, broken in many places, and in some, overhanging the narrow beach below in rude and heavy masses. Huge knots of sea-weed hung upon the jagged and pointed stones, trembling in every breath of wind; and the green ivy clung mournfully round the dark and ruined battlements. Behind it rose the ancient castle, its towers roofless, and its massive walls crumbling away, but telling us proudly of its old might and strength, as when, seven hundred years ago, it rang with the clash of arms, or resounded with the noise of feasting and revelry. On either side, the banks of the Medway, covered with corn-fields and pastures, with here and there a windmill, or a distant church, stretched away as far as the eye could see, presenting a rich and varied landscape, rendered more beautiful by the changing shadows which passed swiftly across it, as the thin and half-formed clouds skimmed away in the light of the morning sun. The river, reflecting the clear blue of the sky, glistened and sparkled as it flowed noiselessly on; and the oars of the fishermen dipped into the water with a clear and liquid sound, as their heavy but picturesque boats glided slowly down the stream."

It was over the same old bridge that poor Pip was pursued by that "unlimited miscreant" Trabb's boy in the days of his "great expectations." He says:—

"Words cannot state the amount of aggravation and injury wreaked upon me by Trabb's boy, when, passing abreast of me, he pulled up his shirt-collar, twined his side hair, stuck an arm akimbo, and smirked extravagantly by, wriggling his elbows and body, and drawling to his attendants: 'Don't know yah; don't know yah, 'pon my soul, don't know yah!' The disgrace [continues Pip] attendant on his immediately afterwards taking to crowing and pursuing me across the bridge with crows, as from an exceedingly dejected fowl who had known me when I was a blacksmith, culminated the disgrace with which I left the town, and was, so to speak, ejected by it into the open country."

There is generally a stiff breeze blowing on the bridge, and the fact may probably have suggested to the artist the positions of the characters in the river scene, one of the plates of *Edwin Drood*, where Mr. Crisparkle is holding his hat on with much tenacity. One other reference to the bridge occurs in the *Seven Poor Travellers*, where Richard Doubledick, in the year 1799, "limped over the bridge here with half a shoe to his dusty foot on his way to Chatham."

After a Pickwickian breakfast in the coffee-room of "broiled ham, eggs, tea, coffee, and sundries," we take a stroll up the High Street. We do not know what the feelings of other pilgrims in "Dickens-Land" may have been on the occasion of a first visit, but we are quite sure that to us it is a perfect revelation to ramble along this quaint street of "the ancient city," returning by way of Star Hill through the Vines, all crowded with associations of Charles Dickens. *Pickwick*, *Great Expectations*, *Edwin Drood*, and many of the minor works of the eminent novelist, had never before appeared so clear to us—they acquire new significance. The air is full of Dickens. At every corner, and almost at the door of every house, we half expect to be met by one or other of the characters who will claim acquaintance with us as their friends or admirers. We are simply delighted, and never tire of repeating our experience in the pleasant summer days of our week's tramp in "Dickens-Land."

Starting from the Bull, and walking along the somewhat arrow but picturesque street towards Chatham,—"the streets f Cloisterham city are little more than one narrow street by hich you get into it and get out of it: the rest being mostly disappointing yards with pumps in them and no thoroughfare—exception made of the Cathedral close, and a paved Quaker settlement, in color and general conformation very like a Quakeress's bonnet, up in a shady corner,"—we pass in

succession the Guildhall, the City Clock, Richard Watts's Charity, the College Gate (Jasper's Gatehouse), Eastgate House (the Nuns' House), and, nearly opposite it, the residence of Mr. Sapsea, which, as we ourselves discover, was also the residence of "Uncle Pumblechook." The latter buildings are about a quarter of a mile from Rochester Bridge, and are splendid examples of sixteenth-century architecture, with carved oaken-timbered fronts and gables and latticed bay-windows. Eastgate House—the "Nuns' House" of *Edwin Drood,* described as "a venerable brick edifice, whose

present appellation is doubtless derived from the legend of its conventual uses"—is especially beautiful, and its "resplendent brass plate on the trim gate" is still so "shining and staring." The date, 1591, is on one of the inside beams, and the fine old place abounds with quaint cosy rooms with carved oak mantel-pieces, and plaster enrichments to the ceilings, as well as mysterious back staircases and means of exit by secret passages. Charles II. is said to have been entertained here by Colonel Gibbons, the then owner, when he visited Chatham and inspected the *Royal George;* but this has been recently disputed. For many years during this century, the house has been occupied as a Ladies' School,

and the old pianos used for practice by the pupils are there still, the keys being worn into holes. We wonder whether Rosa Bud and Helena Landless ever played on them! Looking round, we half expect to witness the famous courting scene in *Edwin Drood*, and afterwards "the matronly Tishe to heave in sight, rustling through the room like the legendary ghost of a dowager in silken skirts, [with her] 'I trust I disturl no one; but there *was* a paper-knife—Oh, thank you, I am sure!'" An excellent local institution, called "The Rochester Men's Institute," has its home here. The house has been immortalized by Mr. Luke Fildes in one of the illustrations to *Edwin Drood* ("Good-bye, Rosebud, darling!"), where, in the front garden, the girls are cordially embracing their charming school-fellow, and Miss Twinkleton looks on approvingly, but perhaps regretfully, at the possible non-return of some of the young ladies. Mrs. Tisher is saluting one of the girls. There is a gate opening into the street, with the lamp over it kept in position by an iron bracket, just as it is now, heaps of ladies' luggage are scattered about, which the housemaid and the coachman are removing to the car outside; and one pretty girl stands in the gateway waving a farewell to the others with her handkerchief.

We feel morally certain that Eastgate House is also the prototype of Westgate House in the *Pickwick Papers*, although, for the purposes of the story, it is therein located at Bury St. Edmund's. The wall surrounding the garden is about seven feet high, and a drop from it into the garden would be uncommonly suggestive of the scene which took place between Sam Weller and his master in the sixteenth chapter, on the occasion of the supposed intended elopement of one of the young ladies of Miss Tomkins's Establishment—which also had the "name on a brass plate on a gate"—with Mr. Charles FitzMarshall, *alias* Mr. Alfred Jingle. The very tree which Mr. Pickwick "considered a very dangerous neighbour in a thunderstorm" is there still—a pretty acacia.

The house opposite Eastgate House was of course Mr. Sapsea's dwelling—"Mr. Sapsea's premises are in the High

Street over against the Nuns' House. They are of about the period of the Nuns' House, irregularly modernized here and there." A carved wooden figure of Mr. Sapsea's father in his rostrum as an auctioneer, with hammer poised in hand, and a

Mr. Sapsea's House.

countenance expressive of "Going—going—gone!" was man years ago fixed over a house (now the Savings Bank) in S Margaret's, Rochester, and was a regular butt for practic jokes by the young officers of the period, although they nev succeeded in their attempts to pull it down. To us the house appears to be an older building than Eastgate House, with much carved oak and timber work about it, and in its prime must have been a most delightful residence. The lower part is now used as business premises, and from the fact that it contains the little drawers of a seedsman's shop, it answers very well to the description of Mr. Pumblechook's "eminently convenient and commodious premises"—indeed there is not a

Mr. Sapsea's Father.

little in common between the two characters. "Mr. Pumblechook's premises in the High Street of the market town [says Pip] were of a peppercorny and farinaceous character, as the premises of a corn chandler and seedsman should be. It appeared to me that he must be a very happy man indeed to have so many little drawers in his shop; and I wondered when I peeped into one or two of the lower tiers, and saw the tied-up brown paper packets inside, whether the flower seeds and bulbs ever wanted of a fine day to break out of those jails, and bloom." Part of these premises is used as a dwelling-house, and Mr. Apsley Kennette, the courteous assistant town-clerk, to whom we were indebted for much kind attention, has apartments on the upper floors of the old mansion, the views from which, looking into the ancient city, are very pretty. There is a good deal of oak panelling and plaster enrichment about the interior, restored by Mr. Kennette, who in the course of his renovations found an interesting wall fresco.

He has had painted most appropriately in gilt letters over the mantel-piece of his charming old panelled chamber of carved and polished oak (with its quaint bay-window looking into the street) the pathetic and sombre lines of Dante Gabriel Rossetti:—

"May not this ancient room thou sitt'st in dwell
In separate living souls for joy or pain;
Nay, all its corners may be painted plain,
Where Heaven shows pictures of some life spent well;
And may be stamped a memory all in vain
Upon the site of lidless eyes in Hell."

The beautiful residence in Maidstone Road, formerly Crow Lane, opposite the Vines, called Restoration House, is the "Satis House" of *Great Expectations*—"Miss Havisham's up-town." "Everybody for miles round had heard of Miss Havisham up-town as an immensely rich and grim lady, who lived in a large and dismal house barricaded against robbers, and who led a life of seclusion." There is a veritable Satis House as well, on the opposite side of the Vines alluded to elsewhere. Restoration House, now occupied by Mr. Stephen

Restoration House.

T. Aveling, is a picturesque old Elizabethan structure, partly covered with ivy, having fine oak staircases, floors, and wainscoted rooms. Charles II. lodged here in 1660, and he subsequently presented to his host, Sir Francis Clarke, several large tapestries, representing pastoral scenes, which the present owner kindly allowed us to see. The tapestry is said to have been made at Mortlake. It was the usual present from royalty in those days—just as Her present Majesty now gives an Indian shawl to a favoured subject. Like many houses o[f] its kind, it contains a secret staircase for escape during time[s] of political trouble.

Mr. Aveling very kindly placed at our disposal the manuscript of an interesting and "true ghost story" written b[y] him relating to Restoration House, which is introduced a[t] the end of this chapter.

Many names in Dickens's novels and tales appear to u[s] as old friends, over the shops and elsewhere in Rochester Looking through the list of Mayors of the city from 1654 t[o] 1887, we notice nearly twenty of the names as having bee[n] given by Dickens to his characters, viz. Robinson, Wad[e] Brooker, Clarke, Harris, Burgess, Head, Weller, Baily, Gordo[n] Parsons, Pordage, Sparks, Simmons, Batten, Saunder[s] Thomson, Edwards, and Budden. The name of Jaspe[r] also occurs as a tradesman several times in the city, but w[e] are informed that this is a recent introduction. In th[e] Cathedral burying-ground occur the names of Fanny Dorr[e] and Richard Pordage. Dartle, we were informed, is an ol[d] Rochester name.

The population of the "four towns" of Rochester, Stroo[d] Chatham, and New Brompton, at the census of 1891, wa[s] upwards of 85,000. The principal industries of Rochest[er] are lime and cement making, "the Medway coal trade," and boat and barge building.

Rochester is very well off for educational institutions. In addition to the Board schools, there is the King's (or Cathedral) Grammar School founded by Henry VIII., a handsome building in the Vines. The tuition fee commences at £15 per annum for boys under 12, and there is a reduction made when there are brothers. There are two or three annual competitive Scholarships tenable for a period of years, and there are also two Exhibitions of £60 a year to University College, Oxford. There is also Sir J. Williamson's Mathematical School in the High Street, founded in 1701, having an income of £1500 a year from endowments, and the teaching, which has a wide range, includes physical science. The fees are very small, commencing at about £5 per annum, and there are foundation Scholarships and "Aveling Scholarships" to the value of £20 per annum.

In addition to the famous Richard Watts's Charity, which is described in another chapter, the city possesses several other important charities, viz.:—St. Catherine's Charity on Star Hill, founded by Simon Potyn in 1316, which provides residences for sixteen aged females, with stipends varying from £24 to £28 each; St. Bartholomew's Hospital in New Road, which was founded in 1078 by Bishop Gundulph for the benefit of lepers returning from the Crusades (the present hospital was erected in 1858, and is supported by voluntary contributions); Sir John Hawkins's Hospital for decayed seamen in Chatham, founded in 1592, and provides for twelve inmates with their wives; and Sir John Hayward's Charity on the Common, founded in 1651, which provides an asylum for twelve poor and aged females, parishioners of St. Nicholas.

Not least noteworthy among the numerous objects of interest in the "ancient city" are the beautiful gardens belonging to several of the houses in the High Street, particularly those of Mr. Syms and Mr. Wildish. The fresh green turf, the profusion of flowers, and the rich growth of foliage and fruit, quite surprise and delight the stranger. Mr. Stephen T. Aveling's garden is a marvel of beauty to be seen in a town. "The Cloisterham gardens blush with ripening fruit."

Some of the old-fashioned cries of street hawkers, as "hot rolls," "herrings," "watercresses," and the like, similar to those in the London of Charles Dickens's early days, still survive at Rochester, and are very noticeable and quaint in the quiet morning.

As illustrative of the many changes which have been brought about by steam, even in the quiet old city o: Rochester, Mr. Syms called attention to the fact that fift years ago he could count twenty-eight windmills on th surrounding heights, but now there are scarcely a dozen t be seen.

In Rochester we heard frequent mention of "Gavelkind, one of the ancient customs of Kent, whereby the lands do no descend to the eldest son alone, but to the whole number c male children equally. Lambarde, the eminent lawyer an antiquary (born 1536), author of *A Perambulation of Kent* says:—"I gather by *Cornelius Tacitus*, and others, th the ancient Germans, (whose Offspring we be) suffered the lands to descend, not to their eldest Sonne alone, but to th

[1] "A Perambulation of Kent: Conteining the Description, Hystori and Customes of that Shire. Written in the yeere 1570 by Willia Lambarde of Lincoln's Inne Gent."

whole number of their male Children: and I finde in the 75th Chapter of *Canutus* Law (a King of this Realm before the Conquest), that after the death of the Father, his Heires should divide both his goods, and his lands amongst them. Now, for as much as all the next of the kinred did this inherit together, I conjecture, that therefore the land was called, either *Gavelkyn* in meaning, *Give all kyn*, because it was given to all the next in one line of kinred, or *Give all kynd*, that is, to all the male Children: for *kynd* in Dutch signifieth yet a male Childe." The learned historian suggests a second possible origin of this curious custom from the writ called "Gavelles," to recover "the rent and service arising out of these lands."

The remarkable custom of "Borough English," whereby the youngest son inherits the lands, also survives in some parts of the county of Kent.

Mr. Robert Langton has done good service by giving in his delightful book, *The Childhood and Youth of Charles Dickens*, an illustration by Mr. W. Hull, of the old Rochester Theatre, which formerly stood at the foot of Star Hill, and in which Jingle and Dismal Jemmy—"rum fellow—does the heavy business—no actor—strange man—all sorts of miseries—dismal Jemmy, we call him on the circuit"—were to play on the morrow after the duel. It exists no more, for the Conservative Association has its club-house and rooms on the site of the building. The theatre is referred to in *Edwin Drood*:—"Even its drooping and despondent little theatre has its poor strip of garden, receiving the foul fiend, when he ducks from its stage into the infernal regions, among scarlet beans or oyster-shells, according to the season of the year." And again in *The Uncommercial Traveller*, on

"Dullborough Town," when the beginning of the end had appeared:—

Old Rochester Theatre, Star Hill.

"It was To Let, and hopelessly so, for its old purposes; and the[r] had been no entertainment within its walls for a long time, except Panorama; and even that had been announced as 'pleasing instructive,' and I knew too well the fatal meaning and the lead[

import of those terrible expressions. No, there was no comfort in the Theatre. It was mysteriously gone, like my own youth. Unlike my own youth, it might be coming back some day; but there was little promise of it."

We did not stay at the Bull during the whole of our visit, comfortable lodgings in Victoria Street having been secured for us by the courtesy of Mr. Prall, the landlady of which, from her kindness and consideration for our comfort, we are pleased to recognize as a veritable "Mrs. Lirriper."

* * * * * *

Among many reminiscences of Charles Dickens obtained at Rochester, the following are the most noteworthy:—

We had an interesting chat with Mr. Franklin Homan, Auctioneer, Cabinet-maker, and Upholsterer of High Street, Rochester. Our informant did a good deal of work for Charles Dickens at Gad's Hill Place, and remarked "he was one of the nicest customers I ever met in my life—so thoroughly precise and methodical. If anything had to be done, he knew exactly what he wanted, and gave his instructions accordingly. He expected every one who served him to be equally exact and punctual."

The novelist wrote to Mr. Homan from America respecting the furnishing of two bedrooms, describing in detail how he wished them fitted up—one was maple, the other white with a red stripe. These rooms are referred to in another chapter. The curtains separating them from the dressing-rooms were ordered to be of Indian pattern chintz. When Dickens came home and saw them complete, he said, "It strikes me as if the room was about to have its hair cut,—but it's my fault, it must be altered;" so crimson damask curtains were substituted.

In the little billiard-room near the dining-room was a one-sided couch standing by the window, which did not seem to please the master of Gad's Hill Place. He said to Mr. Homan one day, "Whenever I see that couch, it makes me think the window is squinting." The result was that Mr. Homan had to make a window-seat instead.

On one occasion, when our informant was waiting in the dining-room for some orders from Miss Hogarth, he saw Dickens walking in the garden with a lady, to whom he was telling the story of how as a boy he longed to live in Gad's Hill Place, and determined to purchase it whenever he had an opportunity.

Mr. Homan mentioned that the act drop painted by Clarkson Stanfield, R.A., for *The Lighthouse* and the scene from *The Frozen Deep*, painted by the same artist, which adorned the hall at Gad's Hill Place, and which fetched such enormous sums at the sale, were technically the property of the purchaser of Tavistock House, but he said, "Perhaps you would like to have them, Mr. Dickens," and so they continued to be the property of the novelist.

The valuation for Probate was made by Mr. Homan, anc he subsequently sold for the executors the furniture anc other domestic effects at Gad's Hill Place. The art collectioı was sold by Messrs. Christie, Manson, and Woods. Ther was a very fine cellar of wine, which included some magnum of port of rare vintage. Mr. Homan purchased a few bottle and gave one to a friend, Dr. Tamplin of London, who ha been kind to his daughter. At a dinner-party some tim afterwards at the Doctor's, a connoisseur being present, th magnum in question was placed on the table, the guests bein unaware from whence it came. Reference was made to th choice quality of the wine. "Yes," said the connoisseur, "it *is* good—very fine. I never tasted the like before, except once at Gad's Hill Place."

Mr. Homan recollects seeing among the plate two oak cases which were not sold, containing the silver figures for dining-table emblematic of spring, summer, and autumn. These were the presents of a Liverpool admirer who wished to remain anonymous. The incident is alluded to in Forster's *Life*, the correspondent being described as "a self-raised man, attributing his prosperous career to what Dickens's writings had taught him at its outset of the wisdom of kindness and sympathy for others, and asking pardon for the liberty he took in hoping that he might be permitted to offer some acknowledgment of what not only had cheered and stimulated him through all his life, but had contributed so much to the success of it." The letter enclosed £500, but Dickens declined this, intimating to the writer that if he pleased to send him any small memorial in another form, he would be glad to receive it.

The funeral was conducted by Mr. Homan, who mentioned that Dickens's instructions in his Will were implicitly followed, as regards privacy and unostentation. It was an anxious time to him, in consequence of the changes which were made in the arrangements, the interment being first suggested to take place at St. Nicholas's Cemetery, then at Shorne, then at Rochester Cathedral, and finally at Westminster Abbey. The mourners, together with the remains, travelled early in the morning by South Eastern Railway from Higham Station to Charing Cross, where a procession, consisting of three mourning-coaches and a hearse, was quietly formed. There was neither show nor public demonstration of any kind. On reaching Westminster Abbey, about half-past nine o'clock, the procession was met by Dean Stanley in the Cloisters, who performed the funeral service. A journalist being by accident in the Abbey at the time of the funeral, Mr. Homan remarked that he became almost frantic when he heard who had just been buried, at having missed such an opportunity.

Mr. Homan possesses several souvenirs of Gad's Hill Place, presented to him by the family, including Charles Dickens's walking-stick, and photographs of the interior and exterior of the house and the châlet.

* * * * * *

We were courteously received by the Rev. Robert Whiston, M.A., who resides at the Old Palace, a beautiful seventeenth-century house, abounding with oak panelling and carving, on Boley Hill, bequeathed in 1674, by Mr. Richard Head, after the death of his wife, to the then Bishop of Rochester and his successors, who were "to hold the same so long as the church was governed by Protestant Bishops." This residence was sold by permission of the Ecclesiastical Commissioners, together with the mansion at Brinley, in order to help to pay for the new palace of Danbury in Essex.

Mr. Whiston was a friend of Charles Dickens, and is one of the oldest inhabitants of Rochester. He was formerly Head-Master of the Cathedral Grammar, or King's, School of Henry VIII., an office which he resigned in 1877. Many years previously, Mr. Whiston published *Cathedral Trusts and their Fulfilment*, which ran through several editions, and was immediately followed by his dismissal from his mastership, on the ground that he had published "false, scandalous and libellous" statements, and had libelled "the Chapter of Rochester and other Chapters, and also the Bishop." Much litigation followed—appeals to the Court of Chancery, the Court of Queen's Bench, and Doctors' Commons, which resulted in his replacement in office; and then a second dismissal, followed by his pleading his own cause for five days at Doctors' Commons against eminent counsel, and after three years of litigation he was fully reinstated in his office. The result at Rochester, for which Mr. Whiston contended, was "an increase of £19 for each of the twenty scholars, and of £35 for each of the four students, a total of £520 a year, and the restoration of the six bedesmen of the Cathedral, with £14 13*s.* 4*d.* a year each, who had disappeared since 1810, making altogether £608 a year." Reforms were effected at other cathedrals, and handsome testimonials—one from Australia—were presented to Mr. Whiston.

A characteristic paper, entitled "The History of a certain Grammar School," in No. 72 of *Household Words*, dated 9th August, 1851, gives a sketch of Mr. Whiston's labours, and of the reforms which he effected. He is thus referred to:—

"But the Reverend Adolphus Hardhead was not merely a scholar and a schoolmaster. He had fought his way against disadvantages, had gained a moderate independence by the fruits of early exertions and constant but by no means sordid economy; and, while disinterested enough to undervalue abundance, was too wise not to know the value of money. He was an undoubted financialist, and never gave a farthing without doing real good, because he always ascertained the purpose and probable effect of his charity beforehand. While he cautiously shunned the idle and undeserving, he would work like a slave, with and for those who would work for themselves; and he would smooth the way for those who had in the first instance been their own pioneers, and would help a man who had once been successful, to attain a yet greater success."

Anthony Trollope, in *The Warden*, also thus refers to this gentleman :—"The struggles of Mr. Whiston have met with sympathy and support. Men are beginning to say that these things must be looked into."

Punch has also immortalized Mr. Whiston, for in the issue of 29th January, 1853, there is a burlesque account with designs of "A stained glass window for Rochester Cathedral.' The design is divided into compartments; each containing a representation in the mediæval fashion of a "Fytte" in "Ye Gestes of Maister Whyston ye Confessour."

Mr. Whiston had dined at Gad's Hill several times, and said that nothing could be more charming than Dickens's powers as a host. Some years after his death, by a fortunate circumstance, a large parcel of letters, written by the novelist came into the hands of Mr. Whiston, who had the pleasure of handing them to Miss Hogarth and Miss Dickens, by whom they were published in the collection of letters of Charles Dickens.

* * * * * *

Thomas Millen of Rochester informed us that he knew Charles Dickens. His (Millen's) father was a hop-farme and about the years 1864-5 lived at Bridgewood House, o the main road from Rochester to Maidstone. One afternoc in the autumn, Dickens, accompanied by Miss Hogarth an his daughters, Mary and Kate, drove along the road, an stopped to admire a pear tree which was covered with rip fruit. Millen happened to be in the garden at the tim and while noticing the carriage, Dickens spoke to him, ar referred to the very fine fruit. Millen said, "Will you ha

me, sir?" to which Dickens replied, "Thank you, you are
ery good, I will." He gave him some pears and some roses.
ickens then said, "You have not the pleasure of knowing me,
d I have not the pleasure of knowing you. I am Charles
ickens; and when you pass Gad's Hill, I shall take it
a favour if you will look in and see my place." Millen
plied, "I feel it to be a great honour to speak to you, sir.
have read most of your works, and I think *David Copper-
ld* is the master-piece. I hope to avail myself of your kind
vitation some day." Dickens laughed, wished Millen
Good-day," and the carriage drove on towards Maidstone.

"Some little time after," said Millen, "I was going to visit
uncle at Gravesend, and drove over with a one-horse trap
way of Gad's Hill. As I came near the place, I saw Mr.
ickens in the road. He said, 'So you are here,' and I
entioned where I was going. He took me in, and we went
rough the tunnel, and by the cedars, to the châlet, which
ood in the shrubbery in front of the house. He showed me
s work there—a manuscript on the table, and also some
oofs. They were part of *Our Mutual Friend*, which was
en appearing in monthly numbers; and on that morning
proof of one of the illustrations had arrived from Mr.
arcus Stone. It was the one in which 'Miss Wren fixes
r idea.' I was then about sixteen or seventeen, and
ckens said, 'You are setting out in life; mind *you* always
your idea.' He asked me what I was going to be, and I
d a farmer. He said, 'Better be that than an author or
et;' and after I had had two glasses of wine, he bade me
ood-bye.'"

* * * * * *

We were kindly favoured with an interview by the Misses

Drage, of No. 1 Minor Canon Row, daughters of the late Rev. W. H. Drage, who was Curate of St. Mary's Church, Chatham, from 1820 to 1828, and lived during that time in apartments at No. 3 Ordnance Terrace, next door to the Dickens family. Afterwards their father was Vicar of St. Margaret's, Rochester, for many years, and resided in their present home. About the year 1850, the Vicar, being interested in the daughter of one of his parishioners, whom he was anxious to get admitted into a public institution in London—a penitentiary or something of the kind—wrote to Miss (now the Baroness) Burdett Coutts, who was a patroness or founder, or who occupied some position of influence in connection therewith. In answer to the reverend gentleman's application, a letter was received from Charles Dickens, then residing at Devonshire Terrace, who appeared to be associated with Miss Burdett Coutts in the management of the institution, proposing to call at Minor Canon Row on a certain day and hour. The letter then concluded with these remarkable words:—"I trust to my childish remembrance for putting your initials correctly."

The letter was properly addressed "The Rev. *W. H.* Drage," and it is interesting to record this circumstance as showing Dickens's habitual precision and excellent memory. The future novelist was about eleven years old when he left Chatham (1823), consequently a period of twenty-seven years or more must have elapsed since he knew his father's neighbour as Curate there; yet, notwithstanding the multiplicity and diversity of his occupations during the interim, his recollection after this long period was perfectly accurate.

It is scarcely necessary to add that the interview took place (probably Dickens came down from London specially), and that the Vicar obtained admission for his *protégée*. The younger Miss Drage, who was in the room at the time of Dickens's visit, particularly noticed what a beautiful head the novelist's was, and in her enthusiasm she made a rough sketch of it while he was talking to her father.

In conversation with the present Mr. Charles Dickens on a subsequent occasion regarding this circumstance, he informed me that there was an institution of the kind referred to, "A Home," at Shepherd's Bush, in which his father took much interest. Forster also says in the *Life* that this Home "largely and regularly occupied his time for several years."

* * * * * *

We heard from a trustworthy authority, *Y. Z.*, at Rochester, some particulars respecting an interesting custom at Gad's Hill Place. On New Year's Eve there was always a dinner-party with friends, and a dance, and games afterwards. Some of the games were called "Buzz," "Crambo," "Spanish Merchant," etc. Claret-cup and other refreshments were introduced later, and at twelve o'clock all the servants came into the entrance-hall. Charles Dickens then went in, shook hands with them all round, wished them a Happy New Year ("A happy new year, God bless us all"), and gave each half-a-sovereign. This custom was maintained for many years, until a man-servant—who used to travel with Dickens—disgracefully betrayed his trust,—robbed his master, in fact,—when it was discontinued, and the name of the man who had thus disgraced himself was never allowed to be mentioned at Gad's Hill.

The same authority spoke of the long walks that Dickens regularly took after breakfast—usually six miles,—but he gave these up after the railway accident at Staplehurst, which, it will be remembered, occurred, on the "fatal anniversary,' the 9th June, 1865. During one of these walks, he fell ir with a man driving a cart loaded with manure, and had a long chat with him, the sort of thing he frequently did (saic our informant) in order to become acquainted with the brogu and feelings of the working people. When Dickens went or his way, one of the man's fellow-labourers said to him, "D you know that that was Charles Dickens who spoke to you? "I don't know who it was," replied the man, "but he was a d—d good fellow, for he gave me a shilling."

Our informant also referred to a conversation betwee Dickens and some of his friends at Gad's Hill, respecting th unhappy marriages of actors. Twenty such marriages wer instanced, and out of these only two turned out happily. H said that Charles Dickens at home was a quiet, unassumin man. He remembers on one occasion his saying, in relatio to a war which was then going on, "What must the feeling of a soldier be, when alone and dying on the battle-field, an leaving his wife and children far away for ever?"

* * * * * *

A TRUE GHOST STORY RELATING TO MISS HAVISHAM'S HOUSE.

"I live in an old red-brick mansion, nearly covered with ivy—on of those picturesque dwellings with high-pitched roofs and ornament gables, which were scattered broadcast over England in the da of good Queen Bess. Every stranger looking at it exclaims, 'Th house must have a history and a ghost!' Many a story has bee told of the ghost which has from time to time been seen, or said t have been seen, within its walls; and many a servant has, from fea refused service in this so-called haunted house.

"On the 28th May, one thousand six hundred and sixty, Charl

the Second sojourned and slept here. This being the eve of 'The Restoration,' a new name was given to the then old house, which name it has since retained. Charles, having knighted the owner (Sir Francis Clarke), departed early the next morning for London.

"There are secret passages *in* the house, and, under ground, *from* the house. From the room in which the king slept, a secret passage through one of the lower panels of the wainscot, leads to various parts of the house. This passage is so well concealed that I occupied the house some years before it was discovered. I had occasion to make a plan of the house, and the inside and outside not agreeing, disclosed the space occupied by the unexplored passage. The jackdaws had forestalled me in my discovery, and had had undisturbed possession for two centuries, having got access through a hole under the eaves of the roof. They had deposited *several bushels* of sticks. They had not been the only tenants, as skeletons and mummies of birds, etc., were also found.

"I came into possession of this old house in December 1875, and on the 27th of April, 1876, slept in it for the first time. At ten o'clock on that night, my family retired to rest; having some letters to write, I sat up later. At a quarter to twelve, I was startled by a loud noise—a sort of rumbling sound, which appeared to proceed from the hall. I left my writing and went to the hall, and found that the noise proceeded from the staircase, but I could see nothing unusual.

"The staircase is one of those so often described as being 'wide enough to drive a carriage and pair up,' with massive oak posts and balustrades. The walls are covered with tapestry, given to the house by 'The Merry Monarch,' after his visit. An oak chest or two, and some high-backed chairs on the landings, picture to one a suitable habitation for a ghost. Fortunately, or unfortunately, I had no belief in ghosts, and commenced an investigation of this extraordinary noise.

"Could it be rats, or mice, or owls? No; the noise was ten times louder than could possibly proceed from these creatures; besides, I knew there were no rats in the house. The clever builder of the house had filled all the space between the ceilings and floors with silver sand, which rendered it impossible for a rat or mouse to make passages. To prick a hole in a ceiling is to have a continuous stream of sand run down, as from an hour-glass.

"The noise was repeated, but much louder (two drum-sticks upon a large drum would not have made more noise), and I was able to localize it, still I could see nothing. I thought some one had fallen on the stairs, and I shouted 'Who is there?' A reply came 'Hush!'—first softly, and then very loud—too loud for a human voice. As no person was visible, I was puzzled, and went up-stairs by a back staircase, and ascertained that none of my family had left their bedrooms, and that certainly no trick was being played me.

"The same rumbling, rolling sound was repeated; and as I stood on the top of the great staircase, I felt a little uncomfortable, but no frightened. The noise seemed to proceed from a large carved oak coffer or chest (as old as the house), which stood on a landing, abou half-way up the stairs. I approached the chest, and from it appeared to come again the word 'Hush!' Could it be the wind whistling through a crack? No; it was far too loud for any such explanation I opened the lid of the chest and found it empty. Again the noise now from *under* the chest. I was just strong enough to move the chest; I turned it over and slid it down the stairs on to the nex landing. Again the noise, and again the 'Hush!' which now appeared to come from the floor where the coffer had stood.

"I felt I would rather have had some one with me to assist in my investigation, and to join me in making the acquaintance of the ghost; but, although my sensations were probably the most uncomfortable I ever experienced, I was determined, if possible, to unearth the mystery.

"The light was imperfect, and I went to another part of the hous for a candle to enable me to examine the floor. In my absence th noise was repeated louder than ever, and not unlike distant thunder On my return, I was saluted with 'Hush!' which I felt convince came from a voice immediately under the floor. By the light of th candle I examined the dark oak boards, and discovered what ap peared to be a trap door about two feet six inches square. The floc at some time had been varnished, and the cracks, or joints of th trap, had been filled and sealed with the varnish. I now hoped had found the habitation of my troublesome and noisy guest. procured a chisel and cut the varnished joint, and found that ther was a trap door, as I supposed. By the aid of a long screwdriver was able to move the door, but at that moment a repetition of th noise, immediately under me, made me hesitate for a moment to try and raise it. With feelings better imagined than described, I raised the lid, and looked into a dark chasm. All was still, and I heard the cathedral bell tolling the hour of midnight. A long African spear was in the corner near me, and I struck this into the opening. I tied a string to the candlestick to lower it into the opening, but at this moment I was startled, and was for the first time nervous, or I may say, frightened; but this had better remain for another chapter.

"So far I have not in the smallest degree exaggerated or over-drawn any one of the matters I have recounted. Every word has been written with the greatest care to truth and accuracy.

"S. T. A."

* * * * * *

To cut our ghost story short, without adding another chapter, Mr. Aveling, on looking into the dark chasm by the neagre light of the lowered candle, beheld, to his amazement, he reflection of his own face in the water of a large cistern inderneath the staircase, the house having formerly been upplied from the "large brewery" a short distance off. The inearthly noise was no doubt caused by air in the pipes, hrough which the water rushed when suddenly turned on by he brewers, who were working late at night. In *Great Expectations* it is stated that:—"The brewery buildings had little lane of communication with it" [the courtyard of atis House], "and the wooden gates of that lane stood open" at the time of Pip's first visit, when Estella showed him over ie premises], "and all the brewery beyond stood open, away the high enclosing wall; and all was empty and disused. he cold wind seemed to blow colder there, than outside the ate; and it made a shrill noise in howling in and out at ie open sides of the brewery, like the noise of wind in the gging of a ship at sea."

CHAPTER IV.

ROCHESTER CASTLE.

"I took up my hat, and went out, climbed to the top of the old Castle, an looked over the windy hills that slope down to the Medway."—*The Seven Poor Travellers.*

TO the lover of Dickens, both the Castle and Cathedral o Rochester appeal with almost equal interest. The Castl however, which stands on an eminence on the right bank o the river Medway, close to the bridge, claims prior attentior and a few lines must therefore be devoted to an epitome of it history in the ante-Pickwickian days.

Tradition says that the first castle was erected by comman of Julius Cæsar, when Cassivelaunus was Governor of Britai "in order to awe the Britons." It was called the "Castle c the Medway," or "the Kentishmen's Castle," and it seem with other antagonisms, to have awed the unfortunate Briton pretty effectively, for it lasted until decay and dissolutio came to it and to them, as to all things. It was replace by a new castle built by Hrofe (509), which in its tur succumbed to the ravages of time.

Gundulph, Bishop of Rochester (1077), whose name sti survives here and there in connection with charities and i ɔther ways in the "ancient city," appears to be entitled to the :redit of having commenced to build the present massive quare Tower or Keep, the surviving portion of a magnificent vhole, sometimes called "Gundulph's Tower," "towards which ıe was to expend the sum of sixty pounds," and this structure anks as one of the most perfect examples of Norman architecure in existence. Other authorities ascribe the erection to

'lo, Bishop of Bayeux and Earl of Kent, half-brother to illiam the Conqueror, who is described by Hasted as "a ·bulent and ambitious prelate, who aimed at nothing less ın the popedom." Later, in the reign of William Rufus, it s accounted "the strongest and most important castle of gland." It was so important that Lambarde, in *A rambulation of Kent*, says:—"It was much in the eie of such as were authors of troubles following within the realme, so that from time to time it had a part almost in every Tragedie."

Mr. Robert Collins, in his compact and useful *Visitors Handbook of Rochester and Neighbourhood*, quoting from another ancient historian, says that "In 1264, King Henry III. [who in 1251 held a grand tournament in the Castle 'commanded that the Shyriffe of Kent do set aboute to finish and complete the great Tower which Gundulpl had left imperfect.'" About 1463, Edward IV. repaire part of the Castle, after which it was allowed to fall int decay. The instructions to the "shyriffe" were no doub necessary; for although £60 would probably go a great wa in the time of Bishop Gundulph, the modern æsthetic builde would do very little indeed for that sum, towards the erectio of such an impregnable fortress as Rochester Castle, th walls of which vary from eight to thirteen feet in thicknes whatever his progenitor may have done in 1077.

The Keep—the last resort of the garrison when all th outworks were taken—is considered so beautiful that it selected, under the article "Castle" in the last edition the *Encyclopædia Britannica*, as an illustration of Norma architecture, showing "an embattled parapet often admittir of chambers and staircases being constructed," and showir also "embattled turrets carried one story higher than tl parapet." There is also a fine woodcut of the Castle p. 198 of vol. v. of that work.

The Keep is seventy feet square and a hundred feet hig built of the native Kentish ragstone and Caen stone; and t adamantine mortar or cement used in its construction w made with sand, evidently procured at the seaside so listance from Rochester, for it contains remains of cardium, ecten, solen, and other marine shells, which would not be ound in river sand. Mr. Roach Smith suggested that pro-ably the sand may have been procured from "Cockle-shell lard," near Sheerness. He called our attention to the fact

at in Norman mortar sand is predominant, and in Roman ortar lime or chalk.

The roof and the chambers are gone,—the Keep remains as nere shell,—and where bishops, kings, and barons came and nt, flocks of the common domestic pigeon, in countless mbers, fly about and make their home and multiply. One nost regrets the freedom which these graceful birds possess, although to grudge freedom to a pigeon is like grudging sunshine to a flower. But though the damage to the walls is really trifling, as they will stand for centuries to come, still the litter and mess which the birds naturally make is considerable and unsightly, and decidedly out of keeping in such a magnificent ruin. The pigeons exhibit what takes place when a species becomes dominant to the exclusion of other species, as witness the pest of the rabbits in New Zealand. With profound respect to his Worship the Mayor and the Corporation of Rochester, to whom the Castle and grounds now belong, the writer of these lines, as a naturalist, ventures to suggest that the Castle should be left to the jackdaws, its natural and doubtless its original tenants, which, although of higher organization, have been driven out by superior numbers in the "struggle for existence," and for whom it is a much more appropriate habitat in keeping with all traditions; and further, that the said pigeons be forthwith made into pies for the use and behoof of the deserving poor of the ancient city of Rochester.

Mention has been made of the fact that the Castle and grounds are the property of the Corporation of Rochester. They were acquired by purchase in 1883 from the Earl of Jersey for £8,000, and the occasion was celebrated by great civic rejoicings.[1] The Corporation are not only to be congratulated on the wisdom of their purchase ("a thing of beauty is a joy for ever"), but also on the excellent manner in which the grounds are maintained—pigeons excepted. The gardens, with closely-cut lawns, abound with euonymus

[1] Mr. Kitton was, by an interesting coincidence, present at the ceremony above referred to, and he has kindly given his impression thereon, which appear at the end of this chapter.

aurustinus, bay, and other evergreens, together with many :hoice flowers. The single red, or Deptford pink (*Dianthus 'Armeria*), grows wild on the walls of the Castle. There is a ;asteful statuette of her Majesty, under a Gothic canopy, near he entrance, which records her Jubilee in 1887. The inscrip- ions on three of the four corners are appropriately chosen rom Lord Tennyson's *Carmen Sæculare*:—

To commemorate the

Jubilee of Queen Victoria,

1887.

L. LEVY, MAYOR.

"Fifty years of ever-broadening commerce!"

"Fifty years of ever-brightening science!"

"Fifty years of ever-widening empire!"

There is free admission to the grounds through a handsome iodern Norman gateway, but a trifling charge of a few pence made for permission to enter the Keep, which has con- enient steps ascending to the top. From the summit of the :eep, there are magnificent views of the valley of the river ledway, the adjacent hills, Rochester, Chatham, and the :cinity. The Cathedral, Jasper's Gatehouse, and Restoration louse, are also noteworthy objects to the lover of Dickens. .s Mr. Philips Bevan says, and as we verified, the views inside : midday, when the sun is streaming down, are "very peculiar id beautiful."

Dickens's first and last great works are both associated ith the Castle, and it is referred to in several other of his ritings. We can fancy, more than sixty years ago, the eager and enthusiastic Pickwickians, in company with their newly-made acquaintance, Mr. Alfred Jingle, seated outside the four-horse coach,—the "Commodore," driven possibly by "Old Chumley,"—dashing over old Rochester Bridge, to "the lively notes of the guard's key-bugle," when the sight of the Castle first broke upon them.

"'Magnificent ruin!' said Mr. Augustus Snodgrass, with all the poetic fervour that distinguished him, when they came in sight of the fine old Castle.

"'What a study for an antiquarian!' were the very words which fell from Mr. Pickwick's mouth, as he applied his telescope to his eye.

"'Ah, fine place!' said the stranger, 'glorious pile—frowning walls—tottering arches—dark nooks—crumbling staircases—'"

Little did poor Mr. Winkle think that within twenty-four hours *his* feeling of admiration for Rochester Castle would be turned into astonishment, for does not the chronicle say that "if the upper tower of Rochester Castle had suddenly walked from its foundation and stationed itself opposite the coffee-room window [of the Bull Hotel], Mr. Winkle's surprise would have been as nothing compared with the perfect astonishment with which he had heard this address" (referring of course to the insult to Dr. Slammer, and the challenge in the matter of the duel).

It was on the occasion of "a visit to the Castle" very soon afterwards that Mr. Winkle confided in, and sought the good offices of, his friend Mr. Snodgrass, in the "affair of honour which was to take place at "sunset, in a lonely field beyond Fort Pitt." Poor fellow! how eagerly he tried, under a mask of the most perfect candour, and how miserably he failed, to arouse the energies of his friend to avert the impending catastrophe.

"'Snodgrass,' he said, stopping suddenly, 'do *not* let me be baulked in this matter—do *not* give information to the local authorities—do *not* obtain the assistance of several peace officers to take either me or Doctor Slammer of the 97th Regiment, at

Interior of Rochester Castle:

resent quartered in Chatham Barracks, into custody, and thus prevent is duel;—I say, do *not*.'

"Mr. Snodgrass seized his friend's hand as he enthusiastically plied, 'Not for worlds!'

"A thrill passed over Mr. Winkle's frame, as the conviction that e had nothing to hope from his friend's fears, and that he was estined to become an animated target, rushed forcibly upon him."

The state of the case having been formally explained to Mr. Snodgrass, they make arrangements, hire "a case of satisfaction pistols, with the satisfactory accompaniments of powder, ball, and caps," and "the two friends returned to their inn." The next ground which they traversed together to pursue the subject was at Fort Pitt. We will follow them presently.

In *The Mystery of Edwin Drood* there is no direct reference to the Castle itself, but the engraving of it, with the Cathedral in the background, after the pretty sketch by Mr. Luke Fildes R.A., will ever be associated with that beautiful fragment.

Another reference is contained in the preface to *Nicholas Nickleby*, where Dickens says:—"I cannot call to mind now how I came to hear about Yorkshire schools when I was a not very robust child, sitting in by-places near Rochester Castle, with a head full of 'Partridge,' 'Strap,' 'Tom Pipes,' and 'Sancho Panza.'"

A sympathetic notice of the Castle is also contained in the *Seven Poor Travellers*. It begins:—

"Sooth to say, he [Time] did an active stroke of work in Rochester in the old days of the Romans, and the Saxons, and the Normans and down to the times of King John, when the rugged Castle—I will not undertake to say how many hundreds of years old then—was abandoned to the centuries of weather which have so defaced the dark apertures in its walls, that the ruin looks as if the rooks and daws had picked its eyes out."

And this, the most touching reference of all, occurs in "One Man in a Dockyard," contributed by Dickens[2] to *Household Words* in 1851:—

[2] This was a joint article; the description of the works of the dockyard being by R. H. Horne, and that of the fortifications and country around by Charles Dickens.

"There was Rochester Castle, to begin with. I surveyed the massive ruin from the Bridge, and thought what a brief little practical joke I seemed to be, in comparison with its solidity, stature, strength, and length of life. I went inside; and, standing in the solemn shadow of its walls, looking up at the blue sky, its only remaining roof, (to the disturbance of the crows and jackdaws who garrison he venerable fortress now,) calculated how much wall of that thickess I, or any other man, could build in his whole life,—say from ight years old to eighty,—and what a ridiculous result would be roduced. I climbed the rugged staircase, stopping now and then o peep at great holes where the rafters and floors were once,—bare s toothless gums now,—or to enjoy glimpses of the Medway hrough dreary apertures like sockets without eyes; and, looking from he Castle ramparts on the Old Cathedral, and on the crumbling emains of the old Priory, and on the row of staid old red-brick ouses where the Cathedral dignitaries live, and on the shrunken ragments of one of the old City gates, and on the old trees with heir high tops below me, felt quite apologetic to the scene in eneral for my own juvenility and insignificance. One of the river oatmen had told me on the bridge, (as country folks do tell of such laces,) that in the old times, when those buildings were in rogress, a labourer's wages 'were a penny a day, and enough too.' ven as a solitary penny was to their whole cost, it appeared to e, was the utmost strength and exertion of one man towards the bour of their erection."

Dickens always took his friends to the Keep of Rochester astle. He naturally considered it as one of the sights of e old city. It was equally attractive to his friends, for a rious adventure is recorded in Forster's *Life*, in connection ith a visit which the poet Longfellow made there in 1842, nd which he recollected a quarter of a century afterwards, d recounted to Forster during a second visit, together with curious experience in the slums of London with Dickens. he first of these adventures is thus described by Forster:—
'One of them was a day at Rochester, when, met by one of

those prohibitions which are the wonder of visitors and the shame of Englishmen, we overleapt gates and barriers, and setting at defiance repeated threats of all the terrors of law, coarsely expressed to us by the custodian of the place, explored minutely the castle ruins." Happily such a circumstance could not now take place, for, by the present excellent regulations of the Corporation of the city of Rochester, every visitor can explore the Castle and grounds to his heart's content.

On arriving at either railway station, Strood or Rochester Bridge, the Castle is the first object to claim attention. Our attention is constantly directed to it during our stay in the pleasant city; it is a landmark when we are on the tramp; and it is the last object to fade from our view as we regretfully take our departure.

* * * * * *

My fellow-tramp favours me with the following note:—

THE DEDICATION OF ROCHESTER CASTLE TO THE PUBLIC.

"I well remember the day of public rejoicing in the picturesque city of Rochester, on the occasion of the ceremony of formally presenting the old Castle and grounds to the inhabitants. I had received instructions from the manager of the *Graphic* newspaper to make sketches of the principal incidents in connection with the day's proceedings, and I reached my destination just in time to obtain from the authorities some idea of the nature of those proceedings. With this object in view, I made my way through the surging crowd to the Guildhall, where, in one of the Corporation rooms, I found a large assembly of local magnates in official attire, including the Mayor, who was vainly endeavouring to properly adjust his sword, an operation in which I had the honour of assisting, much to his Worship's satisfaction, I hope.

"The streets of Rochester were thronged with excited people, and the houses were gaily decked with flags and bunting. When everything was ready, an imposing procession was formed, and proceeded to the Castle grounds,

receded by a military band; on arriving there, an address 'as read from the pagoda to an attentive audience, the ubsequent proceedings being enlivened by musical strains.

"It had been announced that, in the evening, the old Keep ould be illuminated by the electric light, and I made a oint of being present to witness the unusual sight. The ight was very dark, and the ivy-clad ruin could barely be istinguished; presently, a burst of music from the band was immediately followed by a remarkably strong beam of light, which shot into the darkness with such effect as to fairly startle those present. Then it rested on the grey walls of the huge pile, bathing in brightness the massive stones and clinging ivy, the respective colours of each being vividly apparent. But the most striking feature was yet to come. The hundreds of pigeons which inhabited the nooks and crannies of the old Keep, being considerably alarmed by this sudden illumination of their domain, flew with one accord round and round their ancient tenement, now in the full blaze of light, now lost in the inky darkness beyond, and fluttering about in a state of the utmost bewilderment. Methinks even Mr. Pickwick, had he been present in the flesh, would have been equally amazed at this remarkable spectacle."

F. G. K.

CHAPTER V.

ROCHESTER CATHEDRAL.

"That same afternoon, the massive grey square tower of an old Cathedral rises before the sight of a jaded traveller. The bells are going for daily Vesper Service, and he must needs attend it, one would say, from his haste to reach the open Cathedral door. The choir are getting on their sullied white robes, in a hurry, when he arrives among them, gets on his own robe, and falls into the procession filing in to Service. Then, the Sacristan locks the iron-barred gates that divide the Sanctuary from the Chancel, and all of the procession having scuttled into their places, hide their faces; and then the intoned words, 'WHEN THE WICKED MAN—' rise among the groins of arches and beams of roof, awakening muttered thunder."—*Edwin Drood.*

IE readers of Dickens are first introduced to Rochester .thedral, in the early pages of the immortal *Pickwick Papers*, that audacious *raconteur*, Mr. Alfred Jingle:—

"Old Cathedral too—earthy smell—pilgrims' feet worn away the steps—little Saxon doors—confessionals like money-takers' :es at theatres—queer customers those monks—Popes, and Lord :asurers, and all sorts of old fellows, with great red faces, and ken noses, turning up every day—buff jerkins too—matchlocks— :ophagus—fine place—old legends too—strange stories: capital."

But it was through the medium of *Edwin Drood*, and ler the masked name of Cloisterham, that all the novel-ding world beyond the "ancient city" first recognized

Rochester Cathedral

Rochester Cathedral—and indeed the ancient city too—as having been elevated to a degree of interest and importance far beyond that imparted to it by its own venerable history and ecclesiastical associations, numerous and varied as they are. The early portion of the story introduces us to Cloisterham in imperishable language:—

> "An ancient city Cloisterham, and no meet dwelling-place for any one with hankerings after the noisy world. . . . A drowsy city Cloisterham, whose inhabitants seem to suppose, with an inconsistency more strange than rare, that all its changes lie behind it, and hat there are no more to come. . . . In a word, a city of another and a bygone time is Cloisterham, with its hoarse cathedral bell, its hoarse ooks hovering about the cathedral tower, its hoarser and less distinct ooks in the stalls far beneath. . . ."

The particulars in this chapter mainly relate to *The Mystery of Edwin Drood*, which Longfellow thought "certainly one of Dickens's most beautiful works, if not the most beautiful of all," but a few words may not be inappropriate respecting ome of the principal events connected with the Cathedral. t was founded[1] A.D. 604, by Ethelbert, King of Kent, and he first bishop of the See (Bishop Justus) was ordained by Augustine, the Archbishop of the Britons. The See of Rochester is therefore, with the exception of Canterbury, at nce the most ancient and also the smallest in England.

The Cathedral, as well as the city, suffered from the attacks f Ethelred, King of Mercia, and in 1075, "when Arnot, a monk of Bec, came to the See, it was in a most deplorable ondition." Bishop Gundulph, who succeeded him, and by hose efforts the Castle was erected, replaced the old English

[1] It is interesting to record that the foundations of this Church were et with for the first time, in restoring the west front of the Cathedral, 1889.

church by a Norman one (1080), and made other improvements. The Cathedral suffered from fire in 1138 and 1179. Its great north transept was built in 1235, and the great south transept in 1240. In 1423, the parish altar of St. Nicholas, in the nave, was removed to a new Church for the citizens on the north side of the Cathedral. In 1470, the great west window was inserted. The Norman west front has a richly sculptured door of five receding arches, containing figures of the Saviour and the twelve apostles, and statues of Henry I. and his Queen, Matilda. There are monuments in the Cathedral to St. William of Perth, a baker of that town, who was murdered near here by his servant, on his way to the Holy Land (1201), and was canonized, to Bishop Gundulph, Bishop John de Sheppey, Bishop de Merton (the founder of Merton College, Oxford), and to many others.

According to Mr. Phillips Bevan, "the chapter-house is remarkable for its magnificent Decorated Door (about 1344), of which there is a fac-simile at the Crystal Palace. The figures represent the Christian and the Jewish Churches, surrounded by Fathers and Angels. The figure at the top is the pure soul for whom the angels are supposed to be praying."

Various alterations and additions have been made from time to time, the last of which appears to be the central tower, which is terribly mean and inappropriate, and altogether out of place with the ancient surroundings. It was built by Cottingham in 1825.

We pass, at various times, several pleasant hours in the Cathedral and its precincts, admiring the beautiful Norman work, and recalling most delightful memories of Charles Dickens and his associations therewith.

Among the many friends we made at Rochester, was Mr

Syms, the respected Manager of the Gas Company, and an old resident in the city. To this gentleman we are indebted for

several reminiscences of Dickens and his works. He fancies that *The Mystery of Edwin Drood* owed its origin to the following strange local event that happened many years ago. A well-to-do person, a bachelor (who lived somewhere near the site of the present Savings Bank in High St., Rochester, Chatham end), was the guardian and trustee of a nephew (a minor), who was the inheritor of a large property. Business, pleasure, or a desire to seek health, took the nephew to the West Indies, from whence he returned somewhat unexpectedly. After his return he suddenly disappeared, and was supposed to have gone another voyage, but no one ever saw or heard of him again, and the matter was soon forgotten. When, however, certain excavations were being made for some improvements or additions to the Bank, the skeleton of a young man was discovered; and local tradition couples the circumstance with the probability of the murder of the nephew by the uncle.

Mr. Syms thought that the "Crozier," which is probably a set off to the "Mitre," the orthodox hotel where Mr. Datchery put up with his "portmanteau," was probably the city coffee-house, an old hotel of the coaching days, which stood on the site now occupied by the London County Bank. "It was a hotel of a most retiring disposition," and "business was chronically slack at the 'Crozier,'" which probably accounts for its dissolution. Another suggestion is that the "Crozier" may have been "The Old Crown," a fifteenth-century house which was pulled down in 1864. He could not identify the "Tilted Wagon," the "cool establishment on the top of a hill."

It is generally admitted that "Mr. Thomas Sapsea, Auctioneer, &c.," was a compound of two originals well known in Rochester—a Mr. B. and a Mr. F., who had many of the characteristics of the quondam Mayor of Cloisterham

Mr. Sapsea's house is the fine old timbered building opposite Eastgate House, which has been previously alluded to.

The "Travellers' Twopenny" of *Edwin Drood*, where Deputy, *alias* Winks, lodged, Mr. Syms thought to have been a cheap lodging-house well known in that locality, which stood at the junction of Frog Alley and Crow Lane, originally called "The Duck," and subsequently "Kitt's Lodging-house." But, like less interesting and more important relics of the past, this has disappeared, to make way for modern improvements. It had been partly burnt down before. To satisfy ourselves, we go over the ground, which is near Mr. Franklin Homan's furniture establishment.

We are reminded, in reference to *Edwin Drood*, that the chief tenor singer never heads the procession of choristers. That place of honour belongs to the smaller boys of the choir. An enquiry from us, as to what was the opinion of the townsfolk generally respecting Dickens, elicited the reply that they thought him at times "rather masterful."

We are most attentively shown over the Cathedral and its surroundings by Mr. Miles, the venerable verger. This faithful and devoted official, who began at the bottom of the ladder as a choir boy in the sacred edifice at the commencement of the present century, is much respected, and has recently celebrated his golden wedding. Few can therefore be more closely identified with the growth and development of its current history. Pleasant and instructive it is to hear him recount the many celebrated incidents which have marked its progress, and to see the beautiful memorials of past munificence or affection erected by friends or relatives, which he lovingly points out. It is in no perfunctory spirit, or as mere matter of routine, that he performs his office: we really feel that he takes a deep interest in his task, which makes it a privilege to walk under his guidance through the historic building, and into its famous crypt, so especially associated with Jasper and Durdles.

We enter "by a small side door, . . . descend the rugged steps, and are down in the crypt." It is very spacious, and vaulted with stone. Even by daylight, here and there, "the

The Crypt, Rochester Cathedral.

heavy pillars which support the roof engender masses of black shade, but between them there are lanes of light," and we walk "up and down these lanes," being strangely reminded of Durdles as we notice fragments of old broken stone ornaments carefully laid out on boards in several places. Formerly there were altars to St. Mary and St. Catherine in the crypt or undercroft, but Mr. Wildish's local guide-book says:—"They seem not to have been much frequented; consequently these saints were not very profitable to the priests."

We "go up the winding staircase of the great tower, toilsomely turning and turning, and lowering [our] heads to avoid the stairs above, or the rough stone pivot around which they twist." About ninety steps bring us on to the roof of the Cathedral over the choir, and then, keeping along a passage by the parapet, we reach the belfry, and from thence go on by ladder to the bell-chamber, which contains six bells —dark—very—long ladders—trap-doors—very heavy—almost extinguish us when lowering them—more ladders from bell-chamber to roof of tower. The parapet of the tower is very high; we can just see over it when standing on a narrow ledge near the top-coping of the leaded roof. There are a number of curious carved heads on the pinnacles of the tower, and the parapet, to our surprise, appears to be about the same height as the top of the Castle Keep. A panoramic view of Cloisterham presents itself to our view (alas! not by moonlight, as in the story), "its ruined habitations and sanctuaries of the dead at the tower's base; its moss-softened, red-tiled roofs and red-brick houses of the living, clustered beyond."

We are anxious to go round the triforium, but there is no passage through the arches; it was closed, we are told, at the time of the restoration, about fifteen years ago, when the walls of the Cathedral were pinned for safety. The verger, on being asked, said he did not call to mind that Dickens ever went round the triforium or ascended the tower. If this is so, then much of the wonderful description of that "unaccountable sort of expedition," in the twelfth chapter of *Edwin Drood*, must have been written from imagination.

As it is Sunday, and as the summer is nearly over, Mr. Miles, with a feeling akin to that which George Eliot has expressed regarding imperfect work:—

> "but God be praised,
> Antonio Stradivari has an eye
> That winces at false work and loves the true,"—

apologetically explains that one-half the choir are absent on leave, and perhaps we shall not have the musical portion of the service conducted with that degree of efficiency which, as visitors, we may have expected. Nevertheless we attend the afternoon service; and Mendelssohn's glorious anthem, "If with all your hearts," appeals to us with enhanced effect, from the exquisite rendering of it by the gifted pure tenor who takes the solo, followed by the delicate harmonics of the choir, as the sound waves carry them upwards through and around the arches, and from the sublime emotions called into being by the impassioned appeal of the Hebrew prophet.

We study "the fantastic carvings on the under brackets of the stall seats," and examine the lectern described as "the big brass eagle holding the sacred books upon his wings," and in imagination can almost call up the last scene described in *The Mystery of Edwin Drood*, where Her Royal Highness, the Princess Puffer, "grins," and "shakes both fists at the leader of the choir," and "Deputy peeps, sharp-eyed, through the bars, and stares astounded from the threatener to the threatened."

Upon being interrogated as to whether he knew Charles Dickens, our guide immediately answers with a smile—"Knew him! yes. He came here very often, and I knew him very well. The fact is, they want to make me out to be 'Tope.'" And indeed there appears to be such a relevancy in the association, that we frequently find ourselves addressing him as "Mr. Tope," at which he good-humouredly laughs. He further states that Dickens was frequently in Rochester, and especially so when writing *Edwin Drood*, and appeared to be studying the Cathedral and its surroundings very attentively.

The next question we put is:—"Was there ever such a person as Durdles?" to which he replies, "Of course there was,—a drunken old German stonemason, about thirty years ago, who was always prowling about the Cathedral trying to pick up little bits of broken stone ornaments, carved heads, crockets, finials, and such like, which he carried about in a cotton handkerchief, and which may have suggested to Dickens the idea of the 'slouching' Durdles and his inseparable dinner bundle. He used to work for a certain Squire N——." His earnings mostly went to "The Fortune of War,"—now called "The Life-Boat,"—the inn where he lodged.

Mr. Miles does not remember the prototypes of any other "cathedraly" characters—Crisparkle and the rest—but he quite agrees with the general opinion previously referred to as to the origin of Mr. Sapsea. He considers "Deputy" (the imp-like satellite of Durdles and the "Kinfreederel") to be decidedly a street Arab, the type of which is more common in London than in Rochester. He thinks that the fact of the rooms over the gatehouse having once been occupied by an organ-blower of the Cathedral may have prompted Dickens to make it the residence of the choir-master. He also throws out the suggestion that the discovery in 1825 of the effigy of Bishop John de Sheppey, who died in 1360, may possibly have given rise to the idea of the "old 'uns" in the crypt the frequent object of Durdles's search, *e.g.* "Durdles come upon the old chap (in reference to a buried magnate of ancient time and high degree) by striking right into the coffin with his pick. The old chap gave Durdles a look with his open eyes as much as to say, 'Is your name Durdles? Why my man, I've been waiting for you a Devil of a time!' and then he turned to powder. With a two-foot rule always in his pocket, and a mason's hammer all but always in his hand Durdles goes continually sounding and tapping all about and about the Cathedral; and whenever he says to Tope, 'Tope here's another old 'un in here!' Tope announces it to the Dean as an established discovery."

On the south side of the Cathedral is the curious little terrace of old-fashioned houses, about seven in number, called "Minor Canon Row"—"a wonderfully quaint row of red-brick tenements" (Dickens's name for it is "Minor Canon Corner"),—chiefly occupied by the officers and others attached to the Cathedral. Here it was that Mr. Crisparkle dwelt with his mother, and where the little party was held (after the dinner at which Mr. Luke Honeythunder, with his "Curse your souls and bodies—come here and be blessed" philanthropy, was present, and caused "a most doleful breakdown") which included Miss Twinkleton, the Landlesses, Rosa Bud and Edwin Drood, as shown in the illustration, "At the Piano." The Reverend Septimus Crisparkle's mother, who is the hostess (and celebrated for her wonderful closet with stores of pickles, jams, biscuits, and cordials), is beautifully described in the story :—

Minor Canon Row:
Rochester.

"What is prettier than an old lady—except a young lady—whe her eyes are bright, when her figure is trim and compact, when h face is cheerful and calm, when her dress is as the dress of a chir shepherdess: so dainty in its colours, so individually assorted t herself, so neatly moulded on her? Nothing is prettier, thougl the good Minor Canon frequently, when taking his seat at tab opposite his long-widowed mother. Her thought at such times m be condensed into the two words that oftenest did duty together all her conversations: 'My Sept.'"

The backs of the houses have very pretty gardens, an as evidence of the pleasant and healthy atmosphere of tl locality, we notice beautiful specimens of the ilex, arbutu euonymus, and fig, the last-named being in fruit. Tl wall-rue (*Asplenium ruta-muraria*) is found hereabout. Ther too, is a Virginia creeper, but we do not observe one growir on the Cathedral walls, as described in *Edwin Drood.* Jac daws fly about the tower, but there are no rooks, as al stated. Near Minor Canon Row, to the right of Boley H (or "Bully Hill," as it is sometimes called), is the "pav Quaker settlement," a sedate row of about a dozen hous "up in a shady corner."

"Jasper's Gatehouse" of the work above mentioned certainly an object of great interest to the lover of Dicke as many of the remarkable scenes in *Edwin Drood* to place there. It is briefly described as "an old stone gat house crossing the Close, with an arched thoroughfare passi beneath it. Through its latticed window, a fire shines c upon the fast-darkening scene, involving in shadow t pendent masses of ivy and creeper covering the buildin front." There are *three* Gatehouses near the Cathedral, fact which proves somewhat embarrassing to those anxic to identify the original of that so carefully described ıe story. A short description of these may not be uninteresting.

(A) "College Yard Gate," "Cemetery Gate," and "Chertsey's

ıate," are the respective names of what we know as "Jasper's atehouse." It is a picturesque stone structure, weatherıarded above the massive archway, and abuts on the High reet about a hundred yards north of the Cathedral. Some

of the old houses near have recently been demolished, witl
the result that the Gatchouse now stands out in bold relie
against the main thoroughfare of the city. No "penden
masses of ivy" or "creeper" cover it. The Gate was name
"Chertsey" after Edward Chertsey, a gentleman who live

and owned property near in the time of Edward IV., an
the Cathedral authorities still continue to use the old name
"Chertsey's Gate." The place was recently the residence o
the under-porter of the Cathedral, and is now occupied b
poor people. There are four rooms, two below and two above

(B) "Prior's Gate" is a castellated stone structure partly ›vered with ivy, standing about a hundred yards south ˙ the Cathedral, and is not now utilized in any way. here is only one room, approached by a winding stair-.se or "postern stair." The Gate was formerly used a school for choristers, until the new building of the ıoir School was opened in Minor Canon Row about three ·ars ago.

(C) The "Deanery Gatehouse" is the name of a quaint d very cosy old house, having ten rooms, some of which, gether with the staircase, are beautifully panelled; its sition is a little higher up to the eastward of the College ırd Gate, and adjoining the Cathedral, while a gateway ssage under it leads to the Deanery. The house was ›merly the official residence of the Hon. and Reverend non Hotham, who was appointed a Canon in residence in)8, and lived here at intervals until about 1850, when the nonry was suppressed. Of all the Gatehouses, this is the y one suitable for the residence of a person in Jasper's sition, who was enabled to offer befitting hospitality to l. nephew and Neville Landless. Formerly there was an rance into the Cathedral from this house, which is now upied by Mr. Day and his family, who kindly allowed us t inspect it. We were informed that locally it is sometimes led "Jasper's Gatehouse." The interior of the drawing-r m on the upper floor presents a very strong resemblance t Mr. Luke Fildes's illustration, "On dangerous ground." cordingly, to settle the question of identity, I wrote to Fildes, whose interesting and courteous reply to my i uiries is conclusive. Before giving it, however, I may ıtion that my fellow-tramp, Mr. Kitton, suggested, more particularly with reference to another illustration in *Edwi Drood*, viz., "Durdles cautions Mr. Sapsea against boasting,' that, for the purposes of the story, the Prior's Gate is place where the College Yard Gate actually stands.

"11, MELBURY ROAD, KENSINGTON, W.
"*25th October*, 1890.

"DEAR SIR,

"The background of the drawing of 'Durdl cautioning Sapsea,' I believe I sketched from what you ca A., *i.e.* The College Gate. I am almost certain it was n taken from B., the Prior's.

"The room in the drawing, 'On dangerous ground,' imaginary.

"I do not believe I entered any of the Gatehouses.

"The resemblance you see in the drawing to the room in the Deanery Gatehouse (C.), might not be gained by actual observation of the *interior.*

"In many instances an artist can well judge what the nterior may be from studying the *outside.* I only throw his out to show that the artist may not have seen a thing even when a strong resemblance occurs. I am sorry to leave any doubt on the subject, though personally I feel none.

"You see I never felt the necessity or propriety of being locally accurate to Rochester or its buildings. Dickens, of ourse, meant Rochester; yet, at the same time, he chose o be obscure on that point, and I took my cue from him. always thought it was one of his most artistic pieces of ork; the vague, dreamy description of the Cathedral in the pening chapter of the book. So definite in one sense, yet o locally vague.

"Very faithfully yours,

"LUKE FILDES.

"W. R. HUGHES, ESQ."

The College Yard Gate (A) must therefore be regarded the typical Jasper's Gatehouse, but, with the usual novelist's cense, some points in all three Gatehouses have been ilized for effect. So we can imagine the three friends in ccession going up the "postern stair;" and, further on in e story, we can picture that mysterious "single buffer, Dick atchery, living on his means," as a lodger in the "venerable chitectural and inconvenient" official dwelling of Mr. Tope, inutely described in the eighteenth chapter of *Edwin Drood*, "communicating by an upper stair with Mr. Jasper's," watching the unsuspecting Jasper as he goes to and from the Cathedral.

Chapters twelve, fourteen, and twenty-three refer to Jasper's Gatehouse, and its proximity to the busy hum of human life, in very vivid terms, especially chapter twelve:—

"Among these secluded nooks there is little stir or movement after dark. There is little enough in the high tide of the day, but there is next to none at night. Besides that, the cheerfully frequented High Street lies nearly parallel to the spot (the old Cathedral rising between the two), and is the natural channel in which the Cloisterham traffic flows, a certain awful hush pervades the ancient pile, the cloisters, and the churchyard after dark, which not many people care to encounter. . . . One might fancy that the tide of life was stemmed by Mr. Jasper's own Gatehouse. The murmur of the tide is heard beyond; but no wave passes the archway, over which his lamp burns red behind the curtain, as if the building were a Lighthouse. . . .

"The red light burns steadily all the evening in the Lighthouse on the margin of the tide of busy life. Softened sounds and hum of traffic pass it, and flow on irregularly into the lonely precincts; but very little else goes by save violent rushes of wind. It comes on to blow a boisterous gale. . . . John Jasper's lamp is kindled, and his Lighthouse is shining, when Mr. Datchery returns alone towards it. As mariners on a dangerous voyage, approaching an iron-bound coast, may look along the beams of the warning light to the haven lying beyond it that may never be reached, so Mr. Datchery's wistful gaze is directed to this beacon and beyond. . . ."

The sensation of calm in passing suddenly out of the busy High Street of Rochester into the subdued precincts of the Cathedral, as above described, is very marked and peculiar and must be experienced to be realized.

Among the many interesting ancient buildings in "the lonely precincts" may be mentioned the old Episcopal Palace of the Bishops of Rochester. My friend Mr. George Payn

.S.A., Hon. Sec. of the Kent Archæological Society, who now ves there, writes me that:—"it is impossible to say when it as first built, but it was rebuilt *circa* 1200, the Palace which receded it having been destroyed by fire. Bishop Fisher as appointed to the See in 1504, and mainly resided at ochester. The learned prelate here entertained the great rasmus in 1516, and Cardinal Wolsey in 1527. In 1534 shop Fisher left Rochester never to return, being beheaded

Tower Hill, June 22nd, 1535. The front of the Palace has t n coated with rough plaster work dusted over with broken t but the rear walls are in their original state, being wholly posed of rag, tufa, and here and there Roman tiles. The c ars are of the most massive construction, and many of the ns are panelled."

he Monks' Vineyard of *Edwin Drood* exists as "The es," and is one of the "lungs" of Rochester, belonging to the Dean and Chapter, by whom it is liberally leased to the Corporation for a nominal consideration. It was a vineyard, or garden, in the days of the monks, and is now a fine ope space, planted with trees, and has good walks and well-trimmed lawns and borders. Remains of the wall of the city or abbey, previous to the Cathedral, constitute the northern boundary of "The Vines." There are commodious seats fo the public, and it was doubtless on one of these, as represente in the illustration entited "Under the Trees," that Edwi Drood and Rosa sat, during that memorable discussion o their position and prospects, which began so childlike an ended so sadly. "'Can't you see a happy Future?' Fo certain, neither of them sees a happy Present, as the gat opens and closes, and one goes in and the other goes away. A fine clump of old elms (seven in number), called "Th Seven Sisters," stands at the east end of the Vines, nearl opposite Restoration House, and it was under these tre that the conversation took place.

So curiously exact at times does the description fit in wit the places, that we notice opposite Eastgate House th "Lumps of Delight Shop," to which it will be remembere that after the discussion Rosa Bud directed Edwin Drood t take her.

Dickens's last visit to Rochester was on Monday, 6th Jun 1870, when he walked over from Gad's Hill Place with h dogs; and he appears to have been noticed by several perso in the Vines, and particularly by Mr. John Sweet, as he sto leaning against the wooden palings near Restoration Hous contemplating the beautiful old Manor House. These palin have since been removed, and an iron fence substituted. T object of this visit subsequently became apparent, when

Restoration House, Rochester, as it appeared in Dickens's time. (From a sketch by an Amateur.)

was found that, in those pages of *Edwin Drood* written a fe hours before his death, Datchery and the Princess Puffer hel that memorable conference there. "They have arrived at th entrance to the Monks' Vineyard; an appropriate remem brance, presenting an exemplary model for imitation, i revived in the woman's mind by the sight of the place," i allusion of course to a present of "three shillings and sixpence which Edwin Drood gave her Royal Highness on a previou occasion to buy opium.

The extensive promenade called the Esplanade (wher in 1889 we saw the Regatta in which, after a series of annu defeats, Rochester maintained its supremacy), on the ea side of the river Medway, under the Castle walls, pleasantl approached from the Cathedral Close, is memorable as havin been the spot described in the thirteenth chapter whe Edwin and Rosa met for the last time, and mutually agree to terminate their unfortunate and ill-assorted engagement.

"They walked on by the river. They began to speak of the separate plans. He would quicken his departure from England, an she would remain where she was, at least as long as Helena remaine The poor dear girls should have their disappointment broken to the gently, and, as the first preliminary, Miss Twinkleton should l confided in by Rosa, even in advance of the reappearance of M Grewgious. It should be made clear in all quarters that she an Edwin were the best of friends. There had never been so serene a understanding between them since they were first affianced."

We are anxious to identify Cloisterham Weir, frequentl mentioned in *Edwin Drood*, but more particularly as bein the place where Minor Canon Crisparkle found Edwin's watc and shirt-pin. The Weir, we are told in the novel, "is fu two miles above the spot to which the young men [Edwi and Neville] had repaired [presumably the Esplanade] to watch the storm." There is, however, no Weir nearer than Allington, at which place the tide of the Medway stops, and Allington is a considerable distance from Rochester, probably seven or eight miles. How well the good Minor Canon's propensity for "perpetually pitching himself headforemost into all the deep water in the surrounding country," and his "pilgrimages to Cloisterham Weir in the cold rimy mornings," are brought into requisition to enable him to obtain the watch and pin.

"He threw off his clothes, he plunged into the icy water, and swam for the spot—a corner of the Weir—where something glistened which did not move and come over with the glistening water drops, but remained stationary. . . . He brought the watch to the bank, swam to the Weir again, climbed it, and dived off. He knew every hole and corner of all the depths, and dived and dived and dived, until he could bear the cold no more. His notion was that he would find the body; he only found a shirt-pin sticking in some mud and ooze."

Our failure to identify Cloisterham Weir exhibits another instance where, for the purposes of the story, an imaginary place is introduced. To Mr. William Ball is due the credit for subsequently suggesting that Snodland Brook and Snodland Weir may have possibly been in Dickens's mind in originating Cloisterham Weir; so we tramped over to inspect them. Near the village, the brook (or river, for it is of respectable width) is turbid and shallow, but higher up—a mile or so—we found it clearer and deeper, and we heard from some labourers, whom we saw regaling themselves by the side of a hayrick, that a local gentleman had some years ago been in the habit of bathing in the stream all the year round.

The ancient Church of St. Nicholas (1423) is on the north side of the Cathedral. In front of it is a narrow strip of ground, enclosed with iron railings, formerly the burial-ground of the Church, but now disused, referred to in *Edwin Drood* as "a fragment of a burial-ground in which an unhappy sheep was grazing." In this enclosure, which is neatly kept, there

are a weeping willow at each end, and in the centre an exquisite specimen of the catalpa tree (*Catalpa syringifolia*), the floral ornament of the Cathedral precincts. At the time of our visit it is in perfect condition, the large cordate bright green leaves, and the massive trusses of labiate flowers of white, yellow, and purple colours (not unlike those of the *Impatiens noli-me-tangere* balsam, only handsomer) are worth walking miles to see. It is a North American plant, and in its native country sometimes grows to a height of forty feet. The specimen here described is about twenty feet high, and was planted about fifteen years ago.[2]

On the opposite side of the way is the old cemetery of St. Nicholas' Church, originally part of the Castle moat, but which was converted to its present purpose about half a century ago. This quiet resting-place of the dead has intense interest for the over of Dickens, as it was here that he desired to be buried; ınd his family would certainly have carried his wishes into effect, but that the place had been closed for years and no urther interments were allowed. Pending other arrangements .t Shorne, an admirable suggestion was made in the *Times*, which speedily found favour with the nation in its great .ffection for him, namely, that he should rest in Westminster Abbey; and, the Dean of Westminster promptly and wisely esponding to the suggestion, it was at once carried into effect.

As we pause, and look again and again at the sheltered ook in the old cemetery sanctified by his memory, and dorned by rich evergreens and other trees, among which the eeping willow and the almond are conspicuous, we quite nderstand and sympathize with Dickens's love for such a alm and secluded spot.

The Dean and Chapter of Rochester, it will be recollected, ere anxious that the great novelist's remains should be laced in or near their Cathedral, and that wish might have een gratified, except, as just explained, that the public ecreed otherwise. However, they sanctioned the erection, the executors, of a brass, which enriches the wall of the

[2] This was written in 1888; on a subsequent visit to Rochester we re sorry to find that the frost bad made sad havoc with this beautiful

south transept of the edifice, and which has the followin inscription :—

The unfinished novel of *Edwin Drood*, which, as we hav seen, is so inseparably connected with Rochester Cathedra has been *finished* by at least half a dozen authors, probably t their own satisfaction ; but it is a hard matter to the reade to struggle through any one of them. However, there is little *brochure* in this direction which we feel may here b appropriately noticed. It is called, *Watched by the Dead A Loving Study of Charles Dickens's half-told Tale*, 1887, an was written by R. A. Proctor, F.R.A.S., the Astronome whose untimely death from fever in America was announce after our return from our week's tramp. The author ha evidently studied the matter both lovingly and attentivel and starts with the assumption that it is an example of wha he calls " Dickens's favourite theme," which more than an other had a fascination for him, and was apparently regarde by him as likely to be most potent in its influence on other It was that of " a wrong-doer watched at every turn by or of whom he has no suspicion, for whom he even entertains feeling of contempt," and Mr. Proctor has certainly evolved very suggestive and not improbable conclusion to the stor Instances of Dickens's favourite theme are adduced fro *Barnaby Rudge*, where Haredale, unsuspected, steadily wai and watches for Rudge, till, after more than twenty years, "At last! at last!" he cries, as he captures his brother's murderer on the very spot where the murder had been committed; from *The Old Curiosity Shop*, where Sampson and Sally Brass are watched by the Marchioness—their powerless victim as they supposed, and by whom their detection is brought about; from *Nicholas Nickleby*, where Ralph Nickleby is watched by Brooker; and from *Dombey and Son*, where Dombey is watched by Carker, and he in turn is watched by good Mrs. Brown and her unhappy daughter. Instances of this kind also appear in *David Copperfield*, *Bleak House*, and *Little Dorrit*.

Reasoning from similar data, Mr. Proctor concludes that Jasper was watched by Edwin Drood in the person of Datchery, and thus he was to have been tracked remorse-essly "to his death by the man whom he supposed he had lain." The *dénouement* as regards the other characters seems also not improbable. Rosa Bud was to have married Lieu-enant Tartar, and Crisparkle, Helena Landless. Neville was o have died, but not before he had learned to understand the hange which Edwin's character had undergone. As to Edwin Drood himself, "purified by trial, strengthened though addened by his love for Rosa, Edwin would have been one f those characters Dickens loved to draw—a character ntirely changed from a once careless, almost trivial self, to depth and earnestness. "All were to join in changing the ays of dear old Grewgious from the sadness and loneliness f the earlier scenes" in the story, "to the warmth and light f that kindly domestic life for which, angular though he hought himself, his true and genial nature fitted him so horoughly." This attempt to solve *The Mystery of Edwin*

Drood will amply repay perusal. It was probably one of the last works of this very able and versatile author.

It is right to state that Mr. Luke Fildes, R.A., the illustrator of *The Mystery of Edwin Drood*, with whom we have had the pleasure of an interview, entirely rejects this theory. He does not favour the idea that Datchery is Edwin Drood; his opinion is that the ingenuous and kind-hearted Edwin, had he been living, would never have allowed his friend Neville to continue so long under the grave suspicion of murder. Nay more: he is convinced that Dickens intended that Edwin Drood should be killed by his uncle; and this opinion is supported by the fact of the introduction of a "large black scarf of strong close-woven silk," which Jasper wears for the first time in the fourteenth chapter of the story, and which was likely to have been the means of death, *i. e.* by strangulation. Mr. Fildes said that Dickens seemed much surprised when he called his attention to this change of dress—very noticeable and embarrassing to an artist who had studied the character—and appeared as though he had unintentionally disclosed the secret. He further stated that it was Dickens's intention to take him to a condemned cell in Maidstone or some other gaol, in order "that he might make a drawing," "and," said Dickens, "do something better than Cruikshank;" in allusion, of course, to the famous drawing of "Fagin in the condemned cell." "Surely this," remarked our informant, "points to our witnessing the condemned culprit Jasper in his cell before he met his fate." [3]

Mr. Fildes spoke with enthusiasm of the very great kindness

[3] Mr. Charles Dickens informs me that Mr. Fildes is right, and that Edwin Drood was dead. His (Mr. Dickens's) father told him so himself.

.nd consideration which he received from Dickens, and the ›ains he took to introduce his young friend to the visitors at ;ad's Hill, and in London at Hyde Park Place, who were his eniors. He was under an engagement to visit Dickens,—had is portmanteau packed in fact, almost ready to start on his ›urney—when he saw to his amazement the announcement f his death in the newspapers—and it was a very great shock › him. Not long afterwards, Mr. Fildes said, the family, ·ith much kind thoughtfulness, renewed the invitation to him › stay a few days at Gad's Hill Place, and during that time e made the imperishable drawing of "The Empty Chair."

Bearing in mind the above circumstances coming from so igh an authority, a missing link has been supplied, but—*The Iystery of Edwin Drood* is still unsolved!

CHAPTER VI.

RICHARD WATTS'S CHARITY, ROCHESTER.

"Strictly speaking, there were only *six* Poor Travellers; but being a Traveller myself, though an idle one, and being withal as poor as I hope to be, I brought the number up to seven. . . . I, for one, am so divided this night between fact and fiction, that I scarce know which is which."—*The Seven Poor Travellers.*

THE most unique Charity ever described in fiction, or founded on fact, well deserves a few pages to be devoted to a record of its interesting history and present position. We therefore occupy a short time in examining it on Thursday morning, before our visit to the Marshes.

Except for *The Seven Poor Travellers*, which was the title of the Christmas Number of *Household Words* issued in 1854, it is possible that few beyond "the ancient city" would ever have heard, or indeed have cared to hear, anything about the Worshipful Master Richard Watts or his famous Charity; now, as all the world knows, it is a veritable "household word" to readers and admirers of Dickens. In the narrative, he, as the first Traveller, is supposed to have visited Rochester, and passed the evening with the six Poor Travellers, and thus to have made the seventh. After hearing the story of the Charity "from the decent body of a wholesome matronly presence" (this was Mrs. Cackett, a former matron, who is said

:o have been very much astonished at her appearance in the drama of *The Seven Poor Travellers*, which she subsequently

itnessed at the Rochester Theatre), he obtains permission treat the Travellers to a hot supper. The inn at which the 'st Traveller stayed was doubtless our old acquaintance, the ull, "where the window of his adjoining bedroom looked own into the Inn yard, just where the lights of the kitchen redden a massive fragment of the Castle wall." Here wa brewed the "wassail" contained in the "brown beauty," th "turkey" and "beef" roasted, and the "plum-pudding boiled. As Mr. Robert Langton says, "the account of th treat to the poor Travellers is of course wholly fictitiou although it is accepted as sober truth by many people, bot in Rochester and elsewhere."

It is not our purpose to criticize the seven pretty storie which make up this Christmas Number, part of the first c which only relates to Watts's Charity; but we will ventur to affirm that the concluding portion of that story, referrin to "Richard Doubledick," "who was a Poor Traveller wit not a farthing in his pocket, and who came limping dow on foot to this town of Chatham," is one of the most touchin instances of Christian forgiveness ever recorded, and hardene indeed must he be who reads it with dry eyes.

To what extent Dickens himself was affected by this beau tiful tale, is shown by the following extract from a lette addressed by him, on 22nd December, 1854, to the lat Mr. Arthur Ryland, formerly Mayor of Birmingham, no treasured by his widow, Mrs. Arthur Ryland, who kindl allowed a copy to be taken:—

"What you write with so much heartiness of my first Poo Traveller is quite delightful to me. The idea of that litt story obtained such strong possession of me when it cam into my head, that it cost me more time and tears than mo people would consider likely. The response it meets with payment for anything."

It is also interesting to record that many years afterwar Mr. Ryland read this story at one of the Christmas gatherin of the Birmingham and Midland Institute, and subsequentl received from an unknown correspondent—Sergeant A——, of the 106th Light Infantry, then stationed at Umballa, East Indies, who had noticed an account of the reading in a newspaper—a letter under date of 15th July, 1870, asking to be favoured with a copy of the story; "for," said the writer, "we have just started a Penny Reading Society (if I may call it so), and I'm sure that story would be the means of reclaiming many men from their vices—I mean drinking and low company." The story was of course sent, and Mr. Ryland subsequently communicated the circumstances to the present Mr. Charles Dickens, who replied—"I wish my dear father could have seen the sergeant's letter; it would have pleased him, I am sure."

As we proceed along the High Street, on the north side towards Chatham, a walk of only a few yards from the Bull brings us to a curious Tudor stone-built house of two stories, with latticed windows and three-pointed gables. Under a lamp in the centre, which is over the "quaint old door"—the door-sill itself being (as is usual with some old houses) a little below the street, so that we drop by a step or two into the entrance-hall—is a tablet containing the following inscription:—

(CENTRE.)

RICHARD WATTS, ESQUIRE,
by his Will dated 22nd August, 1579,
founded this Charity
for Six Poor Travellers,
who, not being Rogues or Proctors,
May receive gratis for one Night
Lodging, Entertainment,
and Fourpence each.

"In testimony of his munificence, in honour of his memory and inducement to his example, the Charitable Trustees o this City and Borough have caused this stone to be renewe(and inscribed, A.D. 1865."

And on the left and right-hand sides respectively of th(preceding appear smaller tablets, with the following inscrip tions:—

(LEFT.)

The Charitable Trustees
of this City and
Borough appointed
by the Lord High
Chancellor,
16 December, 1836,
are to see
this Charity
executed.

(RIGHT.)

Pagitt *Arms.* Somers

Thomas Pagitt,
second husband of
Mary, Daughter of
Thomas Somers
of Halstow,
Widow of Richard Watts,
Deceased A.D. 1599.

We enter the old-fashioned little parlour, or office, on th left-hand side, "warm in winter and cool in summer. It ha a look of homely welcome and soothing rest. It has remarkably cosy fireside, the very blink of which, gleamin out into the street upon a winter's night, is enough to war all Rochester's heart." The matron receives us politely, an shows us two large books of foolscap size with ruled column one of these containing a record of the visitors to the Charit and the other a list of the recipients thereof. A litt pleasantry is caused by one of us entering his name in th wrong book, but this mistake is promptly rectified by th matron, who informs us that we are scarcely objects for reli as "Poor Travellers." She then kindly repeats to us the two egends respecting the origin of the Charity, the first of which 's tolerably well known, but the other is less familiar. Before ccording these, it may be well to give an extract from the will of Master Richard Watts (a very curious and lengthy document), which was industriously hunted up by the late Ir. Charles Bullard, author of the *Romance of Rochester*, nd by him contributed to the *Rochester and Chatham ournal*, of which it fills a whole column.

The will (dated, as previously stated, August 22nd, 1579) irects, *inter alia*, that "First the Alms-house already erected nd standing beside the Markett Crosse, within the Citty of ochester aforesaid, which Almshouses my Will Purpose nd Desire is that there be reedified added and provided ith such Roomes as be there already provided Six Severall oomes with Chimneys for the Comfort placeing and abideg of the Poore within the said Citty, and alsoe to be made t and convenient places therein for Six good Matrices or ock Bedds and other good and sufficient Furniture to rbour or lodge in poore Travellers or Wayfareing Men ing noe Common Rogues nor Proctors, and they the said ayfareing Men to harbour and lodge therein noe longer n one Night unlesse Sickness be the farther Cause thereof d those poore Folkes there dwelling shall keepe the House ete make the Bedds see to the Furniture keepe the same ete and courteously intreate the said poore Travellers ll to every of the said poore Travellers att their first comei in to have fourpence and they shall warme them at the e of the Residents within the said House if Need be."

he reason for the exception in the testator's will as ards rogues is sufficiently obvious, and therefore all the point of this singular bequest lies in the word "Proctors." Who were they? One of the legends has it that the obsolete word "Proctors" referred to certain sturdy mendicants who swarmed in the south of England, and went about extracting money from the charitable public under the pretence of collecting "Peter's Pence" for the Pope; or, as the compiler of Murray's *Handbook to the County of Kent* suggests, "were probably the bearers of licences to collect alms for hospitals," etc. Possibly the worthy Master Richard Watts objected to the levying of this blackmail; or he may in his walks have been subjected to the proctors' importunities, and consequently in his will rigorously debarred them in all futurity from any share in his Charity.

The other legend is that Master Watts, being grievously sick and sore to die, sent for his lawyer, who in those days acted as proctor as well,—Steerforth in *David Copperfield* calls the proctor "a monkish kind of attorney,"—and bade him prepare his will according to certain instructions. The will was made, but not in the manner directed, and subsequently, on the testator regaining his health, he discovered the fraud which the crafty lawyer or proctor had tried to perpetrate—which was, in fact, to make himself the sole legatee. In his just indignation he made another will, and in it for ever excluded the fraternity of proctors from benefiting thereby. The reader is at liberty to accept whichever of the two legends he chooses. It is right to say that Mr. Roach Smith utterly rejects the second story. He says proctors were simply rogues, although some of them may have been licensed.

The following is a foot-note to Fisher's *History and Antiquities of Rochester and its Environs*, MDCCLXXII.

Watts' Almshouses:
Rochester

"It is generally thought that the reason of Mr. Watts's excluding proctors from the benefit of the Charity, was that a proctor had been employed to make his will, whereby he had given all the estates to himself; but I am inclined to believe that the word proctor is derived from procurator, who was an itinerant priest, and had dispensations from the Pope to absolve the subjects of this realm from the oath of allegiance to Queen Elizabeth, in whose reign there were many such priests."

When the identity of Miss Adelaide Anne Procter, the gifted author of the pure and pathetic *Legends and Lyrics* (who had been an anonymous contributor to *Household Words* for some time under the *nom de plume* of "Mary Berwick"), became known to Charles Dickens, he sent her a charming and kindly letter of congratulation and appreciation, dated 17th December, 1854 (just at the time that the Christmas stories of the *Seven Poor Travellers* were published), which thus concludes:—

"You have given me so much pleasure, and have made me shed so many tears, that I can only think of you now in association with the sentiment and grace of your verses. Pray accept the blessing and forgiveness of Richard Watts, *though I am afraid you come under both his conditions of exclusion.*"

We are informed that the original bequest of the testator was only £36 16*s*. 8*d*. per annum, being the rent of land; but now, owing to the improved letting of the land, for building and other purposes, the Revenues of the Charity are upwards of £4,000 per annum. The "fourpence" of the foundation would be equal to some three shillings and fourpence of our money. The trustees, about sixteen in number

—one of whom has filled the office for fifty years—have very wisely and prudently obtained an extension of their powers; and the Court of Chancery have twice (in 1855 and 1886) sanctioned schemes for the administration of the funds, which have largely benefited Rochester in many ways. As witness of this, there are a series of excellent almshouses on the Maidstone Road (which cost about £6,000), with appropriate entrance-gates and gardens, endowed for the

support and maintenance of townsmen and townswomen. We subsequently go into several of the rooms, all beautifully clean, and in most cases tastefully decorated by the inmates with a few pictures, prints, and flowers, and find that the present occupants are ten almsmen and six women. We have a chat with one of the almsmen,—a hearty old man, once the beadle of St. Margaret's Church,—who rejoices in the name of Peter Weller, and whom we find to be well up in his *Pickwick*. There are a resident head-nurse and three other resident nurses in the establishment, who occasionally go out to nurse the sick in the city. In addition to these almshouses, a handsome new hospital has been erected in the New Road, and partly endowed (£1,000 a year) out of the funds. Contributions are also made annually from the same source towards the support of the Public Baths, and for apprenticing deserving lads. Such is the development of this remarkable Charity.

The matron calls our attention to many interesting names in the Visitors' book. Under date of the 11th May, 1854, are the signatures, in good bold writing, of Charles Dickens and Mark Lemon; and in subsequent entries, extending over many years, appear the names of Wilkie Collins, W. H. Wills, W. G. Wills, Walter Besant, Thomas Adolphus Trollope, J. Henry Shorthouse, Augustus J. C. Hare, and other well-known *littérateurs.* As usual, there are also numerous names of Americans, including those of Miss Mary Anderson and party.

There are many curious remarks recorded in this book, such as an entry dated 26th June, 1857, which says:—"Tossed by, and out of the Bull with a crumpled horn, as no one would lend me five shillings, therefore obliged to solicit the benefit of this excellent charity." There is an admirable testimony in Latin, by the late Bishop of Lincoln, Dr. Wordsworth, to the usefulness of the institution, which, dated 23rd August, 1883, is as follows:—"*Esto perpetua obstantibus Caritatis Commissionariis.*" His Lordship's remark was probably in allusion to the fact that the Charity Commissioners were (as we were afterwards informed) inclined, some time ago, to abolish the Charity, but this proceeding was stoutly and successfully resisted by the trustees. But he most gratifying records which we see in the book consist of several entries by recipients of the Charity themselves, who have subsequently come again after prosperous times in the capacity of visitors, and thus testified to the benefits received.

ere is one:—"Having once enjoyed the Charity, I wish it long life."

A clerk has the responsibility of making a careful selection six from the number of applicants, and this appears to be light task, inasmuch as the "prescribed number of Poor

Travellers are forthcoming every night from year's end t year's end," and sometimes amount to fifty in a day. I selecting the persons to be admitted, care is taken tha

unless under special circumstances, the same person be n admitted for more than one night, and in no case for mo than two consecutive nights. A glance over the regist shows that the names include almost all trades and occup tions; and, as regards the fact of a great many coming from Kentish towns, Dartford, Greenwich, Canterbury, Maidstone, etc., we are informed, in reply to our enquiry, that this is no criterion of the real residence, because the place where the raveller last lodged is always entered. The matron told us story of a clever attempt to obtain admission by a Poor Traveller "with a tin whistle and very gentlemanly hands," who subsequently turned out to be a reporter from the *Echo*, in which paper there afterwards appeared an account of the Charity, called *On Tramp by an Amateur*.

We are shown over the premises—scrupulously neat and lean—and observe that there are excellent lavatories with oot-pans, and a pair of slippers provided for each recipient. We afterwards see the six Poor Travellers who have had their upper, and are comfortably smoking their pipes in a snug oom, and we have a pleasant and interesting chat with them. They are much above the condition of ordinary tramps, and re lodged in six separate bedrooms, or "dormitories" which pen out of a gallery at the back part of the building, very curious structure, remaining just as it was in the ays of Queen Elizabeth. For supper, each man is allowed alf a pound of cooked meat, a pound of bread, and half-a-int of porter, and receives fourpence in money on leaving. is right to state that we heard complaints in the city lating to the evil effects of a number of poor travellers eing attracted to the Charity daily, when but a few can btain relief.

Respecting the Worshipful Master Richard Watts himself ry little is known, except that he was appointed by Queen lizabeth in 1560 to be the surveyor and clerk of the works r the building of Upnor Castle; that he was paymaster to the Wardens of Rochester Bridge for some years previously that he was recorder of Rochester, and represented the city in Parliament from 1563 to 1571, and that he resided a "Satis House," which stood on the site of the modern residence bearing the same name, now occupied by Mrs. Booth a little to the south of the Cathedral, but which must not however, be confounded with the Satis House of *Great Expectations*, this latter, as has been previously explained

Satis House.

being identical with Restoration House, in Crow Lane When Queen Elizabeth visited Rochester in 1573, Watt had the honour of entertaining Her Majesty there, on the last day of her residence in "the ancient city"; and to his expressions of regret at having no better accommodation to offer, the Queen was pleased generously to reply, "Satis," by which name the house has ever since been known. Estella in *Great Expectations*, gives another view of the origin of th name. She says:—"Its other name was Satis; which is Greek, or Latin, or Hebrew, or all three—or all one to me —for enough: but it meant more than it said. It meant, when it was given, that whoever had this house, could want nothing else. They must have been easily satisfied in those

Watts's Monument in Rochester Cathedral.
Over the Memorial Brass of Charles Dickens.

ays, I should think." Archbishop Longley was born there ı 1794.

There is a monument to the proctor-hating philanthropist n the wall of the south transept of the Cathedral over the rass to Charles Dickens, surmounted by a very curious painted marble half-figure effigy with flowing beard, o "worthy Master Richard starting out of it, like a ship's figure-head." Underneath is the following epitaph:—

Sacred to the Memory of
Richard Watts, Esq.,
a principal Benefactor to this City,
who departed this life Sept. 10, 1579, at
his Mansion house on Bully Hill, called SATIS
(so named by Q. ELIZABETH of glorious memory),
and lies interr'd near this place, as by his Will doth
plainly appear. By which Will, dated Aug. 22, and
proved Sep. 25, 1579, he founded an Almshouse
for the relief of poor people and for the reception
of six poor Travelers every night, and for
imploying the poor of this City.

The Mayor and Citizens of this City,
in testimony of their Gratitude and his Merit,
have erected this Monument, A.D. 1736.
RICHARD WATTS, ESQ.,
then Mayor.

Over and over again, in the various roads and lanes which we traverse, in the county famous for "apples, cherries, hops, and women," we have ample opportunities of verifying the experience of Dickens, and indeed of many other observers (including David Copperfield, who met numbers of "ferocious-looking ruffians"), as to the prevalence of tramps, not all of whom appear eligible as recipients of Watts's Charity! Our fraternity seems to be ubiquitous, and had we the purse of Fortunatus, it would hardly suffice to satisfy their requirements. What a wonderfully thoughtful, descriptive, and xhaustive chapter is that on "Tramps" in *The Uncommercial Traveller!* We believe Rochester and Strood Hill must ave been in Dickens's mind when he penned it. Every pecies and every variety of tramp is herein described,—'he surly Tramp, The slinking Tramp, The well-spoken oung-man Tramp, The John Anderson Tramp, Squire 'ouncerby's Tramp, The show Tramp, The educated Tramp, 'he tramping Soldier, The tramping Sailor, The Tramp andicraft man, Clock-mending Tramps, Harvest Tramps, Iopping Tramps and Spectator Tramps—but perhaps the iost amusing of all is the following:—

"The young fellows who trudge along barefoot, five or six together, eir boots slung over their shoulders, their shabby bundles under eir arms, their sticks newly cut from some roadside wood, are not ninently prepossessing, but are much less objectionable. There is tramp-fellowship among them. They pick one another up at sting stations, and go on in companies. They always go at a fast ing—though they generally limp too—and there is invariably one the company who has much ado to keep up with the rest. They nerally talk about horses, and any other means of locomotion than ılking: or, one of the company relates some recent experiences of e road—which are always disputes and difficulties. As for example. as I'm a standing at the pump in the market, blest if there don't me up a Beadle, and he ses, 'Mustn't stand here,' he ses. 'Why t?' I ses. 'No beggars allowed in this town,' he ses. 'Who's a ggar?' I ses. 'You are,' he ses. 'Who ever see *me* beg? Did *t?*' I ses. 'Then you're a tramp,' he ses. 'I'd rather be that ın a Beadle,' I ses. (The company express great approval.) 'ould you?' he ses to me. 'Yes, I would,' I ses to him. 'Well,' ses, 'anyhow, get out of this town.' 'Why, blow your little vn!' I ses, 'who wants to be in it? Wot does your dirty little vn mean by comin' and stickin' itself in the road to anywhere? ıy don't you get a shovel and a barrer, and clear your town out people's way?' (The company expressing the highest approval d laughing aloud, they all go down the hill.)"

It is worthy of consideration, and it is probably more thar a mere coincidence, to observe that some of the reform which have been effected in the management of the nov munificent revenues of Richard Watts's Charity were in stigated as a sequence to the appearance of Dickens' imperishable stories, published under the title of *The Seve Poor Travellers.* The Rev. Robert Whiston, with whom w chatted on the subject, is of opinion that the late Lor Brougham is entitled to the credit for reforms in this an other charities.

CHAPTER VII.

AN AFTERNOON AT GAD'S HILL PLACE.

It was just large enough, and no more; was as pretty within as it was without, and was perfectly arranged and comfortable."—*Little Dorrit.*

This has been a happy home. . . . I love it. . . ."—*The Cricket on the Hearth.*

\ NEVER-TO-BE-FORGOTTEN day was Saturday, the twenty-fth of August, 1888, a day remarkable, as were many of the osing days of the summer of that year, for its bright, sunny, ıd cheerful nature. The sky was a deep blue—usually :scribed as an Italian sky—broken only by a few fleecy, ımulus clouds, which served to bring out more clearly the :h colour of the background. There was a fine bracing air ıming from the north-west, for which the county of Kent is ımous. Truly an enjoyable day for a holiday! and one at Dickens himself would have loved to describe. So after lesultory stroll about the streets of Rochester, one of many lightful strolls, we make our first outward tramp, and that course to Gad's Hill. By the way, much attention has en devoted to the consideration of the derivation of the me, "Gad's Hill." It is no doubt a corruption of "God's ll," of which there are two so-called places in the county, and there is also a veritable "God's Hill" a little furthe south, in the Isle of Wight.

Crossing Rochester Bridge, we enter the busy town o Strood, pass through its long thoroughfare, go up the Dove Road,—which was the ancient Roman military road after wards called Watling Street, until a little above Strood i turned slightly to the left, passing through what is nov Cobham Park,—and leave the windmill on Broomhill to th right. The ground rises gently, the chalk formation bein

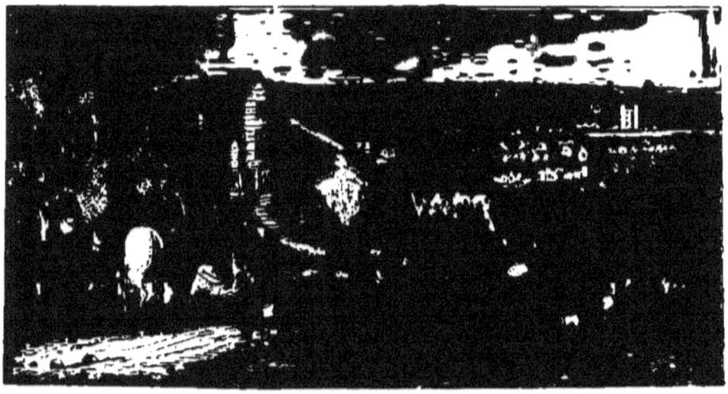

Rochester from Strood Hill.

exposed here and there in disused pits. A portion of tl road higher up is cut through the Thanet sands, which re on the chalk. Again and again we stop, and turn to admi the winding valley of the Medway. As we get more in the country and leave the town behind, we find the roadsid still decked with summer flowers, notably the fine dark bl Canterbury bell—the nettle-leaved Campanula (*Campanu Trachelium*)—and the exquisite light-blue chicory (*Cichoriu Intybus*); but the flowers of the latter are so evanescent th when gathered, they fade in an hour or two. This beauti starlike-blossomed plant is abundant in many parts of Kent. We pass on the right the pretty high-standing grounds of Mr. Hulkes at the "Little Hermitage," and notice the obelisk further to the right on still higher land, erected about fifty years ago to the memory of Charles Larkin (a name very suggestive of "the eldest Miss Larkins") of Rochester,— "a parish orator and borough Hampden"—by his grateful fellow-citizens.

A walk of less than three miles brings us to the "Sir John Falstaff"—"a delightfully old-fashioned roadside inn of the coaching days, which stands on the north side of the road a little below 'Gad's Hill Place,' and which no man possessed of a penny was ever known to pass in warm weather."

Mr. Kitton relates in *Dickensiana* the following amusing story of a former waiter at the "Falstaff":—

"A few days after Dickens's death, an Englishman, deeply grieved at the event, made a sort of pilgrimage to Gad's Hill —to the home of the great novelist. He went into the famous 'Sir John Falstaff Inn' near at hand, and in the effusiveness of his honest emotions, he could not avoid taking the country waiter into his confidence.

"'A great loss this of Mr. Dickens,' said the pilgrim.

"'A very great loss to us, sir,' replied the waiter, shaking his head; 'he had all his ale sent in from this house!'"

One of the two lime-trees only remains, but the well and bucket—as recorded by the *Uncommercial Traveller* in the chapter on "Tramps"—are there still, surrounded by a protective fence.

We have but little time to notice the "Falstaff," for our admiring gaze is presently fixed on Gad's Hill Place itself, the house in which Dickens resided happily—albeit trouble

F G Kitton

came to him as to most men—from the year 1856 till his death in 1870. Everybody knows the story of how, as a little boy, he cherished the idea of one day living in this house, and how that idea was gratified in after-life. It is from the *Uncommercial Traveller*, in the chapter on "Travelling Abroad," and the repetition is never stale. He says:—

"So smooth was the old high road, and so fresh were the horses, and so fast went I, that it was midway between Gravesend and Rochester, and the widening river was bearing the ships, white-sailed or black-smoked, out to sea, when I noticed by the wayside a very queer small boy.

"'Holloa!' said I to the very queer small boy, 'where do you ve?'

"'At Chatham,' says he.

"'What do you do there?' says I.

"'I go to school,' says he.

"I took him up in a moment, and we went on. Presently, the ery queer small boy says, 'This is Gad's Hill we are coming to, here Falstaff went out to rob those travellers, and ran away.'

"'You know something about Falstaff, eh?' said I.

"'All about him,' said the very queer small boy. 'I am old (I n nine), and I read all sorts of books. But *do* let us stop at the top the hill, and look at the house there, if you please!'

"'You admire that house?' said I.

"'Bless you, sir,' said the very queer small boy, 'when I was not ore than half as old as nine, it used to be a treat for me to be ought to look at it. And now, I am nine, I come by myself to ok at it. And ever since I can recollect, my father, seeing me fond of it, has often said to me, 'If you were to be very per-vering, and were to work hard, you might some day come to live it.' Though that's impossible!' said the very queer small boy, awing a low breath, and now staring at the house out of window th all his might.

"I was rather amazed to be told this by the very queer small boy; that house happens to be *my* house, and I have reason to believe at what he said was true."

Gadshill Place

Mrs. Lynn Linton, the celebrated novelist, who resided at Gad's Hill as a child, has very kindly given us her personal recollections of it sixty years ago, and of the interesting circumstances under which Charles Dickens subsequently purchased the property;—which will be found at the end of this chapter.

Before seeking permission to enter the grounds of Gad's Hill Place, which are surrounded by a high wall, and screened xternally by a row of well-topped lime-trees, we retrace our teps for a few minutes, in order to refresh ourselves with a iomely luncheon, and what Mr. Richard Swiveller would call "modest quencher," at the Sir John Falstaff. It may be ertain that not much time is consumed in this operation. Ve then take a good look at the remarkable house opposite, he object of our pilgrimage, which has been made well nown by countless photographs and engravings. It is a omfortable, but a not very attractive-looking red-brick house f two stories, with porch at entrance, partly covered with ivy. ll the front windows, with the exception of the central ones, re bayed, and there are dormer windows in the roof, which is ırmounted by a bell-turret and vane. What a strange ıscination it has for admirers of Dickens when seen for the rst time! According to Forster, in his *Life* of the novelist, ıe house was built in 1780 by a well-known local character amed James Stevens, who rose to a good position. He was ıe father-in-law of the late Professor Henslow, the Botanist, f Cambridge. Dickens paid for it the sum of £1,790, and the urchase was completed on Friday, 14th March, 1856. The resent owner is Major Austin F. Budden,[1] of the 12th Kent

[1] Since this was written, Gad's Hill Place has been purchased by the on. F. G. Latham. Major Budden has resigned his commission

Artillery Volunteers, who, we find, in the course of subsequent conversation, had also done good municipal service, having filled the office of Mayor of Rochester for two years,—from 1879 to 1881,—and that he was elected at the early age of twenty-eight.

We ring the bell at the gate which shuts the house out from view, and are promptly answered by a pleasant-speaking housemaid, who takes our cards on a salver, and ushers us into the library. We are requested to enter our names in the visitors' book, and this is done with alacrity. We are under the impression that we shall only be allowed to see the hall and study, a privilege allowed to any visitor on presentation of a card; but fortunately for us the courteous owner appears and says that, as he has half an hour to spare, he will show us entirely over the house. He is better than his word, and we, delighted with the prospect, commence our inspection of the late home of the great novelist with feelings of singular pleasure, which are altogether a new sensation. Do any readers remember, when perusing the Waverley novels in their youth, a certain longing (as the height of their ambition, possibly gratified in after-life) to see Abbotsford the home of the "Wizard of the North"? *That* is a feeling akin to the one which possesses us on the present occasion a feeling of veneration almost amounting to awe as we recall

---

locally, and now holds a commission in the Limerick City Artillery Militia. It is very pleasant to place on record that in subsequent visits to "Dickens-Land" I was always received with friendly kindness by Major and Mrs. Budden, whose hospitality I often enjoyed. Their enthusiasm for the late owner of Gad's Hill Place, and their willingness to show every part of their beautiful residence to any one specially interested, was most gratifying to a lover of Dickens. Like the novelist Mrs. Budden is fond of private theatricals, and has published a little book on *Mrs. Jarley's Wax-Works and How to Use Them.*

ınd seem to realize, not only the presence of Charles Dickens ıimself, but of the many eminent literary, artistic, and his-rionic characters—his contemporaries—who assembled here, ınd shared the hospitality of the distinguished owner. ' Dickens penetrates here—where does not his genial sunshine ›enetrate ?"

Turning over the leaves of the visitors' book, Major Budden :alls our attention to the signatures of Americans, who :onstitute by far the majority of visitors. Among the more ecent appears the name of that accomplished actress, Miss Mary Anderson—herself a great admirer of Charles Dickens —who came accompanied by a party of friends. We also ɔund her name, with the same party, in the visitors' book at Richard Watts's Charity in Rochester. Major Budden spoke lso of the great enthusiasm always exhibited by our Ameri-an friends in regard to Dickens, some of whom had told him ıore than once that it was the custom to instruct their hildren in a knowledge of his works: they read them, in ıct, in the schools.

The library, or study, is a very cosy little room, made famous y Mr. Luke Fildes's picture of "The Empty Chair." It is tuated on the west side of the porch, looking to the front, ith the shrubbery in the distance; and among the most ɔnspicuous objects contained in it are the curious counter-it book-backs devised by Dickens and his friends, and ranged as shelves to fit the door of the room. They umber nearly eighty, and a selection is given below of a w of the quaintest titles, viz.:—

The Quarrelly Review. 4 vols.

King Henry the Eighth's Evidences of Christianity. 5 vols.

Noah's Arkitecture. 2 vols.

"THE EMPTY CHAIR":
Gad's Hill
Ninth of June 1870
F G Kitton
from the Drawing by
S. L. Fildes

Chickweed.

Groundsel (by the Author of Chickweed).

Cockatoo on Perch.

History of a Short Chancery Suit. 21 vols.

Cats' Lives. 9 vols.

Hansard's Guide to Refreshing Sleep (many volumes).

The Wisdom of our Ancestors—I. Ignorance. II. Superstition. III. The Block. IV. The Stake. V. The Rack. VI. Dirt. VII. Disease.

Several of the titles were used for a similar purpose at avistock House, London—Dickens's former residence.

We cannot help, as we sit down quietly for a few minutes, ondering how much of *Little Dorrit*, *Hunted Down*, *A Tale f Two Cities*, *Great Expectations*, *The Uncommercial Traveller*, *ur Mutual Friend*, and *The Mystery of Edwin Drood* (which ere all issued between 1856 and 1870) was written in this mous room, to say nothing of those heaps of exquisite tters which so helped, cheered, interested, or amused many correspondent, and have delighted the public since.

In the hall, which has the famous parquet floor laid down y Dickens, is still hanging the framed illumination, artistally executed by Owen Jones, and placed there immediately ter Dickens became the "Kentish freeholder on his native ath" as he called it. It is as follows:—

This House,

GAD'S HILL PLACE,

stands on the summit of Shakespeare's Gad's Hill,
ever memorable for its association with
Sir John Falstaff, in his noble fancy.

"But, my lads, my lads, to-morrow morning by four o'cloc early at Gad's Hill. There are pilgrims going to Canterbur with rich offerings, and traders riding to London with f

Counterfeit Book-backs on Study Door.

purses; I have vizards for you all; you have horses fc yourselves." [2]

[2] It has been suggested that the lines above quoted might give one th impression that they are those of Falstaff. This, of course, is not th

From the hall we enter the dining-room, a cheerful apartment looking on to the beautiful lawn at the back, which has at the end the arched conservatory of lilac-tinted glass at top, in which the novelist took so much interest, and where he hung some Chinese lanterns, sent down from London the day before his death. We are informed that in this building he signed the last cheque which he drew, to pay his subscription to the Higham Cricket Club. The door of the dining-room is faced with looking-glass, so that it may reflect the contents of the conservatory. Among these are two or three New Zealand tree-ferns which Dickens himself purchased. In the dining-room Major Budden pointed out the exact spot where the fatal seizure from effusion on the brain took place, on the afternoon of Wednesday, 8th June, 1870, and where Dickens

---

ase. They are spoken by Poins, when in company with Falstaff, Prince Henry, and others. They occur in Act I. Scene ii. of *King Henry IV.*, Part 1.

A Note to Charles Knight's Edition of Shakespeare, contained in the Illustrations to Act I." of the same Play, states that Gad's Hill appears to have been a place notorious for robbers before the time of Shakespeare, r Stevens discovered an entry of the date of 1558 in the books of the Stationers' Company, of a ballad entitled, "The Robbery at Gad's Hill." nd the late Sir Henry Ellis, of the British Museum, communicated to r. Boswell, Editor of Malone's Shakespeare, a narrative in the handriting of Sir Roger Manwood, Chief Baron of the Exchequer, dated 5th uly, 1590, which shows that Gad's Hill was at that period the resort of a and of well-mounted robbers of more than usual daring, as appears from e following extract :—

"In the course of that Michaelmas term, I being at London, many bberies were done in the bye-ways at Gad's Hill, on the west part of ochester, and at Chatham, down on the east part of Rochester, by rse thieves, with such fat and lusty horses, as were not like hackney rses nor far-journeying horses; and one of them sometimes wearing vizard grey beard, he was by common report in the country called 'ustice Grey Beard;' and no man durst travel that way without great mpany."

lay: first on the floor to the right of the door on entering and afterwards to the left, when the couch was brought dowr (by order of Mr. Steele, the surgeon of Strood, as we subse quently learned), upon which he breathed his last.

The drawing-room faces the front, and, like the dining room, has been lengthened, and opens into the conservatory In fact, Dickens was always improving Gad's Hill Place There is a memorable reference to the conservatory by Forster in the third vol. of the *Life*. He says:—

"This last addition had long been an object of desire witl him, though he would hardly, even now, have given himsel the indulgence but for the golden shower from America He saw it first in a completed state on the Sunday before hi death, when his youngest daughter was on a visit to him.

"'Well, Katey,' he said to her, 'now you see POSITIVEL' the last improvement at Gad's Hill,' and every one laughe at the joke against himself. The success of the new con servatory was unquestionable. It was the remark of al around him, that he was certainly, from this last of hi improvements, drawing more enjoyment than from any of it predecessors, when the scene for ever closed!"

This room is a long one, and, in common with all th others, gives us, under the auspices of the brilliantly fin day, some idea of the late owner's love of light, air, an cheerfulness. That the situation is also a healthy an bracing one is confirmed by the fact, that in a letter writte on board the *Russia*, bound for Liverpool, on the 26th Apri 1868, after his second American tour, he speaks of havin made a "Gad's Hill breakfast."

Our most considerate cicerone next takes us into severa of the bedrooms, these being of large size, and having a littl dressing-room marked off with a partition, head-high, so that no cubic space is lost to the main chamber. As illustrative of Charles Dickens's care for the comfort of his friends, it is said that in the visitors' bedrooms there was always hot water and a little tea-table set out, so that each one could at any time make for himself a cup of the beverage "that cheers but not inebriates." The views from these rooms are very charming. Mr. W. T. Wildish afterwards told us, that luring the novelist's life-time, Mr. Trood, the landlord of the Sir John Falstaff, once took him over Gad's Hill Place, and he was surprised to find Dickens's own bath-room covered with cuttings from *Punch* and other comic papers. I have ince learned that this was a screen of engravings which had riginally been given him.

The gardens, both flower and vegetable, are then pointed ut—the approach thereto from the back lawn being by neans of a flight of steps—as also the rosary, which occupies portion of the front lawn to the westward. The roses are f course past their best, but the trees look very healthy.

In the flower garden we are especially reminded of ickens's love for flowers, the China-asters, single dahlias, nd zinnias being of exceptional brightness. As to the iolets, which are here in abundance, both the Neapolitan nd Russian varieties, the Major shows us a method of ltivating them, first in frames, and then in single rows, so at he can get them in bloom for nearly nine months in e year!

Adjoining the lawn and vegetable garden is "the much-veted meadow," which the master of Gad's Hill obtained by change of some land with the trustees of Sir Joseph illiamson's Mathematical School at Rochester, and in which he planted "a number of limes and chestnuts, anc other quick-growing trees." Four grass walks meet in th centre of the vegetable garden, where there is a fine ol mulberry tree.

It is stated in Forster's *Life* of the novelist (Vol. iii p. 188) that Dickens obtained the meadow by exchange o some land "with the Trustees of Watts's Charity." But thi is not right. The distinguished historian of the Common wealth, and the faithful friend of the novelist all througl his life, is so habitually accurate, that it is an exceptiona circumstance for any one to be able to correct him. Howeve I am indebted to Mr. A. A. Arnold, of Rochester, for th following authentic account of the transaction.

Dickens was always anxious to obtain this meadow (whic consists of about fourteen acres), and, believing that th Trustees of Sir Joseph Williamson's Mathematical Schoc at Rochester were not empowered to sell their land, h purchased a field at the back of his own shrubbery fror Mr. Brooker, of Higham, with a view—as appears from th following characteristically courteous and business-like lette —to effect an exchange.

"GAD'S HILL PLACE,
"HIGHAM BY ROCHESTER, KENT.
"*Monday, Thirtieth June*, 186

"GENTLEMEN,

"Reverting to a proposal already made in gener terms by my solicitor, Mr. Ouvry, of Lincoln's Inn Field to Messrs. Essel and Co., I beg to submit my applicatio to you in detail.

"It is that you will have the kindness to consider th feasibility of exchanging the field at the back of my propert here (marked 404 in the accompanying plan), for the plot of land marked 384 in the said plan.

"I believe it will appear to you, on inquiry, that the land I offer in exchange for the meadow is very advantageously situated, and is of greater extent than the meadow, and would be of greater value to the Institution, whose interests you represent. On the other hand, the acquisition of the

Gad's Hill Place from the rear.

meadow as a freehold would render my little property more compact and complete.

"I have the honor to be, Gentlemen,

"Your faithful and obedient Servant,

"CHARLES DICKENS.

"To the Governors of
Sir Joseph Williamson's Free School,
"Rochester."

The offer fell through at the time; but it was renewed i 1868 in a different form, and eventually the field was sol (by permission of the Charity Commissioners) to Charle Dickens at an "accommodation" price—£2,500—which reall exceeded its actual market value.

But to resume our inspection. The whole of the bac of the house, looking southward, is covered by a Virgini creeper (*Ampelopsis quinquefolia*) of profuse growth, whic

must be an object of singular beauty in the autumn wh the crimson tints appear. As it now stands it is beautiful green, and there is scarcely more than a leaf or two he and there marking autumnal decay. The two famo hawthorn trees were blown down in a gale some yea ago.

In a quiet corner under a rose-tree (*Gloire de Dijo* flanked by a *Yucca* in bloom, the bed underneath consisti of deep blue lobelia, is a touching little memorial to a favourite canary. This consists of a narrow little board, made like a head-stone, and set aslant, on which is painted in neat letters the following epitaph :—

This is
the grave of
DICK,
the best of birds,
born
AT BROADSTAIRS,
Midsummer, 1851,
died
AT GAD'S HILL PLACE,
4th October, 1866.

No one can doubt who was the author of these simple lines. "Dick," it should be said, "was very dear both to Dickens and his eldest daughter," and he has been immortalized in Forster's *Life*. There is a very humorous account given of the attacks which the cats in the neighbourhood made upon him, and which were frustrated by an organized defence. The following is the passage :—

"Soon after the arrival of Dickens and his family at Gad's Hill Place, a household war broke out, in which the commander-in-chief was his man French, the bulk of the forces engaged being his children, and the invaders two cats." Writing to Forster, Dickens says :—"'The only thing new in this garden is that war is raging against two particularly tigerish and fearful cats (from the mill, I suppose), which are always glaring in dark corners after our wonderful little Dick. Keeping the house open at all points, it is impossible to shut them out, and they hide themselves in the most terrific manner: hanging themselves up behind draperies, like bats, and tumbling out in the dead of night with frightful caterwaulings. Hereupon French borrows Beaucourt's gun, loads the same to the muzzle, discharges it twice in vain, and throws himself over with the recoil, exactly like a clown. . . . About four pounds of powder and half a ton of shot have been fired off at the cat (and the public in general) during the week. The funniest thing is, that immediately after I have heard the noble sportsman blazing away at her in the garden in front, I look out of my room door into the drawing-room, and am pretty sure to see her coming in after the birds, in the calmest manner possible, by the back window.'"

Passing on our way the large and well-lighted servants' hall, over which is the bachelors' room,—whence in days gone by that rare literary serial, *The Gad's Hill Gazette*,[3] issued from a little printing press, presented by a friend to the sixth son of the novelist, who encouraged his boy's literary tastes,—we next see the stables, as usual, like everything else, in excellent order. A small statue of Fame blowing her golden trumpet surmounts the bachelors' room, and looks down upon us encouragingly.

[3] At an interview with Mr. H. F. Dickens some time afterwards, he told me the story of the origin of *The Gad's Hill Gazette*. There was a good deal of sand exposed at the back of the house, and the sons of the novelist—who like other boys were full of energy,—were fond of playing at "burying" each other. Their father naturally feared that this kind of play might have some disastrous effects, and develop into burying in earnest. So he said one day to his sons, "Why not establish a newspaper, if you want a field for your energies?" *The Gad's Hill Gazette* was the result. At first the tiny journal was written on a plain sheet and copies made; then a Manifold Writer was used; and afterwards came the Printing Press.

Our attention is then turned to the well, which is stated o be two hundred and seventeen feet deep, in the shed, or umping-room, over which is the Major's mare, "Tell-tale," heerfully doing her daily twenty minutes' task of drawing vater, which is pumped up to the cistern on the roof for the upply of the house. There is said to be never less than wenty feet of water in the well.

It may be interesting to mention that Gad's Hill Place

the title of my estate, sir, my place down in Kent"), which in the parish of Higham, and about twenty-six miles from ondon, stands on an elevation two hundred and fifty feet ove mean sea-level. The house itself is built on a bed the Thanet sands. The well is bored right through these nds, which Mr. W. H. Whitaker, F.R.S., of H. M. Geoical Survey (who has kindly given me some valuable ormation on the subject), states "may be about forty feet ck, and the water is drawn up from the bed of chalk beneath. This bed is of great thickness, probably six hundred or seven hundred feet, and the well simply reaches the level at which the chalk is charged with water, *i.e.* something a little higher than the level of the neighbouring river." The chalk is exposed on the lower bases of Gad's Hill, such as the Railway Station at Higham, the village of Chalk, the town of Strood, etc.

There are humorous extracts from letters by Dickens in Forster's *Life* respecting the well, which may appropriately be introduced. He says:—

"We are still (6th of July) boring for water here, at the rate of two pounds per day for wages. The men seem to like it very much, and to be perfectly comfortable." . . . And again, "Here are six men perpetually going up and down the well (I know that somebody will be killed), in the course of fitting a pump; which is quite a railway terminus—it is so iron, and so big. The process is much more like putting Oxford Street endwise, and laying gas along it, than anything else. By the time it is finished, the cost of this water will be something absolutely frightful. But of course it proportionately increases the value of the property, and that's my only comfort. . . . Five men have been looking attentively at the pump for a week, and (I should hope) may begin to fit it in the course of October." The depression caused by the prospect of the "absolutely frightful" cost of the water seems to have continued to the end of the letter, for it thus concludes:—"The horse has gone lame from a sprain, the big dog has run a tenpenny nail into one of his hind feet, the bolts have all flown out of the basket carriage, and the gardener says all the fruit trees want replacing with new ones."

Two of the Major's dogs are chained in the places formerly occupied by Dickens's dogs, "Linda" and "Turk."

The Porch, Gad's Hill Place.

The chains are very long, and allow the animals plenty of room for exercise. The space between the two permitted a person to walk past without their being able to come near him; and, as an instance of Dickens's thoughtful kindliness even to the lower animals, two holes were made in the wall so that the dogs could get through in hot weather, and lie in the shade of the trees on the other side. On the back gate entering into the lane at the side of the house was painted, "Beware of the dogs!" This caution appears to have been very necessary, for we heard more than once the story of an intrusive tramp who trespassed, and going too near the dogs, got sadly mauled. Dickens, with characteristic goodness, sent him at once to Chatham Hospital, and otherwise healed his wounds.

We are next conducted round the grounds, and have an opportunity of examining the front of the house more in detail. The porch is flanked by two cosy seats, the pretty little spade-shaped shields, and lateral angular ornamental supports on the back of which, we are informed, were constructed of pieces of wood from Shakespeare's furniture given to Dickens by a friend. A large variegated holly grows on either side of the porch, and a semi-circular gravel walk leads to the door. There is a closely-cut lawn in front, and opposite the hollies are two fine specimens of *Aucuba Japonica*—the so-called variegated laurel.

It will be remembered that the master of Gad's Hill had a tunnel excavated under the Dover Road (which runs through the property), so as to approach the "shrubbery" previously referred to, without having to cross the open public road. We did not learn who constructed the tunnel, but it was designed either by his brother, Mr. Alfred L. Dickens, who died at Manchester in 1860, or by his brother-in-law, Mr. Henry Austin. The entrance to the tunnel is by a flight of about twenty steps, flanked by two beautifully-grown specimens of

The Cedars, Gad's Hill.

Cedrus deodara, the "deodar," or god-tree of the Himalayas. The tunnel itself is cut through the sands, and, being only a little longer than the width of the road, it is not at all dark, but very pleasant and cool on a hot day. A corresponding flight of steps leads us into the shrubbery, which is shut off from the main road by iron railings only. Both ends of the tunnel are covered with ivy, which has the effect of partially concealing the openings. Readers of Forster's *Life* will recollect that the Swiss châlet presented to Dickens by his friend Fechter the actor, and in which he spent his last afternoon, formerly stood in the shrubbery. The châlet now stands in the terrace-garden of Cobham Hall.

Before we reach the exact place we have an opportunity of examining the two stately cedar trees (*Cedrus Libani*) which are the arboreal gems of the place. Major Budden informs us that they are about one hundred and twenty-eight years old, and were planted in their present position when they had attained about twenty years' growth. Some idea of their luxuriance may be formed when it is mentioned that the girth of each tree exceeds sixteen feet, and the longest branch of one of them measures eighty-four feet in length. In consequence of the habit of these trees "fastigiating" at the base, a very numerous series of lateral ramifying branches is the result. These branches spread out in terraces, and the rich green foliage, covered with exudations of resin, seems as though powdered silver had been lightly dusted over it. Each tree extends over a circular area of about eighty feet of ground in diameter. Under one of the cedars is the grave of "the big and beautiful Linda," Dickens's favourite St. Bernard dog. One of the trees has been injured, a large ıranch over-weighted with snow having broken off some 'ears ago.

Two or three noble ash trees also grace this spot, running traight up in a column some thirty-five feet before shooting ut a canopy of branches and leaves. There are also a few Scotch firs, the trunks well covered with ivy, and a pretty pecimen of the variegated sycamore. The undergrowth of aurel, laurustinus, briar, privet, holly, etc., is very luxuriant ere, and the vacant ground is closely covered with the wood nemone (*Anemone nemorosa*), which must form a continuous nass of pearly white flowers in spring-time.

The ground formerly occupied by the châlet is pointed ut to us, its site being marked by a bed of rich scarlet asturtiums. It will be recollected that Dickens describes the nterior of the building in a letter to an American friend, which is thus recorded in Forster's *Life*:—

"Divers birds sing here all day, and the nightingales all ight. The place is lovely and in perfect order. . . I have put ve mirrors in the châlet where I write, and they reflect and efract, in all kinds of ways, the leaves that are quivering at he windows, and the great fields of waving corn, and the ail-dotted river. My room is up among the branches of he trees; and the birds and the butterflies fly in and out, nd the green branches shoot in at the open windows, and he lights and shadows of the clouds come and go with he rest of the company. The scent of the flowers, and ndeed of everything that is growing for miles and miles, is nost delicious."

But the glory of Gad's Hill Place is reserved for us until ie close of our visit, when Major Budden very kindly takes s up to the roof, which is approached by a commodious flight of steps; and here, on this exceptionally fine day, we are privileged to behold a prospect of surpassing beauty. Right away to the westward is the great Metropolis, its presence being marked by the usual pall of greyish smoke. Opening from the town, and becoming wider and wider as the noble river approaches its estuary, is the Thames, now conspicuous by numerous vessels, showing masts and white and brown sails, and here and there by the smoky track of a steamer.

We remember how often the city and the river have been the scene of many and many an exploit in Dickens's novels. Northward are the dreary marshes, the famous "meshes" of *Great Expectations*, hereafter to be noticed. Then far to the eastward runs the valley of the Medway, the picturesque city of Rochester thereon being crowned by those conspicuous landmarks, its magnificent Castle and ancient Cathedral. In the background is the busy town of Chatham, its heights being capped by an enormous square and lofty building erected by the sect called "Jezreelites," whatever that may be. We were informed that the so-called "immortal" leader had just died, and it has since been reported that the gloomy building is likely to be converted into a huge jam factory. Beyond, and nearly seven miles off, is the high land called "Blue Bell," about three hundred feet above mean sea-level, and all along to the south the undulating grounds and beautiful woodland scenery of Cobham Park complete the picture.

As Major Budden points out in detail these many natural beauties of the district, we can quite understand and sympathize with Dickens's love for this exquisite spot; and we

View from the Roof
of Dickens's House
at Gad's Hill

heartily congratulate the present owner of Gad's Hill Plac on the charming historical property which he possesses, an which, so far as we can perceive (all honour to him), i kept in the same excellent condition that characterized i during the novelist's lifetime. What is particularly strikin about it is at once its compactness, completeness, an unpretentiousness.

Descending to the library, whence we started nearly thre hours previously, we refresh ourselves with a glass of wate from the celebrated deep well—a draught deliciously co and clear—which the hospitable Major presses us to "dilute (as Professor Huxley has somewhere said) in any way w please, but which we prefer to drink, as Dickens himse drank it—pure. Before we rise to leave the spot we have s long wished to see, and which we have now gone over to o hearts' content, we sadly recall to memory for a moment th "last scene of all that ends this strange, eventful history —that tragic incident which occurred on Thursday, 9th Jun 1870, when there was an "empty chair" at Gad's Hill Plac and all intelligent English-speaking nations experienced personal sorrow.

And so with many grateful acknowledgments to our kir and courteous host, who gives us some nice flowers ar cuttings as a parting souvenir, we take our leave, havir derived from our bright sunny visit to Gad's Hill Place th "wave of pleasure" which Mr. Herbert Spencer describes "raising the rate of respiration,—raised respiration beir an index of raised vital activities in general." In fine, t impression left on our minds is such as to induce us feel that we understand and appreciate more of Dicken old home than any illustration or written description of it, however excellent, had hitherto adequately conveyed to us. We have seen it for ourselves.

* * * * * *

The reminiscences which follow are from Mrs. Lynn Linton and three of Charles Dickens's nearest neighbours.

GAD'S HILL SIXTY YEARS AGO.

The early love which Charles Dickens felt for Gad's Hill House, and his boyish ambition to be one day its owner, had been already anticipated by my father. As a boy and young man, my father's heart was set on this place; and when my grandfather's death put him in sufficient funds he bought it. Being a beneficed clergyman, both of whose livings were in the extreme north of England, he could not live in the house; but he kept it empty for many years, always hoping to get leave of absence from the Bishop for a term long enough to justify the removal of his large family from Keswick to Rochester. In 1831 a five years' leave of absence was granted; and we all came up by coach to this Mecca of my father's love. We were three days and three nights on the road; and I remember quite distinctly the square court-yard and outside balcony of the old Belle Sauvage Inn, where we put up on our arrival in London. I remember, too, the powerful scent of the Portugal laurel and the bay-tree which grew on the right-hand side of Gad's Hill House as we entered—brought out by the warm damp of the late autumn afternoon. In our time all the outhouses had leaden figures on the top. There was a cupola with an alarm bell, which one night was rung lustily, to the terror of the whole neighbourhood, and the ashamed discovery among ourselves that rats were not burglars. In the shrubbery were two large leaden figures of Pomona and Vertumnus, standing on each side of the walk leading up to the arbour. We had then two arbours—one opposite the house at the end of the green walk, and another in a dilapidated state further in the shrubbery. They were built of big flint stones, many of which had holes in them, where small birds made their nests. I remember in one was a tomtit which was quite tame, and used to fly in and out while we were watching it. The two cedars, which I believe are still there, were a little choked and overshadowed by a large oak-tree, which my father cut down. Between seventy and eighty coaches, "vans," and mail-carts passed our house during the day, besides private carriages, specially those of travellers posting to or from Dover. Regiments, too, often passed on their way to Gravesend, where they embarked for India; and ships' companies, paid off, rowdy and half-tipsy, made the road really dangerous for the time being. We used to lock the two gates when we heard them coming, shouting and singing up the hill; and we had to stand many a mimic siege from the blue-jackets trying to force their way in. Sweet-water grapes grew and ripened in the open air over the wash-house; and the back of the house was covered with a singularly fine and luscious jargonelle pear. The garden was rich in apples. We had many kinds, from the sweet and pulpy nonsuch, to the small tight little pearmain and lemon pippin. We had nonparcils, golden pippins, brown nd golden russets, Ribstone pippins, and what we called a ort-wine apple—the flesh red, like that of the "blood-ranges." The small orchard to the right was as rich in herry-trees, filberts, and cobnuts. In the garden we had a g-tree, and the mulberry-tree, which is still there, was in ıll bearing in our time. The garden altogether was won-erfully prolific in flowers as well as fruits—roses as well as :rawberries and apples; and the green-house was full of rapes. Nightingales sang in the trees near the house, and ıe shrubbery was full of song birds. We had a grand view 'om the leads, where we used sometimes to go, and whence remember seeing a farmyard fire over at Higham—which re they said had been caused by an incendiary. There 'as a Low Church clergyman in the neighbourhood who ıight have been Chadband or Stiggins. He was fond of ɔme girls we knew, and called them his "lambs." He used ɔ put his arm round their waists, and they sat on his knees uite naturally. I myself heard him preach at Shorne gainst the institution of pancakes on Shrove Tuesday. He ıid it was not only superstitious but irreligious; as pancakes ıeant "pan Kakon," all evil. This I, then a girl of thirteen r so, heard and remember. When my father died his :operty had to be sold, as he did not make an eldest son. Ir. W. H. Wills, the trusty friend of Charles Dickens, and litor of *Household Words* and *All The Year Round*, was so a friend of mine. We met at a dinner, and he spoke me about Gad's Hill, but as if he wanted to buy it for mself. He was afraid to mention Charles Dickens's name, st we should ask too much. So he told me afterwards. I ıd been left executrix under my father's will, being then the only unmarried daughter; and I took the news to our solicitor and co-executor, Mr. Loaden. He wrote to Mr. Wills, and the sale was effected. We scored a little triumph over the "ornamental timber." Mr. Dickens objected to our price; the case was submitted to an arbitrator, and we got more than we originally asked. But there was never one moment of pique on either side, nor a drop of bad blood as the consequence. It was always a matter for a laugh and a joke between Mr. Wills and myself. When we first went to Gad's Hill there was a fish-pond at the back; but my father had it filled up, lest one of his adventurous little ones should tumble in. Officers used to come up from Chatham to the Falstaff, and have pigeon matches in our big field; and one of the sights which used to delight our young eyes, was the gallant bearing and gay uniforms of the Commandant at Chatham, when he and his staff rode by. We were great walkers in those days, and used to ramble over Cobham Park, and round by Shorne, and down to the dreary marshes beyond Higham. But this was not a favourite walk with us and we girls never went there alone. The banks on the Rochester road—past Davies's Straits—were full of sweet violets, white and purple; and the fungi, lichens, flowers, and ferns about Shorne and Cobham yet linger in my memory as things of rarest beauty. We always thought that the coachman, "Old Chumley," as he was called, was old Weller. He was a fine, cheery, trustworthy man; and once when my father was in London, he had one of my sisters and myself—girls then about fifteen and thirteen—put under his charge to be delivered to him at the end of the journey. The dear old fellow took as much care of us as if he had been our father himself. I remember my brothers gave him a new whip, and he was very fond of us all.

E. L. L.

* * * * * *

* * * We had at a subsequent visit to Gad's Hill Place, on the invitation of our hospitable friends, Major and Mrs. Budden, the pleasure of a long and interesting conversation with Mr. James Hulkes, J.P., of the Little Hermitage, Frindsbury, a Kentish man, who came to live here more than sixty years ago, and who was thus a very near neighbour of Charles Dickens during the whole of the time that he resided at Gad's Hill Place. We were shown into a delightful oom at the back of the house, overlooking the shrubberies f the mansion—in the distance appearing the high ground n which stands the monument to Charles Larkin. The room s a happy combination of part workshop, with a fine lathe nd assortment of tools fitted round it—part study, with a ice collection of books, engravings and pictures (some of unting scenes) on the walls—and part naturalist's den, with ases of stuffed birds and animals, guns and fishing-rods—e fragrant odour of tobacco breathing friendly welcome to visitor of smoking proclivities. The varied tastes of the wner were sufficiently apparent, and a long chat of over two ours seemed to us but a few minutes.

Mr. Hulkes said he just remembered the road from Strood Gad's Hill being cut through the sands down to the chalk. was for some time afterwards called "Davies's Straits," ter the Rev. George Davies, the then Chairman of the urnpike Road Board, and the term indicated the difficulty d expense of the operation. Before the new road was cut, the old highway constituting this part of the Dover Road was very hilly and dangerous.

Reverting to the subject of Charles Dickens, our relator remarked, "I fear I cannot be of much use to you by giving information about Mr. Dickens, as I only knew him as a kind friend, a very genial host, and a most charming companion; to the poor he was always kind—a deserving beggar never went from his house unrelieved." What indeed could be said more! These few simple words, spoken sc earnestly after a period of nearly twenty years, sufficed tc bring before us the lost neighbour whose memory was sc warmly cherished by his surviving friend.

John Forster, in the *Life*, speaks of Mr. Hulkes as bein "one of the two nearest country neighbours with whom th [Dickens] family had become very intimate," and mention that both Mr. and Mrs. Hulkes were present at the wedding o the novelist's second daughter, Kate, with Mr. Charles Alsto Collins. Mr. Hulkes spoke of the pleasant parties at Gad' Hill Place, at which he met Mr. Forster, Mr. Wilkie Collin Mr. Percy Fitzgerald, Mr. Marcus Stone, Mr. H. F. Chorle and many others; and observed that, on the occasion c charades and private theatricals there, Charles Dickens wa always in fine form. He showed us an original manuscrip programme (of which we were allowed to take a copy written on half-a-sheet of foolscap; and from the fact tha "*Gad's Hill Gazette* Printing Office" appears in the corn it would seem that it was printed on the occasion for th guests. It is as follows:—

December 31st, 1863.

"A night's exploit on Gad's Hill."—*Shakespeare.*

Her Majesty's Servants

will have the honour of presenting

Three Charades!!!

Each Charade is a word of two syllables, arranged in three Scenes. The first scene is the first syllable; the second is the second syllable; the third scene is the entire word.

(*At the end of each Charade the audience is respectfully invited to name the word.*)

Charade 1!

Scene I.—The awful end of the Profligate Sailor.
Scene II.—On the way to foreign parts.
Scene III.—Miss Belinda Jane and the faithful policeman (Division Q).

Charade 2!!

Scene I.—Archery at Castle Doodle.
Scene II.—Fra Diavolo a Dread Reality.
Scene III.—The Choice of a too Lowly Youth.

Charade 3!!!

Scene I.—The Pathetic History of the Poor Little Sweep.
Scene II.—Mussulman Barbarity to Christians.
Scene III.—Merry England.

Gad's Hill Gazette Printing Office.

The various parts were taken by Dickens and his family, and the entire word of the last Charade is supposed to be "May Day."

In connection with charades, Mr. Hulkes alluded to

Dickens's remarkable facility for "guessing a subject fixed on when he was out of the room, in half a dozen questions;" and related the story of how at the young people's game of "Yes and No," he found out the proper answer to a random question fixed upon by Mr. Charles Collins, one of the company, in his absence, which was, "The top-boot of the left leg of the head post-boy at Newman's Yard, London." The squire sometimes took a stroll with his neighbour, but observed "he was too fast a walker for me—I couldn't keep up with him!"

Mr. Hulkes possesses a nearly complete "file" (from 1862 to 1866) of the *Gad's Hill Gazette*, to which he was one of the subscribers, and which was edited by the novelist's son, Mr. Henry Fielding Dickens, and, as before stated, printed at Gad's Hill Place. It chronicled the arrivals and departures, the results of cricket matches and billiard games, with interesting gossip of events relating to the family and the neighbourhood. Occasionally there was a leading article, and now and then an acrostic appeared. Among the subscribers were the novelist and his family, The Lord Chief Justice, The Dean of Bristol, Lady Molesworth, Mrs. Milner Gibson, M. Stone, A. Halliday, J. Hulkes, C. Kent, W. H. Wills, H. F. Chorley, Edmund Yates, etc. The number for January 20th, 1866, contains a humorous correspondence on the management of the journal between "Jabez Skinner" and "Blackbury Jones." Mr. H. F. Dickens kindly allows a copy of the number for December 30th, 1865, to be reproduced, which is interesting as giving an account of the Staplehurst accident, and also the notice issued when the journal was discontinued.

THE

GAD'S HILL GAZETTE

Edited by H.F. Dickens

December 30th 1865 Price 2d

We are very glad to meet our subscri-bers again after such a long lapse of time, and we hope that they will patronise us in the same kind and indul-gent manner as they did, last season. In the circulars, we announced that some great improvements were to be made in the Gazette– We are sorry that they cannot appear in this number (as our suppliers of type have dis-appointed us) but we hope that next week, we shall be able to publish this journal in quite a different form. Hoping that our subscribers will ex-cuse us this week, we beg to wish them all A Merry Christmas & a Happy New Year!

Christmas at Gad's Hill.

During the past week, Gad's Hill has re-sounded with the sounds of festivity and mer-riment.

(Continued on the next page)

As is usually the case, the house has been filled with the guests who have come to taste of Mr Dickens' hospita-
-lity. These consisted of Mr, Mad, and Master Fechter, Mr & Mrs C. Collins, Mr Mrs and Master C. Dickens junr, Mr Morgan (who suddenly appeared on Christ mas Day, having just returned from A merica) Mr M. Stone, Mr Chorley and Mr Dickenson.

The latter gentleman has not yet en-
-tirely recovered from the effects of a most disastrous railway accident in which he was a sufferer, and had it not been for the courage and intrepidity of Mr Dickens, he would not now be s pending his Christmas at Gad's Hill. A short time before the accident occurred, Mr Dickenson had a dispute with a French gentleman about the opening of the window when the former offered to change places, if the open window was disagreeable to his fel-
-low traveller - this they did.—

Then came the accident, accompanied by all its frightful incidents.The French gentleman was killed, Mr Dickenson was stunned and hurled with great violence under the debris of a carriage.

Mr Dickens, who was in another compart-ment, managed to crawl out of the window and then, caring little for his own safety, busied himself in helping the wounded. Whilst engaged in doing this, he passed by a carri-age, underneath which he saw a gentleman (Mr Dickenson) lying perfectly still, and bleed-ing from the eyes, ears, nose and mouth.

He was immediately taken to the town of Staplehurst where he so far recovered as to be able to return to London, that evening.

Next morning he was suffering from a very severe concussion of the brain and was ill for many weeks—But to our subject.

On Christmas Day, Mr, Mrs & Miss Mal-leson came to dinner. At about 9, an ex tempore dance began and was kept up till about 2 o'clock Tuesday mor-ning. During the week, billiards has been much resorted to. (See next page)

All the visitors are still here, except Mr Fechter and family who left on De-cember 26th, and Mr Morgan (who is to return on 31st. Talking of Mr Fech-ter, our readers will be glad to hear that he has made a most decided suc-cess in his new piece entitled —The Master of Ravenswood—

Sporting Intelligence.
Billiards

Of all the matches that have been played during the past week the most important was a Great Handicap on Christmas Day, the prize being a pew-ter Annexed is an account of it.

Stone	Scratch	C Dickens jun	20	Harry	30
Fechter	5	Dickenson	20	C Dickens	35
Morgan	10	Collins	30	Plorn	40

Our space will not allow us to enter into the minute details of this match suffice it to say that Mr Dickenson won but that as regards good play, he was excelled by Mr Stone (who, however, was so heavily weighted that he could not win. Great credit is due to Mr Ch Dickens junr for the way in which he handicapped the men.

On Saturday 30th a match is to be play-ed between The Earl of Darnley and Mr M Stone.

Gad's Hill Gazette Office.
January— 1867.

In a circular issued last August, we announced hat a final number of the Gad's Hill Gazette was to be pub lished this Xmas. We are grieved however to state, that the hortening of the Wimbledon School holidays (in which es-ablishment the Editor is a pupil) has rendered this impossi ble.

It is with feelings of the deepest regret that we find our-selves obliged to conclude the publication of our Journal in his sudden and unexpected manner, but we feel sure that he great indulgence of the Public will overlook this, as it as done many other great errors in the Gad's Hill Gazette.

In conclusion, we beg to take leave of our Subscribers in ur public capacity of Editor, thanking them for their kind-ess in supporting our Journal, and wishing them all

—"A Happy New Year."—

A. F. Dickens

(Signed) Sole Editor

Mrs. Hulkes had a number of pleasant recollections of Gad's Hill Place, and of Charles Dickens and his family. "As a girl," said this lady, "I was an admiring reader of his works, and I longed to see and know the author; but little did I think that my high ambition would ever be gratified." That a warm friendship existed between his admirer and Charles Dickens, who subsequently became her near neighbour, is evidenced by the fact that, in reply to her request, he allowed this lady the great privilege of reading the catastrophe of that exquisitely-pathetic and nobly-altruistic story of *A Tale of Two Cities*, some weeks before its publication, as appears from the following letter :—

"GAD'S HILL PLACE,
"HIGHAM BY ROCHESTER, KENT.
"*Sunday evening, Sixteenth Oct.*, 1857.

"MY DEAR MRS. HULKES,

"My daughter has shown me your note, and it has impressed me with the horrible determination to become a new kind of Bluebeard, and lay an awful injunction of secrecy on you for five mortal weeks.

"Here is the remainder of the *Tale of Two Cities.* Not half-a-dozen of my oldest and most trusty literary friends have seen it. It is a real pleasure to me to entrust you with the catastrophe, and to ask you to keep a grim and inflexible silence on the subject until it is published. When you have read the proofs, will you kindly return them to me?

"With my regard to Mr. Hulkes,

"Believe me always,
"Faithfully yours,
"CHARLES DICKENS.

"MRS. HULKES."

Mrs. Hulkes said that when Dickens went to Paris in 1863, he jokingly said to her, "I am going to Paris; what shall I bring you?" She replied, "A good photograph of yourself, as I do not like the one you gave me; and I hear the French people are more successful than the English, or their climate may help them." And he brought a photograph of himself, of which there were only four printed. It now graces Mrs. Hulkes' drawing-room, and represents the novelist very life-like in full face, head and bust. The photograph was taken by Alphonse Maze, and has been exquisitely engraved in Mr. Kitton's *Charles Dickens by Pen and Pencil.*

Mrs. Hulkes mentioned a curious and interesting circumstance. On the night before the funeral of her friend, Miss Dickens sent down to the Little Hermitage to ask if she could kindly give her some roses. Mrs. Hulkes cut a quantity from one of the trees in the garden (Lamarque, she believes), and the tree never bloomed again, and soon after died. No doubt, as she observed, it bled to death from the excessive cutting. It was the second case only of the kind in her experience as a rose-grower during very many years.

Charles Dickens also took interest in his friend's son (their only child, who has since finished his University career), and this gentleman prizes as a relic a copy of *A Child's History of England,* which was presented to him, with the following inscription written in the characteristic blue ink —"Charles Dickens. To his little friend, Cecil James Hulkes. Christmas Eve, 1864." In a letter to Miss Hogarth, written from New York, on Friday, 3rd January, 1868, he says:—"I have a letter from Mrs. Hulkes by this post, wherein the boy encloses a violet, now lying on the table before me. Let her know that it arrived safely and retaining its colour."

There are many interesting relics of Gad's Hill Place now in the possession of the family at the Little Hermitage, notably Charles Dickens's seal with his crest, and the initials C. D., his pen-tray, his desk, a photograph of the study on 8th June, 1870 (a present from Miss Hogarth), the portrait above referred to, an arm-chair, a drawing-room settee, a dressing-table, and a library writing-table.

* * * * * *

On another occasion we were favoured with an interview by Mr. J. N. Malleson, of Brighton, who formerly resided at the Great Hermitage, Higham, and who was a neighbour of Charles Dickens for many years. Mr. Malleson came to the Great Hermitage in 1859, and a day or two after Christmas Day in that year—having previously been a guest at the wedding of Dickens's second daughter Kate, with Mr. Charles Alston Collins—he met the novelist, who, stopping to chat pleasantly, asked his neighbours where they dined at Christmas? "Oh, Darby and Joan," said our informant. Dickens laughingly replied:—"That shall never happen again"; and the following year, and every year afterwards, except when their friend was in America, Mr. and Mrs. Malleson received and accepted invitations to dine at Gad's Hill Place. On the exception in question, the family of Dickens dined at the Great Hermitage.

* * * * * *

In the autumn of the year 1889 we had a most interesting chat with Mr. William Stocker Trood, at his residence Spearcehay Farm, Pitminster, pleasantly situated in the vale of Taunton, for many years landlord of the Sir John Falstaff at Gad's Hill. The first noteworthy circumstance to record is that his name is not *Edwin* Trood, as commonly supposed, but William Stocker, as above stated, Stocker being an old family name. This fact disposes of the supposition that the former two names, with the alteration of a single letter, gave rise in Dickens's mind to the designation of the principal character in *The Mystery of Edwin Drood.* The name of "Trood" is by the substitution of one letter easily converted into Drood, and that word is perhaps more euphonious with "Edwin" as prefixed to it; but "William Stocker" is not by any means easily converted into "Edwin." The idea that "Edwin Drood" is derived from "William Stocker Trood" may therefore be dismissed as a popular fallacy. It may be mentioned, however, *en passant*, that Mr. Trood had a brother named Edward, who sometimes visited him at the Falstaff, and also a son who bore the name of his uncle.

We found our informant to be wonderfully genial, hale and hearty, although in his eighty-fifth year. He had a perfect ecollection of Charles Dickens, and remembered his first coming to Gad's Hill Place. Before the house was properly urnished and put in order, both Mr. and Mrs. Dickens somemes slept at the Falstaff; and afterwards, when visitors ere staying at Gad's Hill Place, and the bedrooms there ere full, some of them slept at the Inn; in particular, John orster, Wilkie Collins, and Marcus Stone. He said Mr. Dickens was a very nice man to speak to, and Mrs. Dickens as a very nice lady. They were always kind and pleasant neighbours, but Mr. Dickens did not talk much. Said Ir. Trood:—"When I was at Higham, Mr. Dickens used to y no one could put in a word; I had all the talk to myself." The sons were all very pleasant; in fact, he liked the family very much indeed.

Mr. Trood sometimes acted as local banker to Charles Dickens, and used to cash his cheques for him. Only the day before his death, he cashed a cheque for £22, and was subsequently offered £24 for it by an admirer of Dickens who desired the autograph; but to his credit it should be mentioned that he did not accept the offer.

Our informant next spoke of the wonderful partiality of Dickens to cricket; he would stand out all night if he could watch a cricket match. The matches were always played in Mr. Dickens's field, and the business meetings of the club were held monthly at the Falstaff. Mr. Trood was Treasurer of the club. Occasionally there was a dinner.

A circumstance was related which made a profound impression on our friend. The family at Gad's Hill Place were very fond of music, and on one occasion there were present as visitors two great violinists, one a German and the other an Italian, and it was a debated question among the listeners outside the gates, where the music could be distinctly heard, which played the better. Mr. Trood had just returned from Gravesend in the cool of the summer evening, about ten o'clock, and stood in the road opposite listening, "spell-bound," to the delightful music. Miss Dickens played the accompaniments.

Mr. Trood spoke with a lively and appreciative recollection of the Christmas sports that were held in a field at the back of Gad's Hill Place, and of the good order and nice feeling that prevailed at those gatherings, although several thousand people were present. Among the games that were played the wheeling of barrows by blind-folded men seemed to tickle him most.

Our octogenarian friend also spoke of the great love of Dickens for scarlet geraniums. Hundreds of the "Tom Thumb" variety were planted in the beds on the front lawn and in the back garden at Gad's Hill Place.

Soon after the terrible railway accident at Staplehurst, Dickens came over to the Falstaff and spoke to Mr. Trood, who congratulated him. Said Dickens, "I never thought I should be here again." It is a wonderful coincidence to record, that a young gentleman named Dickenson, who subsequently became intimate with the novelist, changed places (so as to get the benefit of meeting the fresh air) with a French gentleman in the same carriage who was killed, and Mr. Dickenson escaped! The accident happened on the 9th June, 1865, and Dickens died on the "fatal anniversary," 9th June, 1870.

Mr. Trood confirmed his daughter's (Mrs. Latter's) account of the *fraças* with the men and performing bears, given in another chapter, adding, "That *was* a concern."

* * * * * *

The beautiful city of Exeter is not far from Taunton, and we naturally avail ourselves of the opportunity of stopping there for a few hours, and stroll over to see the village of Alphington. It was here, in the year 1839, that Charles Dickens took and furnished Mile End Cottage for his father and mother and their youngest son. He thus describes the event in a letter to Forster:—"I took a little house for them this morning (5th March, 1839), and if they are not pleased with it I shall be grievously disappointed. Exactly a mile beyond the city on the Plymouth road there are two white cottages: one is theirs, and the other belongs to their landlady. I almost forget the number of rooms, but there is an excellent parlour with two other rooms on the ground floor, there is really a beautiful little room over the parlour which I am furnishing as a drawing-room, and there is a splendid garden. The paint and paper throughout is new and fresh and cheerful-looking, the place is clean beyond all description, and the neighbourhood I suppose the most beautiful in this most beautiful of English counties." The negotiations with the landlady and the operation of furnishing the house are most humorously pourtrayed in the same letter.

The cottage is also described in *Nicholas Nickleby*, which he was writing at the time. Mrs. Nickleby, in allusion to her old home, calls it "the beautiful little thatched white house one storey high, covered all over with ivy and creeping plants, with an exquisite little porch with twining honeysuckles and all sorts of things."

Fifty years have passed since the parents of the novelist went to live at Alphington, which, notwithstanding the subsequent growth of the city, still continues to be a pretty suburb with fine views of the Ide Hills to the westward, and Heavitree to the eastward. Our efforts to obtain any reminiscence of the Dickens family in the village were quite unsuccessful—so long a time had elapsed since their departure—although to oblige us, the vicar of the place kindly made enquiries and took some interest in the matter.

CHAPTER VIII.

CHARLES DICKENS AND STROOD.

So altered was the battle-ground, where thousands upon thousands had been killed in the great fight."—*The Battle of Life.*

Keep me always at it, I'll keep you always at it, you keep somebody else always at it. There you are, with the Whole Duty of Man in a commercial country."—*Little Dorrit.*

'HE town of Strood,—the Roman *Strata*,—which stands on ıe left bank of the river Medway, has, like the city of ochester, its interesting historical associations. Its Church, edicated to St. Nicholas, stands high on the north side of ıe London road leading to Gad's Hill, and has a brass of . Glover and his three wives. At one time there was a ɔspital for travellers, founded by Bishop Glanville (*temp.* ichard I.), near the Church. The most interesting remains e, however, those of the Temple Farm, distant about half mile south, formerly (*temp.* Henry II.) the mansion of the nights Templars of the Teutonic order, to whom it, together th the lands thereto belonging, was given by that monarch. ıe gift was confirmed by King John and by Henry III. 227); but the unfortunate brethren of the order did not ain possession more than a century, for in the reign of lward II. they were dispossessed of their lands and goods, under pretence of their leading a vicious course of life, but in reality to satisfy the avarice of their dispossessors. The present building dates from about James I., has one fine room overlooking the river, and underneath is a spacious vault called by Grose the "Preceptory," excavated out of the chalk, and having fine groined stone arches and aisles—the walls are of very great thickness. Near Frindsbury Church—in which are three most interesting wall-paintings of St. William the Baker of Perth, St. Lawrence, and another figure, all three discovered on the jambs of the Norman windows only a few years ago—stands the Quarry House, a handsome olc red-brick mansion, "described as more Jacobean thar Elizabethan," built in the form of a capital E, each storey slightly receding behind the front level of that beneath it the top tapering into pretty gables, the effect being enhancec by heavy buttresses.

There is a dreadful legend of the ancient people of Strooc common to several other parts of the kingdom, *e.g.* Austc in Dorsetshire, which the quaint and diligent Lambardc quoting from Polydore Virgil, evidently regarded as serious and takes immense pains to confute! It relates to St Thomas à Becket and his contention with King Henry II whereby he began to be looked upon as the King's enemy and as such began to be "so commonly neglected, contemned and hated :—

"That when as it happened him upon a time to come t *Stroude*, the Inhabitants thereabouts (being desirous to dis pite that good Father) sticked not to cut the tail from th horse on which he road, binding themselves thereby with perpetuall reproach: for afterward (by the will of God) it s happened, that every one which came of that kinred of me

Temple Farm:
Strood-

which plaied that naughty prank, were borne with tails, even as brute beasts be."

Surely had the credulous historian lived in Darwinian times, he might have recorded this as a splendid instance of "degeneration"!

In a lecture delivered here some years ago, the Rev. Canon

Scott Robertson, Editor of *Archæologia Cantiana*, gave a graphic picture of "Strood in the Olden Times." To this we are much indebted for the opportunity of giving an abstract of several of the most interesting details.

In the thirteenth century Strood and Rochester were the scene of a severe struggle between Simon de Montfort, Earl of Leicester, the leader of the Barons in their war against Henry III. to resist the aggressive encroachments of the King on the liberties of the subject, and the supporters of that monarch.

Simon de Montfort, who was a Strood landowner, and possessed of other large properties in Kent, took the lead, followed by several other nobles, in the siege of Rochester.

heir first obstacle was the fortified gate-house at the Strood id of Rochester Bridge, and for some time their efforts were vain, till at length, by means of small ships filled with flammable matter, set on fire and driven towards the centre the wooden bridge, causing "actual or expected ignition of e timbers," the King's soldiers were dismayed and retreated. he Earl of Gloucester simultaneously reached the south end of the city, and the Barons took possession thereof, sacking the town, monastery, and Cathedral Church. The garrison of the Castle shut themselves up in the strong Norman Keep, and held it till relieved by Prince Edward, the King's son.

The Castle was subsequently taken by Simon de Montfort after the Battle of Lewes (1264), where Henry III. was taken prisoner and brought to Rochester, and a Proclamation was issued transferring the custody of the Royal Castle to the Barons.

At the Battle of Evesham (1265) Simon de Montfort was slain; and the King, on becoming master of the situation, imposed a fine, equivalent to about £1,500 of our money, on Strood, because it was the headquarters of Simon during his assault on Rochester. The fine caused much ill-feeling between the two towns, which lasted until the reign of Edward I. Such was Strood in the olden times.

Long years have since passed, and the amenities of an industrial age have succeeded to these turmoils. The town of Strood appears to be flourishing, and now possesses large engineering works, cement manufactories, flour mills, and other extensive industries.

Allusion has been previously made to a very entertaining *brochure*, entitled *Charles Dickens and Rochester*, by Mr. Robert Langton, F. R. Hist. Soc. of Manchester (himself, we believe, a Rochester man). In it there is scarcely any reference to Strood, although the sister-town, Chatham, is freely mentioned. Our enquiries at Strood, on the Tuesday and subsequently, resulted in the discovery of many most interesting memorials of Charles Dickens in connection with that town, enough almost to fill a small volume. There was a general impression that Dickens had no great liking for Strood, and yet it was a doctor from that town who was one of his most intimate friends, and who attended him in his last illness; it was a builder in Strood who executed most of the alterations and repairs at Gad's Hill Place; it was a Strood contractor who gave him the souvenir of old Rochester Bridge; it was at Strood that an eminent local scientist lived, who was incidentally, but very importantly, associated with him in the movement connected with the Guild of Literature and Art; and it was at a quiet roadside inn at Strood that he sometimes called to refresh himself after one of those long walks, alone or with friends, for which he was famous.

Let us reverse the order of the above, and give a recollection from the last-mentioned. The "Crispin and Crispianus" is a very old-fashioned inn, which stands on the north side of the London road just out of Strood, and was, as we were informed, erected some centuries ago. It is a long building, of brick below, with an overhanging upper floor and weather-boarded front, surmounted by a single dormer window. The sanded floor of the common parlour is, as the saying goes, "as clean as a new pin." Round the room is a settle terminating with arms at each side of the door, which is opposite the fireplace. Mrs. Masters, the cheerful and obliging landlady, who has lived here thirty years, describes Dickens to us (as we sit in the seat he used now and then to occupy), when on one of his walks, as habited in low shoes not over-well mended, loose large check-patterned trousers that sometimes got entangled in the shoes when walking, a brown coat thrown open, sometimes without waistcoat, a belt instead of braces, a necktie which now and then got round towards his ear, and a large-brimmed felt hat, similar to an

American's, set well at the back of his head. In his hand he carried by the middle an umbrella, which he was in the habit of constantly swinging, and if he had dogs (a not unfrequent

occurrence), he had a small whip as well. He walked in the middle of the road at a rapid pace, upright, but with his eyes cast down as if in deep thought. When he called at the Crispin for refreshment, usually a glass of ale (mild sixpenny—bitter ale was not drawn in those days), or a little cold brandy and water, he walked straight in, and sat down at the corner of the settle on the right-hand side where the arm is, opposite the fire-place ; he rarely spoke to any one, but looked round as though taking in everything at a glance. (In *David Copperfield* he says, " I looked at nothing, that I know of, but I saw everything.") Once he and a friend were sheltering there during a thunderstorm (by a coincidence, a storm occurs at the time we are here), and while Dickens stood looking out of the window he saw opposite a poor woman with a baby, who appeared very worn, wet, and ravel-stained. She too was sheltering from the rain.

"Call her in here," said Dickens. Mrs. Masters obeyed.

" Now," said he, " draw her some brandy."

" How much ? " she asked.

" Never mind," he answered, " draw her some."

The landlady drew her four-pennyworth, the quantity enerally served.

" Now," said Dickens to the woman, " drink that up," which he did, and soon seemed refreshed. Dickens gave her a hilling, and remarked to Mrs. Masters that " now she will go n her way rejoicing." The story is a trivial one, but the nits make the aggregate, and it sufficiently indicates his indness of heart and thoughtfulness for others.

In some of his walks Dickens was accompanied either by is sister-in-law, Miss Hogarth, or by friends who were staying t " Gad's " (or the " Place," as it was sometimes called). Irs. Masters, whose recollections of Dickens are very vivid, aid—" Lor ! we never thought much about him when he as alive ; it was only when his death took place that we nderstood what a great man he was." Alas ! it is not the rst instance that " a prophet is not without honour, save in his wn country, and in his own house." The news of his death as a great shock to Mrs. Masters, who heard of it from

Edward, son of Mr. W. S. Trood, the landlord of the Sir John Falstaff, as he was bearing the intelligence to Rochester within half-an-hour after the event.

In passing we should mention, that the Crispin and Crispianus has been immortalized in the chapter on "Tramps," in *The Uncommercial Traveller*, where, in reference to the handicrafts of certain tramps, Dickens imagines himself to be a travelling clockmaker, and after adjusting "t'ould clock" in the keeper's kitchen, "he sees to something wrong with the bell of the turret stable clock up at the Hall [Cobham Hall]. . . . Our task at length accomplished, we should be taken into an enormous servants'-hall, and there regaled with beef and bread, and powerful ale. Then, paid freely, we should be at liberty to go, and should be told by a pointing helper to keep round over yinder by the blasted ash, and so straight through the woods till we should see the town-lights right afore us. . . . So should we lie that night at the ancient sign of the Crispin and Crispianus [at Strood], and rise early next morning to be betimes on tramp again." [1]

[1] Since our tramp in Dickens-Land, Messrs. Winch and Sons have, with liberality and good taste, restored the old sign at this historic hostelry with which the memory of Charles Dickens is associated. It has been suggested that the sign may possibly have had its origin from the Battle of Agincourt fought on the day of "Saints Crispin-Crispian," 25th October, 1415. Victories in more recent times have been thus commemorated on sign-boards, such as the *Vigo* expedition, and the fights at Portobello, Trafalgar, Waterloo, Alma, and elsewhere, and the heroes who won them thus celebrated.

The sign, which is very well painted, represents the patron saints of the shoe-making fraternity, the holy brothers, Crispin and Crispian, at work on their cobbler's bench. The legend runs that it was at Soissons, in the year 287, while they were so employed "labouring with their hands," that they were seized by the emissaries of the Emperor Maximinian, and led away to torture and to death. The sign is understood to have been faithfully copied from a well-known work preserved to this day, at the

We are also indebted to Mrs. Masters for an introduction to our next informant, Mr. J. Couchman, master-builder and undertaker of Strood, who, though advanced in years and tried by illness, is very free and chatty; and from him and his son we obtained some interesting facts. He had worked for Charles Dickens at Gad's Hill Place, from the date of his going there ("which," says Mr. Couchman, "was on Whitsun Monday, 1856,") until the 11th June, 1870, two days after the sad occurrence "which eclipsed the gaiety of nations."

From Mr. Couchman's standpoint as a tradesman, it is interesting to record his experience of Dickens in his own words. "Mr. Dickens," he says, "was always very straightforward, honourable, and kind, and paid his bills most regularly. The first work I did for him was to make a dog-kennel; I also put up the châlet at Gad's Hill. When it was forwarded from London, which was by water, Mr. Fechter [whose name he did not at first remember] sent a Frenchman to assist in the erection. The châlet consisted of ninety-four pieces, all fitting accurately together like a puzzle. The Frenchman did not understand it, and could not make out the fitting of the pieces. So I asked Mr. Henry [Mr. Henry Fielding Dickens, the novelist's sixth son, the present Recorder of Deal] if he understood French. He said 'Yes,' and told me the names of the different pieces, and I managed it without the Frenchman, who stayed the night, and went away next day." In conversation, we suggest that the circumstance of the châlet having been made in Switzerland may have embarrassed the Frenchman, he not having been accustomed to that kind of work. In his letter to Forster of the

---

urch of St. Pantaléon at Troyes.—Abstract of a note in the *Rochester* *d Chatham Journal*, October 5th, 1889.

7th June, 1865, Dickens says:—"The châlet is going on excellently, though the ornamental part is more slowly put together than the substantial. It will really be a very pretty thing; and in the summer (supposing it not to be blown away in the spring), the upper room will make a charming study. It is much higher than we supposed."

Mr. Couchman also took down the châlet after Charles Dickens's death, and erected it at the Crystal Palace at Sydenham, where it remained for a short time, and was subsequently presented to the Earl of Darnley by several members of the Dickens family. His lordship afterwards ordered him to fit it up at Cobham Hall, where, as previously stated, it now stands. The woods of which it is constructed he believed to be Baltic oak and a kind of pine, the lighter parts being of maple or sycamore. We saw it subsequently.

Several contracts were entered into by Mr. Couchman with Charles Dickens for the extension and modification of Gad's Hill Place, notably during the year 1861. We are favoured with a sight of an original specification signed by both parties which is as follows:—

"Specification of works proposed to be done at Gad's Hill House Higham, for C. Dickens, Esq.

"*Bricklayer.*—To take off slates and copings and heighten brick walls and chimneys, and build No. 2 new chimneys with stock and picking bricks laid in cement. No. 2 chimney bars, to cope gable ends with old stone. No. 2 hearthstones. No. 2 plain stone chimney-pieces. No. 2—2 ft. 6 in. Register stoves. To lath and plaster ceiling, side walls, and partitions with lime and hair two coats, and set to slate the new roof with good countess slates and metal nails.

"*Carpenter.*—To take off roof, to lay floor joist with 7 × 2½ in yellow battens; to fix roof, ceiling, joist and partitions of good f timber, 4 ft. × 2 ft.; to use old timber that is sound and fit for use; to close board roof, lead flat and gutters; to lay 1 in. × 9 in. white deal floors, to skirt rooms with 8 in. × $\frac{3}{4}$ in. deal; to fix No. 4 pairs of $1\frac{3}{4}$ in. sashes and frames for plate-glass as per order. *All the sashes to have weights and pulleys for opening.* To fix No. 2—6 ft. 6 in. × 2 ft. 6 in. $1\frac{1}{2}$ in., four panel doors, and encase frames with all necessary mouldings; to fix window linings, and $1\frac{1}{2}$ in. square framings and doors for No. 2 dressing-rooms; to fix No. 2, 7 in. rim locks, No. 2 box latches, sash fastenings, sash weights, to fix 4 in. O. G. iron eaves, gutter with cistern heads, and 3 in. iron leading pipes.

"*Plumber, Glazier, and Painter.*—To take up old lead guttering, and lay new gutters and lead flats with 6lb. lead, ridge and flushings with 5lb. lead; to paint all wood and iron-work that requires painting 4 coats in oil, the windows to be glazed with good plate glass; to paper rooms and landings when the walls are dry with paper of the value of 1*s.* 6*d.* per piece, the old lead to be the property of the plumber. *The two cisterns to be carried up and replaced on new roof, the pipes attached to them to be lengthened as required by the alterations; and a water tap to be fitted in each dressing-room.*

"All old materials not used and rubbish to be carted away by the contractor. All the work to be completed in a sound and workmanlike manner to the satisfaction of C. Dickens, Esq., for the sum of £241. The roof to be slated and flat covered with lead in one month from commencing the work. The whole to be completed—paper excepted—and all rubbish cleared away by the 30th day of November, 1861.

"(Signed) J. COUCHMAN,
"Builder.

"*High Street, Strood,*
"*Sep. 20th,* 1861."

Then follows in Dickens's own handwriting:—

"*The above contract I accept on the stipulated conditions; the specified* time, *in common with all the other conditions, to be strictly observed.*

"(Signed) CHARLES DICKENS.

"*Gad's Hill Place,*
"*Saturday,* 21*st Sep.*, 1861."

What is most interesting to notice in the above specification, is the careful way in which Dickens appears to have mastered all the details, and the very sensible interlineations given in italics which he made, (1) as to the sashes and weights, (2) as to the two cisterns, and especially (3) in the final memorandum as to *time*.

It is also worthy of remark, that the work *was* completed in the specified time, the bill duly sent in, and the next day Dickens sent a cheque for the amount.

Another contract, amounting to £393, was executed by Mr Couchman, for extensions at Gad's Hill. On its completion Mr. Dickens paid him by two cheques. He went up tc London to the Bank (Coutts's in the Strand) to cash them The clerk just looked at the cheques, the signature apparentl being very familiar to him, and then put the usual questior —"How will you have it?" to which he replied, "Notes please."

It appears that, as is frequently the case in large establishments, orders were sometimes given by the servants for worl which the master knew nothing about until the bill wa presented; and to prevent this, Dickens issued instruction to the tradesmen that they were not to execute any wor for him without his written authority. The following is a illustration of this new arrangement:—

"GAD'S HILL PLACE,
"HIGHAM BY ROCHESTER, KENT.
"*Thursday*, 5*th Nov.*, 1858.

"MR. COUCHMAN,

"Please to ease the coach-house doors, and to put u some pegs, agreeably to George Belcher's directions.

"CHARLES DICKENS."

It should be mentioned that George Belcher was the coachman at the time.

Mr. Couchman recalls an interesting custom that was maintained at Gad's Hill. There were a number of tin check plates, marked respectively 3*d.* and 6*d.* each, which enabled the person to whom they were given to obtain an equivalent in refreshment of any kind at the Sir John Falstaff. The threepenny checks were for the workmen, and the sixpenny ones for the tradesmen. The chief housemaid had the distribution of these checks to persons employed in the house, the head-gardener to those engaged in the gardens, and the coachman to those in the stables. On one occasion, our informant remembers when his men were engaged upon some work at Gad's Hill, such checks were given out to them, and that he also had one offered to him; but, recollecting that his position as a master scarcely entitled him to the privilege, he stated his objections to the housemaid, who said in reply that it was a pity to break an old custom, he had better have one. "So," says our informant, "I had a sixpenny ticket with the others, and obtained my refreshment."

He has in his photographic album a carte-de-visite of Charles Dickens, by Watkins. It is the well-known one in which the novelist is represented in a sitting position, dressed in a grey suit; and the owner considered it a very good likeness. He also showed us a funeral card which he thought had been sent to him by the family of Dickens at the time of his death, but judging by its contents, this seems impossible. It is, however, well worth transcribing:—

To the Memory of

Charles Dickens

(England's most popular author),
who died at his Residence,
Higham, near Rochester, Kent,
June 9th, 1870.
Aged 58 years.

He was a sympathizer with the poor, suffering, and oppressed; and by his death one of England's greatest writers is lost to the world.

Mr. Couchman confirms the verbal sketch of Dickens as drawn by his neighbour, Mrs. Masters, and states that Dickens used to put up his dogs ("Linda" and "Turk"), "boisterous companions as they always were," in the stables whenever he came to see him on business.

Mr. William Ball, J.P., of Hillside, Strood, kindly favoured us with many interviews, and generally took great interest in the subject of our visit to "Dickens-Land," rendering invaluable assistance in our enquiries. This gentleman is th son of Mr. John H. Ball, the well-known contractor, wh removed old Rochester Bridge; he is also a brother-in-law o the late gifted tenor, Mr. Joseph Maas, to whom a handsom memorial tablet, consisting of a marble medallion of th deceased, over which is a lyre with one of the string broken, has since been erected on the east wall of the sout transept of Rochester Cathedral. By Mr. Ball's considerat courtesy and that of his daughters, we are allowed t see many interesting relics of Charles Dickens and Gad

Hill.[2] When Mr. Ball's father removed the old bridge in 1859, it will be remembered that he offered to present the novelist with one of the balustrades as a souvenir, the offer being gracefully and promptly accepted, as the following letter testifies :—

"GAD'S HILL PLACE,
"HIGHAM BY ROCHESTER, KENT.
"*Thursday, eighth June,* 1859.

"SIR,

"I feel exceedingly obliged to you for your kind and :onsiderate offer of a remembrance of old Rochester Bridge ; hat will interest me very much. I accept the relic with nany thanks, and with great pleasure.

"Do me the favor to let it be delivered to a workman who /ill receive instructions to bring it away, and once again ccept my acknowledgments.

"Yours faithfully,
"CHARLES DICKENS.

"MR. JOHN H. BALL."

[2] Enthusiastic admirers of Dickens will doubtless envy me the possion of some remarkable memorials of the great writer. My friend r. Ball is kind enough to present me with a very curious souvenir of e novelist : his old garden hat ! Mr. Ball's father obtained it from the rdener at Gad's Hill Place, to whom it had been given after his master's ath. The hat is a "grey-bowler," size 7¼, maker's name "Hillhouse," nd Street, and is the same hat that he is seen to wear in the photoaph of him leaning against the entrance-porch, an engraving of which pears on page 183. Many hats from Shakespeare and Gesler have come historical, and there is no reason why Dickens's should not in : future be an equally interesting personal relic. The gift was accomnied by a couple of collars belonging to the novelist, with the initials :. D." very neatly marked in red cotton. The collar is technically own as a "Persigny," and its size is 16. Last, not least, a small bottle "very rare old Madeira" from Gad's Hill, which calls to mind pleasant :ollections of "the last bottle of the old Madeira," opened by dear old l. Gills in the final chapter of *Dombey and Son.* Needless to say, the nsumption of the valued contents of Dickens's bottle is reserved for a y special and appropriate occasion.

The present Mr. William Ball, then a young lad, was the bearer of the gift, and on being asked by us why he didn't ask to see the great novelist, replies, "Yes, I ought to have done so, but I was afraid of the dogs!"

The balustrade, which was placed on the back lawn at Gad's Hill, was mounted on a square pedestal, on the sides of which were representations of the four seasons, and a sun-dial crowned the capital. Something like it, but a little modified, appears in one of Mr. Luke Fildes's beautiful illustrations to the original edition of *Edwin Drood*, entitled "Jasper's Sacrifices." Three more of the balustrades now ornament Mr. Ball's garden at Hillside.

Mr. Ball the elder was invited to send in a tender for the construction of the tunnel at Gad's Hill previously mentioned, but it was not accepted, as appears from a letter addressed to him by Mr. Alfred L. Dickens (Charles Dickens's brother), of which we are allowed to take a copy:—

"8, RICHMOND TERRACE,
"WHITEHALL, S.W.
"*August 30th*, 1859.

"DEAR SIR,

"I am very sorry that absence from home has prevented my replying to your note as to the tender for the Gad's Hill tunnel before.

"I much regret that the amount of your tender is so much higher than my estimate, that I cannot recommend my brother to accept it.

"I am,
"Dear Sir,
"Yours faithfully,
"ALFRED L. DICKENS.

"MR. BALL."

Among the Dickens relics at Hillside, we are shown by Mr. Ball the pretty set of five silver bells presented by his friend Mr. F. Lehmann, to the novelist, who always used them when driving out in his basket pony-phaeton. They are fastened on to a leather pad, and make a pleasant musical sound when shaken. They are of graduated sizes, the largest being somewhat smaller than a tennis-ball, and appear to be in the key of C: comprising the Tonic, Third, Fifth, Octave, and Octave of the Third.

There is also a hall clock with maker's name—"Bennett, Cheapside, London." This was the "werry identical" clock respecting which Dickens wrote the following characteristically humorous letter to Sir John Bennett:—

"MY DEAR SIR,

"Since my hall clock was sent to your establishment to be cleaned it has gone (as indeed it always had) perfectly well, but has struck the hours with great reluctance, and after enduring internal agonies of a most distressing nature, it has now ceased striking altogether. Though a happy release for the clock, this is not convenient to the household. If you can send down any confidential person with whom the clock can confer, I think it may have something on its works that it would be glad to make a clean breast of.

"Faithfully yours,

"CHARLES DICKENS."

Included among the relics are a very handsome mahogany fire-screen in three folds, of red morocco, with Grecian key-border, a musical Canterbury, and a bookcase. But the most interesting object from an art point of view is an India proof copy, "before letters," of Sir Edwin Landseer's beautiful picture of "King Charles's Spaniels," the original of which is said to have been painted for the late Mr. Vernon in two days, and is now in the National Gallery. The engraving of the picture is by Outram. It has the initials in pencil "E. L.," and a little ticket on the frame—"Lot 445," that being the number in the auctioneer's catalogue.

The following is the story as recently told by Mr. W. P. Frith, R.A., in his most interesting and readable *Autobiography and Reminiscences*, 1887:—

"His" [Sir Edwin's] "rapidity of execution was extraordinary. In the National Gallery there is a picture of Two Spaniels, of what is erroneously called the Charles II. breed (the real dog of that time is of a different form and breed altogether, as may be seen in pictures of the period), the size of life, with appropriate accompaniments, painted by him in two days. An empty frame had been sent to the British Institution, where it was hung on the wall, waiting for its tenant—a picture of a lady with dogs—till Landseer felt the impossibility of finishing the picture satisfactorily. Time had passed, till two days only remained before the opening of the Exhibition. Something must be done; and in the time named those wonderfully life-like little dogs were produced."

Mr. Ball has also an interesting photograph of the "Last Lot," some bottles of wine, evidently taken on the occasion of the sale at Gad's Hill Place after Dickens's death, the auctioneer being represented with his hammer raised ready to fall and a smile upon his face. Among the crowd, consisting principally of London and local dealers, may be seen two local policemen with peaked caps, and auctioneer's porter in shirt-sleeves and aprons. The sale took place in a large tent at the back of the house and close to the well, which can be readily seen through an opening in the tent.

The next person whom we meet at Strood is Mr. Charles Roach Smith, F.S.A., the eminent archæologist, who has achieved a European reputation, and from whom we get many interesting particulars relating to Dickens. We heard some idle gossip at Rochester to the effect that Mr. Roach Smith always felt a little "touchy" about the satire on archæology in *Pickwick*, *in re* "Bill Stumps, his mark." That, however, we took *cum grano salis*, because this gentleman, from his delightful conversation and frank manner, is evidently above any such littleness. He is, however, free to confess, that Dickens had not much love for Strood, but infinitely preferred Chatham.

There had been but little personal intercourse between Dickens and Mr. Roach Smith, though each respected the other. Our informant says that, soon after the novelist came to Gad's Hill Place, Mrs. Dickens called and left her husband's card, which he, whether rightly or not, took as an intimation that the acquaintance was not to be extended. He spoke with all the enthusiasm of a man of science, and rather bitterly too, of a certain reading given by Dickens at Chatham to an overflowing house, whereas on the same evening a distinguished Professor of Agriculture (a Mr. Roberts or Robinson, we believe), who came to instruct the people at Ashford (one of the neighbouring towns) by means of a lecture, failed to secure an audience, and only got a few pence for admissions. The learned Professor subsequently poured forth his troubles to Mr. Roach Smith, from whom he obtained sympathy and hospitality. We venture to remind our good friend that the public in general much prefer amusement to instruction, at which he laughs, and says that in this matter he perfectly agrees with us. He expresses his strong opinion as to Dickens's reading of the "Murder of Nancy" (*Oliver Twist*), which he characterizes as "repulsive and indecent."

The most important communication made to us by Mr. Roach Smith is that contained in volume ii. of his recently published *Reminiscences and Retrospections, Social and Archæological*, 1886. As this interesting work may not be generally accessible, it is as well to quote the passage intact. It has reference to the Guild of Literature and Art, for the promotion of which Dickens, Lord Lytton, John Forster, Mark Lemon, John Leech, and others, gave so much valuable time and energy, in addition to liberal pecuniary support. The following is the extract:—

"Of Mr. Dodd I knew much. He was one of my earliest friends when I lived in Liverpool Street—I may say, one of my earliest patrons; and the intimacy continued up to his death, a few years since. The story of his connection with the movement for a dramatic college, and of his rapid separation from it, a deposition by order of the projectors and directors, forms a curious episode in the history of our friendship; and especially so, as I had an important, though unseen, part to sustain.

"In the summer of 1858 I was summoned to Mr. Dodd's residence at the City Wharf, New North Road, Hoxton, to give consent to be a trustee, with Messrs. Cobden and Bright, for five acres of land, which Mr. Dodd was about to give for the building of a dramatic college, which had been resolved on at a public meeting, held on the 21st of July in this year, in the Princess's Theatre, Mr. Charles Kean acting as chairman. 'I give this most freely,' said Mr. Dodd to me, 'for it is to the stage I am indebted for my education ; to it I owe whatsoever may be good in me.' That there was much good in him, thousands can testify ; and thousands yet to come will be evidence to his benevolence. Of course, I felt pleased in being selected to act as a trustee for this gift. I conceived, and I suppose I was correct, that Mr. Dodd intended that his gift was strictly for a dramatic college, and for no other purpose, then or thereafter. Having expressed my willingness and resolution to be faithful to the trust, I said, 'I presume, Mr. Dodd, you stipulate for a presentation ?' He looked rather surprised ; and asked his solicitor, who sat by him, how they came to overlook this ? Both of them directly agreed that this simple return should be required.

"I must leave such of my readers as feel inclined, to search in the public journals for the correspondence between the directors and Mr. Dodd up to the 13th of January, 1859, when, at a meeting held in the Adelphi Theatre, Lord Tenterden in the chair, it was stated that Mr. Dodd evinced, through his solicitor, a disposition to fence round his gift with legal restrictions and stipulations, which apprised the committee of coming difficulty ; and the meeting unanimously agreed to decline Mr. Dodd's offer of land. Previously and subsequently to this, Mr. Dodd was most discourteously commented on and attacked in the newspapers, the editors of which, however, sided with him. I was told that the stipulation for a presentation was the great offence ; but I should think that the provision made against the improper use of the land must have been the real grievance. In the very last letter I received from Mr. Dodd, not very long anterior to his death, he says that Mark Lemon told him that Charles Dickens had said he had never occasion to repent but of two things, one being his conduct to Mr. Dodd. That Dickens, Thackeray, and others sincerely believed they were taking the best steps for accomplishing their benevolent object, there can be no doubt; their judgment, not their heart, was wrong. The scheme was based upon a wrong principle, as was shown by its collapse in less than twenty years, after the expenditure of very large subscriptions, and the patronage of the Queen. Articles in *The Era* of the 22nd July, 1877, leave no doubt, while they clearly reveal the causes of failure."

It may be mentioned that the Mr. Henry Dodd above referred to, appears to have been a large city contractor, or something of that kind. According to Mr. Roach Smith, what with him led on to fortune was a long and heavy fall of snow, which had filled the streets of the city of London, and rendered traffic impossible. The city was blocked by snow, and there was no remedy at hand. Mr. Dodd boldly undertook a contract to remove the mighty obstruction in a given time. This he did thoroughly and within the limited number of days. Afterwards he appears to have undertaken brick-making and other works on a very large scale. In the opinion of Mr. Roach Smith, Mr. Dodd was the origin of the "golden dustman" in *Our Mutual Friend*, whom every reader of Dickens remembers as Mr. Nicodemus, *alias* Noddy Boffin.

Speaking of Dickens's readings, our informant relates a conversation with Charles Dickens's sixth son, Mr. Henry Fielding Dickens. The former gentleman asked the latter whose model he took?

"Oh, my father's," said Mr. Henry Dickens.

"I would not take any man's model," said Mr. Roach Smith, "I would take my own." And judging from the perfect intonation and thoroughly musical rhythm of his voice, there is no doubt whatever that his model, whoever it may have been, was one of very high standard.

We have since learnt that Mr. Roach Smith is the President of the Strood Elocution Society, an almost unique institution of its kind. It has been established upwards of thirteen years; and at the weekly meetings "the various readers are subjected to an exhaustive and salutary criticism by the members present." Mr. Roach Smith has always taken immense interest in the progress of this Society. Miss Dickens occasionally helped at the above meetings.

Mr. Roach Smith kindly favours us with the following extract from the third and forthcoming volume of his *Retrospections* with reference to the late Mr. J. H. Ball, of Strood, which may appropriately be here introduced:—

"Although I have said that I was the gainer by our acquaintance, yet now and then I had a chance of serving him. Soon after the death of the great novelist, Charles Dickens, and when people were speculating as to what would become of his residence at Gad's Hill, Mr. Ball, wishing to purchase it, commissioned me to call on the executrix, Miss Hogarth, and offer ten thousand pounds, for which he had written a cheque. I accordingly went, and sent in my card. Miss Hogarth, fortunately, could not see me; she was hastening to catch the train for London, the carriage being at the door, and not a moment to be lost; but she would be happy to see me on her return in a day or two. I then wrote to Mr. Forster, the other executor; and received a reply that the place was not for sale. I kept him ignorant of the sum that

Mr. Ball was willing to give, and thus saved my friend some thousands of pounds, . . . for the house and land were not worth half the money."

After some further conversation with our kind octogenarian friend, who insists on showing us hospitality notwithstanding

his sufferings from a trying illness, we take our departure with many pleasant memories of our visit.[3]

[3] This was written soon after our first visit to Strood at the end of August, 1888. Within little more than two years afterwards, on Thursday, 7th August, 1890, I had the mournful pleasure of being present at the funeral of my friend, which took place at Frindsbury Church on that day,

We have, after one or two unsuccessful attempts, the good fortune to meet with Mr. Stephen Steele, M.R.C.S. and L.S.A.,

---

in the presence of the sorrowing relatives and of a large concourse of admirers, both local and from a distance. There were also present many representatives of distinguished scientific societies, including Dr. John Evans, F.R.S., Treasurer of the Royal Society, and President of the Society of Antiquaries.

The kindness which I received from Mr. Roach Smith, to whom I presented myself in the first instance as a perfect stranger, and which was extended during the period of two years that I was privileged to enjoy his friendship, and at times his hospitality, would be ill requited if I did not here place on record my humble tribute of appreciation. Born about the commencement of the present century at Landguard Manor House, near Shanklin, Isle of Wight, after a somewhat diversified educa-tion and experience, he finally settled in London as a wholesale druggist, from which business he retired in 1856, and came to live at Temple Place, Strood. The bent of his mind was, however, distinctly in favour of rchæology, and in this science, which he commenced in the early years f his business, his work has been enormous. In the matter of the identi-ication of Roman remains he was *facile princeps*, and for many years tood without a rival, his investigations and explorations extending over England and Europe. His principal works are *Collectanea Antiqua*, even volumes; *Illustrations of Roman London; Catalogue of London Antiquities; Richborough, Reculver, and Lymne*, and numberless contri-utions scattered over the journal of the Society of Antiquaries, the *Archæologia Cantiana*, and other publications. He was an enthusiastic hakespearean, the author of the *Rural Life of Shakespeare*, and of a ittle work on *The Scarcity of Home-Grown Fruits*. He also published wo volumes of *Retrospections: Social and Archæological*, and was ngaged at his death in completing the third volume. He contributed nany articles to Dr. William Smith's *Classical Dictionaries*, and other imilar works.

He was elected a Fellow of the Society of Antiquaries so far back as 836, and at the time of his death was an Honorary Member or Fellow of t least thirty learned societies of a kindred nature in Great Britain and n the continent, and had been honoured by his colleagues and admirers n having his medal struck on two occasions.

"He was," says one of the highest of living scientists and writers, "one f the chief representatives of the *science* of archæology as understood in s broadest and widest sense. He has never been a mere collector of emains of ancient art, regarded only as curiosities, but has always had in iew their use as exponents of the great unwritten history—the history of of Bridge House, Esplanade, Strood, who was admitted a member of the medical profession so far back as the year 1831, and has therefore been in practice nearly sixty years. It will be remembered that this experienced surgeon was sent for by Miss Hogarth, to see Dickens in his last illness. He is good enough to go over and describe to us in graphic and sympathetic language the whole of the circumstances attending that sorrowful event. Previously to doing so, he gives us some interesting details of his recollections of Charles Dickens. Dr. Steele had occupied the onerous post of Chairman of the Liberal Association at Rochester for thirty years, and believes that in politics Dickens was a Liberal, for he frequently prefaced his remarks in conversation with him on any subject of passing interest by the expression, "We Liberals, you know—"

As a matter of fact, Dickens discharged his conscience of his political creed in the remarks which followed his address

---

the people—which is not to be obtained from other sources; his writings have tended to the same end. Hence he stands as one of the foremost amongst those few of the present day who understand the science in its best and widest sense, his works being referred to as *the* authority at home and abroad."

Speaking with his friend and companion for many years, Mr. George Payne, F.S.A., Hon. Sec. to the Kent Archæological Society, on my last visit, about several personal characteristics of our mutual friend, such as his persistent energy and his indomitable disposition to stoically resist the infirmities of approaching age, and decline any assistance in helplessness, and especially as to the *quæstio vexata*, "Bill Stumps, his mark," Mr. Payne expressed his opinion, that at the bottom of his heart Mr. Roach Smith may probably have had a feeling that Dickens in some way (however unintentionally) slighted the science of archæology, which he (Mr. Roach Smith) had all his life tried to elevate.

A most distinguished antiquarian, a thoroughly honourable man, a versatile and accomplished gentleman, and a kind-hearted and liberal friend, the town of Strood, to which he was for so many years endeared, will long and deservedly mourn his loss.

as President of the Birmingham and Midland Institute,[4] delivered 27th September, 1869, when he said—"My political creed is contained in two articles, and has no reference to any party or persons. My faith in the 'people governing' is, on the whole, infinitesimal; my faith in the 'people governed'

is, on the whole, illimitable." At a subsequent visit to Birmingham on the 6th January, 1870, when giving out the

[4] It is interesting to place on record here, that the germ of Charles Dickens's "Readings," which afterwards developed so marvellously both in England and America, originated in Birmingham. On the 27th December, 1853, he read his *Christmas Carol* in the Town Hall in aid of the funds of the Institute. On the 29th he read *The Cricket on the Hearth*, and on the 30th he repeated the *Carol* to an audience principally composed of working men. The success was overwhelming.

prizes at the Institute, he further emphasized his political faith in these words:—"When I was here last autumn, I made a short confession of my political faith—or perhaps, I should better say, want of faith. It imported that I have very little confidence in the people who govern us—please to observe 'people' with a small 'p,'—but I have very great confidence in the People whom they govern—please to observe 'People' with a large 'P.'"

A few days after Charles Dickens's first visit, my friend Mr. Howard S. Pearson, Lecturer on English Literature at the Institute, addressed a letter to him on the subject of the remarks at the conclusion of his Presidential Address, and promptly received in reply the following communication, which Mr. Pearson kindly allows me to print, emphasizing his (Dickens's) observations:—

"GAD'S HILL PLACE,
"HIGHAM BY ROCHESTER, KENT.
"*Wednesday, 6th October*, 1869.

"SIR,

"You are perfectly right in your construction of my meaning at Birmingham. If a capital P be put to the word People in its second use in the sentence, and not in its first, I should suppose the passage next to impossible to be mistaken, even if it were read without any reference to the whole spirit of my speech and the whole tenor of my writings.

"Faithfully yours,
"CHARLES DICKENS.

"H. S. PEARSON, ESQUIRE."

Dr. Steele had dined several times at Gad's Hill Place, and was impressed with Dickens's wonderful powers as a host. He never absorbed the whole of the conversation to himself, but listened attentively when his guests were speaking, and endeavoured, as it were, to draw out any friends who were not generally talkative. He liked each one to chat about his own hobby in which he took most interest. Our informant was also present at Gad's Hill Place at several theatrical entertainments, and especially remembers some charades being given. After the performance of the latter was over, Dickens walked round among his guests in the drawing-room, and enquired if any one could guess the "word." Says the doctor, "We never seemed to do so, but there was always a hearty laugh when we were told what it was. There was a good deal of company at Gad's Hill at Christmas time."

À propos of private theatricals at Gad's Hill Place, Mr. T. Edgar Pemberton, in *Charles Dickens and the Stage*, calls attention to the fact that "Mr. Clarkson Stanfield's *Lighthouse* Act drop subsequently decorated the walls of Gad's Hill Place; and although it took the painter less than a couple of days to execute, fetched a thousand guineas at the famous Dickens Sale in 1870." A cloth painted for *The Frozen Deep*, which was the next and last of these productions, also had a foremost place in the Gad's Hill picture-gallery.

Dr. Steele mentions a conversation once with Dickens about Gad's Hill and Shakespeare's description of it. He (the doctor) considers that Shakespeare could not have described it so accurately if he had not been there, and Dickens agreed with him in this opinion. Possibly he may have stayed at the "Plough," which was an inn on the same spot as, or close to, the "Falstaff." The place must have been much wooded at that time, and Shakespeare might have been there on his way

R

to Dover. A note in the *Rochester and Chatham Journal*, 1883, states that "Shakespeare's company made a tour in Sussex and Kent in the summer of 1597."

Dr. Steele, in common with his friend Charles Dickens, strongly deprecated the action of certain parties in Rochester, by voting at a public meeting something to this effect:—"That the Theatre was an irreligious kind of institution, and, in the opinion of the meeting, it ought to be closed."

The doctor observes that Dickens was not much of a Church-goer. He went occasionally to Higham, and used to give the vicar assistance for the poor and distressed. Dickens and Miss Hogarth asked Dr. Steele to point out objects of charity worthy of relief, and they gave him money for distribution.

He remarks that Dickens did not care much about associating with the local residents, going out to dinners, &c. Most of the principal people of Rochester would have been glad of the honour of his presence as a guest, but he rarely accepted invitations, preferring the quietude of home.[5]

As regards readings, our informant says he is under the impression that Dickens must have had some lessons or hints from some one of experience (possibly his friend Fechter, the actor), as he noticed from time to time a regular improvement which was permanently maintained. On the subject of the American War, he thinks Dickens's sympathies were decidedly with the South. With respect to the American Readings, Dr. Steele expresses his opinion that the excitement, fatigue, and worry consequent thereon had considerably shortened Dickens's life, if it had not pretty well killed him

[5] Miss Hogarth informs me that her brother-in-law frequently dined out in the neighbourhood, accompanied by his daughter and herself.

e considered him a most genial sort of man; "he always ɔked you straight in the face when speaking."

Before referring to the closing chapter in Dickens's life, we .ve some interesting talk respecting Venesection,—*à propos* that memorable occasion on the ice at Dingley Dell, when ıIr. Benjamin Allen was holding a hurried consultation with r. Bob Sawyer on the advisability of bleeding the company nerally, as an improving little bit of professional practice," and Dr. Steele gives us his opinion thereon, and on some ints connected with the medical profession. He was a ıdent of Guy's and St. Thomas's Hospitals, and was under e distinguished physicians Drs. Addison and Elliotson. He nsidered the characters of Bob Sawyer and Ben Allen not all overdrawn. They were good representations of the edical students of those days. He believed the practice of enesection commenced to be general about the year 1811, : his father was a medical practitioner before him, and he es not remember his (the father's) telling him that he actised it before that time. Says our friend, "We used to eed regularly in my young days, and in cases of pneumonia d convulsions we never thought of omitting to bleed. e should have considered that to have done so would have en a grave instance of irregular practice. And," he adds, bleed in cases of convulsions now." The doctor did not ink well of the change at the time, but, speaking generally, says Venesection had had its turn, and has now given ace to other treatment.

The events in connection with the fatal illness of Dickens : then touchingly related as follows:—

"I was sent for on Wednesday, the eighth of June, 1870, to end at Gad's Hill Place, and arrived about 6.30 p.m. I found

Dickens lying on the floor of the dining-room in a fit. He was unconscious, and never moved. The servants brought a couch down, on which he wás placed. I applied clysters and other remedies to the patient without effect. Miss Hogarth, his sister-in-law, had already sent a telegram (by the same messenger on horseback who summoned me) to his old friend and family doctor, Mr. Frank Beard, who arrived about midnight. He relieved me in attendance at that time, and I came again in the morning. There was unhappily no change in the symptoms, and stertorous breathing, which had commenced before, now continued. In conversation Miss Hogarth and the family expressed themselves perfectly satisfied with the attendance of Mr. Beard and myself. I said, 'That may be so, and we are much obliged for your kind opinion; but we have a duty to perform, not only to you, my dear madam, and the family of Mr. Dickens, but also to the public. What will the public say if we allow Charles Dickens to pass away without further medical assistance? Our advice is to send for Dr. Russell Reynolds.' Mr. Beard first made the suggestion.

"The family reiterated their expression of perfect satisfaction with the treatment of Mr. Beard and myself, but immediately gave way, Dr. Russell Reynolds was sent for, and came in the course of the day. This eminent physician without hesitation pronounced the case to be hopeless. He said at once on seeing him, 'He cannot live.' And so it proved. At a little past 6 o'clock on Thursday, the 9th of June, 1870 Charles Dickens passed quietly away without a word—about twenty-four hours after the seizure."

Such is the simple narrative which the kind-hearted octogenarian surgeon, whom it is a delightful pleasure t

Rochester: from Strood Pier:

meet and converse with, communicates to us, and then cordially wishes us "good-bye."

* * * * * *

There is an annual pleasure fair at Strood, instituted, it is said, so far back as the reign of Edward III. It takes place during three days in the last week of August, and as it is going on while we are on our tramp, we just look in for a few minutes, the more especially as we were informed by Mr. William Ball, and others who had seen him, that Dickens used to be very fond of going there at times in an appropriate disguise, where perhaps he may have seen the prototype of the famous "Doctor Marigold." The fair is now held on a large piece of waste ground near the Railway Station. There are the usual set-out of booths, "Aunt Sallies," shooting-galleries, "Try your weight and strength, gentlemen" machines, a theatre, with a tragedy and comedy both performed in about an hour, and hot-sausage and gingerbread stalls in abundance. But the deafening martial music poured forth from a barrel-organ by means of a steam-engine belonging to the proprietor of a huge "Merry-go-round," and the wet and muddy condition of the ground from the effects of the recent thunderstorm, make us glad to get away.

A MYSTERIOUS DICKENS-ITEM.

Mr. C. D. Levy, Auctioneer, etc., of Strood, was good enough to lend me what at first sight, and indeed for some time afterwards, was supposed to be a most unique Dickens-item. It came into his possession in this way. At the sale of Charles Dickens's furniture and effects, which took place at Gad's Hill in 1870, Mr. Levy was authorized by a custome to purchase Dickens's writing-desk, which, however, he was unable to secure. In transferring the desk to the purchaser at the time of the sale, a few old and torn papers tumbled out, and being considered of no value, were disregarded and scattered. One of these scraps was picked up by Mr. Levy, and proved on further examination to be a sheet of headed note-paper having the stamp of "Gad's Hill Place, Higham by Rochester, Kent."—On the first page were a few rough sketches drawn with pen and ink, which greatly resembled some of the characters in *The Mystery of Edwin Drood*—Durdles, Jasper, and Edwin Drood. At the side was a curious row of capital letters looking like a puzzle. On the second and third pages were short-hand notes, and on the fourth page a few lines written in long-hand, continued on the next page,—wonderfully like Charles Dickens's own handwriting,—being the commencement of a speech with reference to a cricket match. The sheet of paper had evidently been made to do double duty, for after the sketches had been drawn on the front page, the sheet was put aside, and when used again was turned over, so that what ordinarily would have been page 4 became page 1 for the second object. No "Daniel" in Strood or Rochester had ever been able to decipher the mysterious hieroglyphics, or make known the interpretation thereof, during twenty years, or give any explanation of the sketches. But everybody thought that in some way or other they related to *The Mystery of Edwin Drood*—and possibly contained a clue to the solution of that exquisite fragment. So, as a student and admirer of Dickens, Mr. Levy kindly left the matter in my hands to make out what I could of it. Reference was accordingly had to several learned pundits in the short-hand systems of "Pitman,"

"Odell," and "Harding," but without avail; and eventually Mr. Gurney Archer, of 20, Abingdon Street, Westminster (successor to the old-established and eminent firm of Messrs. W. B. Gurney and Sons, who have been the short-hand writers to the House of Lords from time immemorial), kindly transcribed the short-hand notes, which referred to a speech relating to a cricket match, a portion of which had already been written out in long-hand, as above stated,—but there was not a word in the short-hand about Edwin Drood!

So far, one portion of the mystery had been explained—not so the sketches, which were still believed to contain the key to *The Mystery of Edwin Drood.* As a *dernier ressort*, application was made to the fountain-head—to Mr. Luke Fildes, R.A., the famous illustrator of that beautiful work. He received me most courteously, scrutinized the document closely; we had a long chat about Edwin Drood generally, the substance of which has been given in a previous chapter—but he admitted that the sketches failed to give any solution of the mystery.

The document was subsequently sent by Mr. Kitton to Mrs. Perugini, who at once replied that it had caused some merriment when she saw it again, as she remembered it very well. It had been done by her brother, Mr. Henry Fielding Dickens, when a young man living at home at Gad's Hill—that the short-hand notes referred to his speech at a dinner after one of the numerous cricket matches held there, and that the sketches were rough portraits of some of the cricketers. The capital letters at the side referred to a double acrostic. The heads of the speech had been suggested by his father as being desirable to be brought before the cricket club, which at that time was in a rather drooping condition.

Now although the original theory about this curious document entirely broke down, and not an atom has been added to what was already known about *The Mystery of Edwin Drood*, still there is one subject of much interest which the document has brought to light. The short-hand is the same system, "Gurney's," as that which Charles Dickens wrote as a reporter in his early newspaper days—a system not generally used now, but which he subsequently taught his son to write. Of the many sheets which Dickens covered with notes in days gone by not one remains. But there are two manuscripts by Dickens in Gurney's system of short-hand, now in the Dyce and Forster collection at South Kensington, which relate to some private matters in connection with publishing arrangements. The document is certainly interesting from this point of view (*i.e.* the system which Dickens used), and from its reference to life at Gad's Hill, and especially to cricket, the favourite game mentioned many times in this book, in which the novelist took so much interest. Mr. Henry Fielding Dickens, with whom I had on another occasion some conversation on the subject of this souvenir of his youth at Gad's Hill, remarked that many more important issues had hung upon much more slender evidence. It was done about the year 1865-6, before he went to college.

At our interview Mr. H. F. Dickens told me the details of the following touching incident which happened at one of the cricket matches at Gad's Hill. His father was as usual attired in flannels, acting as umpire and energetically taking the score of the game, when there came out from among the bystanders a tall, grizzled, and sun-burnt Sergeant of the Guards. The Sergeant walked straight up to Mr. Dickens, saying, "May I look at you, sir?" "Oh, yes!" said the novelist, blushing up to the eyes. The Sergeant gazed intently at him for a minute or so, then stood at attention, gave the military salute, and said, "God bless you, sir." He then walked off and was seen no more. In recounting this anecdote, Mr. H. F. Dickens agreed with me that, reading between the lines, one can almost fancy some lingering reminiscences similar to those in the early experience of Private Richard Doubledick.

CHAPTER IX.

CHATHAM:—ST. MARY'S CHURCH, ORDNANCE TERRACE, THE HOUSE ON THE BROOK, THE MITRE HOTEL, AND FORT PITT. LANDPORT:—PORTSEA, HANTS.

"The home of his infancy, to which his heart had yearned with an intensity of affection not to be described."—*The Pickwick Papers.*

"I believe the power of observation in numbers of very young children to be quite wonderful for its closeness and accuracy. Indeed, I think that most grown men who are remarkable in this respect, may, with greater propriety, be said not to have lost the faculty than to have acquired it; the rather, as I generally observe such men to retain a certain freshness, and gentleness, and capacity of being pleased, which are also an inheritance they have preserved from their childhood."—*David Copperfield.*

THE naval and military town of Chatham, unlike the Cathedral city of Rochester, has, at first sight, few attractions for the lover of Dickens. Mr. Phillips Bevan calls it "a dirty, unpleasant town devoted to the interests of soldiers, sailors, and marines." We are not disposed to agree entirely with him; but we must admit that it has little of the picturesque to recommend it—no venerable Castle or Cathedral to attract attention, no scenes in the novels of much importance to visit, no characters therein of much interest to identify. Mr. Pickwick's own description of the four towns of Strood, Rochester, Chatham, and Brompton, certainly applies more nearly to Chatham than to the others; but things have improved in many ways since the days of that veracious chronicler, as we are glad to testify :—

"The principal productions of these towns," says Mr. Pickwick, "appear to be soldiers, sailors, Jews, chalk, shrimps, officers, and dockyard men. The commodities chiefly exposed for sale in the public streets are marine stores, hard-bake, apples, flat-fish, and oysters. The streets present a lively and animated appearance, occasioned chiefly by the conviviality of the military. . . .

"The consumption of tobacco in these towns," continues Mr. Pickwick, "must be very great; and the smell which pervades the streets must be exceedingly delicious to those who are extremely fond of smoking. A superficial traveller might object to the dirt, which is their leading characteristic; but to those who view it as an indication of traffic and commercial prosperity, it is truly gratifying."

And yet for all this, there are circumstances to be noticed of the deepest possible interest connected with Chatham, and spots therein to be visited, which every pilgrim to "Dickens-Land" must recognize. At Chatham,—"my boyhood's home," as he affectionately calls it,—many of the earlier years of Charles Dickens (probably from his fourth to his eleventh) were passed; here it was "that the most durable of his earlier impressions were received; and the associations around him when he died were those which at the outset of his life had affected him most strongly."

Admirers of the great novelist are much indebted to Mr. Robert Langton, F. R. Hist. Soc., for his *Childhood and Youth of Charles Dickens*, a book quite indispensable to a tramp in this neighbourhood, the charming illustrations by the late Mr. William Hull, the author, and others rendering the identification of places perfectly easy. Dickens says, "If anybody knows to a nicety where Rochester ends and Chatham begins, it is more than I do." "It's of no consequence," as Mr.

Toots would say, for the High Street is one continuous thoroughfare, but as a matter of fact, a narrow street called Boundary Lane on the north side of High Street separates the two places.

A few words of recapitulation as to early family history[1]

[1] So far as I am aware, nothing has been done to trace the genealogy of the Dickens family, and it may therefore be of interest to place on record the title of, and an extract from, a very scarce and curious thin quarto volume (pp. 1—28) in my collection. Sir Walter Scott was immensely proud of his lineage and historical associations, but it would be a wonderful thing if we could trace the descent of Charles Dickens from King Edward III.

In the *Rambler in Worcestershire* (Longmans, 1854), Mr. John Noake, the author, in alluding to the parish of Churchill, Worcestershire, says :— "The Dickens family of Bobbington were lords of this manor from 1432 to 1657, and it is said that from this family Mr. Dickens, the author, is descended."

[TITLE.]

A

POSTHUMOUS POEM

of the

late THOMAS DICKENS, ESQ.,

Lieut.-Colonel in the First Regiment of Foot Guards,
Dedicated, by permission,
to his Royal Highness, the Duke of Gloucester,
to which is added
The genealogy of the Author from King Edward III.;
also
A few grateful stanzas to the Deity, three months
previous to his death, *Sep. 21st*, 1789.

CAMBRIDGE:
Printed by J. Archdeacon, Printer to the University.
And may be had of the Editor, C. DICKENS, LL.D., near Huntingdon,
and of T. PAYNE AND SON, Booksellers, London.
MDCCXC.

Above the title is written in ink: "Peter Cowling to Charles Robert may be useful here. John Dickens, who is represented as "a fine portly man," was a Navy pay-clerk, and Elizabeth his

---

Dickens, 3rd son to Sam. Trevor Dickens, this 10th August, 1807, and from said Chas. R. Dickens to his loved father, on the 16th June, 1832."

[EXTRACT.]

Genealogy of the late Thomas Dickens, Esq.

KING EDWARD III.

LIONEL, Duke of Clarence	his Son
PHILIPPA, married to EDMUND MORTIMER, Earl of March	his Daughter
ROGER, Earl of March	her Son
ANN, who married RICHARD, Duke of York and Earl of Cambridge	his Daughter
RICHARD, Duke of York	her Son
GEORGE, Duke of Clarence, brother to Edward IV.	his Son
Countess of SALISBURY	his Daughter
Viscount MONTAGUE	her Son
Lady BARRINGTON	his Daughter
Sir Francis BARRINGTON	her Son
Lady MASHAM	his Daughter
William MASHAM, ESQ.	her Son
Sir FRANCIS MASHAM	her Son
JOHANNA MASHAM, who married Counsellor Hildesley	his Daughter
JOHN HILDESLEY, ESQ.	her Son
MARY HILDESLEY, who married the Reverend SAMUEL DICKENS	his Daughter
THOMAS DICKENS, ESQ., the Author	her Son

Opposite GEORGE, Duke of Clarence, is written in ink, "Drown'd in a Butt of Malmsey Madeira," and following THOMAS DICKENS, ESQ., the Author, also written in ink—

"Lieut.-Gen. Sir SAML. T. DICKENS, K.C.H.	his Son
Capt. SAML. T. DICKENS, R.N.	his Son"

And following the last-mentioned names written in pencil—

"Admiral SAMUEL TREVOR DICKENS, R.N.	my Son"

Also written in pencil underneath the above—

"qy. CHARLES DICKENS the Novelist."

wife (*née* Barrow), who is described as "a dear good mother and a fine woman," the parents of the future genius, resided in the beginning of this century at 387, Mile End Terrace, Commercial Road, Landport, Portsea,[2] "and is so far in Portsea as being in the island of that name." Here Charles Dickens was born, at twelve o'clock at night, on Friday, 7th February, 1812. He was the second child and eldest son of a rather numerous family consisting of eight sons and daughters, and was baptized at St. Mary's, Kingston (the parish church of Portsea), under the names of Charles John Huff*h*am; the last of these is no doubt a misspelling, as the name of his grandfather, from whom he took it, was Huffam, but Dickens himself scarcely ever used it. In the old family Bible now in possession of Mr. Charles Dickens it is Huffam in his father's own handwriting. The Dickens family left Mile End Terrace on 24th June, 1812, and went to live in Hawke Street, Portsea, from whence, in consequence of a change in official duties of the elder Dickens, they removed to Chatham in 1816 or 1817, and resided there for six or seven years, until they went to live in London.

Bearing these circumstances in mind, it is very natural that we should determine on an early pilgrimage to Chatham, and Sunday morning sees us at the old church—St. Mary's—where Dickens himself must often have been taken as a child, and where he saw the marriage of his aunt Fanny with James Lamert, a Staff Doctor in the Army,—the Doctor Slammer of *Pickwick*,—of whom Mr. Langton says:—"The regimental

[2] In a copy—in my collection—of the second edition 8vo of "*The History and Antiquities of Rochester and its Environs*, embellished with engravings (pp. i—xvii, 1—419), printed and sold by W. Wildash, Rochester, 1817," there occurs in the list of subscribers—about four hundred in number—the name:—DICKENS MR. JOHN, CHATHAM.

surgeon's kindly manner, and his short odd way of expressing himself, still survive in the recollections of a few old people." Dr. Lamert's son James, by a former wife, was a great crony of young Charles Dickens, taking him to the Rochester theatre, and getting up private theatricals in which they both acted.

Surely there is a faint description of those times in the second chapter of *David Copperfield*:—

St. Mary's Church, Chatham.

"Here is our pew in the church. What a high-backed pew! With a window near it, out of which our house can be seen, and *is* seen many times during the morning's service by Peggotty, who likes to make herself as sure as she can that it's not being robbed, or is not in flames. But though Peggotty's eye wanders, she is much offended if mine does, and frowns to me, as I stand upon the seat, that I am to look at the clergyman. But I can't always look at him—I know him without that white thing on, and I am afraid of his wondering why I stare so, and perhaps stopping the service to enquire—and what am I to do? It's a dreadful thing to gape, but I must do something. I look at my mother, but *she* pretends not to see me. I look at a boy in the aisle, and *he* makes faces at me. I look at the sunlight coming in at the open door through the porch, and there I see a stray sheep—I don't mean a sinner, but mutton—half making up his mind to come into the church. I feel that if I looked at him any longer, I might be tempted to say something out loud; and what would become of me then!"

The church, now undergoing reconstruction, is not a very presentable structure, and has little of interest to recommend it, except a brass to a famous navigator named Stephen Borough, the discoverer of the northern passage to Russia (1584), and a monument to Sir John Cox, who was killed in an action with the Dutch (1672). The name of Weller occurs on a gravestone near the church door.

We cross the High Street, proceed along Railway Street, formerly Rome Lane, pass the Chatham Railway Station (near which is a statue of Lieutenant Waghorn, R.N., "pioneer and founder of the Overland Route," born at Chatham, 1800, and died 1850),[3] and find ourselves at Ordnance Terrace, a conspicuous row of two-storied houses, prominently situated on the higher ground facing us, beyond the Station. In one of these houses (No. 11—formerly No. 2) the Dickens family resided from 1817 to 1821. The present occupier is a Mr. Roberts, who kindly allows us to inspect the interior. It has the dining-room on the left-hand side of the entrance and the drawing-room on the first floor, and is altogether a pleasantly-situated, comfortable, and respectable dwelling. No. 11, "the second house in the terrace," is overgrown with a Virginia creeper, which, from its possible association with Dickens's earliest years, may have induced him to plant the now

[3] A most interesting paper entitled "The Life and Labours of Lieutenant Waghorn," appeared in *Household Words* (No. 21), August 17th, 1850.

magnificent one which exists at Gad's Hill. "Here it was," says Forster, "that his first desire for knowledge, and his greatest passion for reading, were awakened by his mother, who taught him the first rudiments, not only of English, but also, a little later, of Latin. She taught him regularly every day for a long time, and taught him, he was convinced, thoroughly well." Mr. Langton also says that "It was during his residence here that some of the happiest hours of the childhood of little Charles were passed, as his father was in a fairly good position in the Navy Pay Office, and they were a most genial, lovable family." Here it was that the theatrical entertainments and the genial parties took place, when, in addition to his brothers and sisters and his cousin, James Lamert, there were also present his friends and neighbours, George Stroughill, and Master and Miss Tribe.

Mr. Langton further states that "Ordnance Terrace is known to have formed the locality and characters for some of the earlier *Sketches by Boz*." "The Old Lady" was a Miss Newnham, who lived at No. 5, and who was, by all accounts, very kind to the Dickens children. The "Half-pay Captain" was also a near neighbour, and he is supposed to have supplied one of the earliest characters to Dickens as a mere child. Some of the neighbours at the corner house next door (formerly No. 1) were named Stroughill,—pronounced Stro'-hill (there was, it will be remembered, a *Struggles* at the famous cricket-match at All-Muggleton)—and the son, George, is said to have had some of the characteristics of Steerforth in *David Copperfield*. He had a sister named Lucy, probably the "Golden Lucy," from her beautiful locks, and who, according to Mr. Langton, "was the special favourite and little sweetheart of Charles Dickens." She was possibly the

No. 11, Ordnance Terrace, Chatham. *Where the Dickens Family lived* 1817-21.

prototype of her namesake, in the beautiful story of the *Wreck of the Golden Mary.*

About the year 1821 pecuniary embarrassments beset and tormented the Dickens family, which were afterwards to be "ascribed in fiction" in the histories of the Micawbers and the Dorrits, and the family removed to the House on the Brook. In order to follow their steps in perfect sequence, we have to

The House on the Brook, Chatham. *Where the Dickens Family lived* 1821-3.

return by the way we came from the church, cross the Hig Street, and proceed along Military Road, so as to visit tl obscure dwelling, No. 18, St. Mary's Place, situated in tl valley through which a brook, now covered over, flows fro the higher lands adjacent, into the Medway.

The House on the Brook—"plain-looking, whitewash plaster front, and a small garden before and behind"—ne: door to the former Providence (Baptist) Chapel, now t

Drill Hall of the Salvation Army, is a very humble and unpretentious six-roomed dwelling, and of a style very different to the one in Ordnance Terrace. Here the Dickens family lived from 1821 to 1823. The Reverend William Giles, the Baptist Minister, father of Mr. William Giles, the schoolmaster, formerly officiated at the chapel. This was the Mr. Giles who, when Dickens was half-way through *Pickwick*, sent him a silver snuff-box, with an admiring inscription to the "Inimitable Boz." Dickens went to school at Mr. Giles's

Giles's School, Chatham.

Academy in Clover Lane (now Clover Street), Chatham, and boys of this and neighbouring schools were thus nicknamed :—

"Baker's Bull-dogs,
"Giles's Cats,
"New Road Scrubbers,
"Troy Town Rats."

It was in the House on the Brook that he acquired those readings and imaginings" which in "boyish recollections" he describes as having been brought away from Chatham :—

"My father had left a small collection of books in a little room up-stairs, to which I had access (for it adjoined my own), and which nobody else in our house ever troubled. From that blessed little room *Roderick Random*, *Peregrine Pickle*, *Humphry Clinker*, *Tom Jones*, *The Vicar of Wakefield*, *Don Quixote*, *Gil Blas*, and *Robinson Crusoe*, came out, a glorious host to keep me company. They kept alive my fancy, and my hope of something beyond that place and time,—they and the *Arabian Nights*, and the *Tales of the Genii*,—and did me no harm; for whatever harm was in some of them was not there for me. *I* knew nothing of it."

It is very probable that his first literary effort, *The Tragedy of Misnar, the Sultan of India*, "founded" (says Forster), "and very literally founded, no doubt, on the *Tales of the Genii*," was composed after perusal of some of the works above referred to, but it is to be feared that it was never even rehearsed. The circumstances of the family had so changed for the worse, that here were neither juvenile parties nor theatrical entertainments.

A view from one of the upper windows of the house in St. Mary's Place gives the parish church and churchyard precisely as described in that pathetic little story, *A Child's Dream of a Star*. Charles Dickens was the child who "strolled about a good deal, and thought of a number of things," and his little sister Fanny—or his younger sister Harriet Ellen—was doubtless "his constant companion" referred to in the story.

We leave with feelings of respect the humble but famous little tenement, its condition now sadly degraded; proceed along the High Street, and soon reach "The Mitre Inn and Clarence Hotel," a solid-looking and comfortable house of entertainment, at which Lord Nelson and King William IV., when Duke of Clarence, frequently stayed, and (what is more to our purpose) where we find associations of Charles Dickens. There are a beautiful bowling-green and grounds at the back, approached by a series of terraces well planted with flowers, and the green is surrounded by fine elms which constitute quite an oasis in the desert of the somewhat prosaic Chatham.

Mitre Inn, Chatham.

[The Mitre is thus immortalized in the "Guest's Story" of the *Holly Tree Inn*:—

"There was an Inn in the Cathedral town where I went to school, which had pleasanter recollections about it than any of these. I took next. It was the Inn where friends used to put up, and where we sed to go to see parents, and to have salmon and fowls, and be pped. It had an ecclesiastical sign—the 'Mitre'—and a bar that eemed to be the next best thing to a Bishopric, it was so snug. I oved the landlord's youngest daughter to distraction—but let that ass. It was in this Inn that I was cried over by my rosy little sister, because I had acquired a black-eye in a fight. And though she had been, that holly-tree night, for many a long year where all tears are dried, the Mitre softened me yet."

About the year 1820 the landlord of the Mitre was Mr. John Tribe, and his family being intimate with the Dickenses, young Charles spent many pleasant evenings at the "genial parties" given at this fine old inn. Mr. Langton mentions that the late Mr. Alderman William Tribe, son of Mr. John Tribe, the former proprietor, perfectly recollected Charles Dickens and his sister Fanny coming to the Mitre, and on one occasion their being mounted on a dining-table for a stage, and singing what was then a popular duet, *i.e.*—

"Long time I've courted you, miss,
And now I've come from sea;
We'll make no more ado, miss,
But quickly married be.
Sing Fal-de-ral," &c.

The worthy alderman is also stated to have had in his possession a card of invitation to spend the evening at Ordnance Terrace, addressed from Master and Miss Dickens to Master and Miss Tribe, which was dated about this time.

In consequence of the elder Dickens being recalled from Chatham to Somerset House, to comply with official requirements, the family removed to London in 1823,[4] "and took up its abode in a house in Bayham Street, Camden Town." Dickens thus describes his journey to London in "Dullborough Town," one of the sketches in *The Uncommercial Traveller*:—

[4] See Note to Chapter ii. p. 38.

"As I left Dullborough in the days when there were no railroads in the land, I left it in a stage-coach. Through all the years that have since passed, have I ever lost the smell of the damp straw in which I was packed—like game—and forwarded, carriage paid, to the Cross Keys, Wood Street, Cheapside, London? There was no other inside passenger, and I consumed my sandwiches in solitude and dreariness, and it rained hard all the way, and I thought life sloppier than I had expected to find it. . . ."

Mr. W. T. Wildish, the proprietor of the *Rochester and Chatham Journal*, kindly favours us with some interesting information which has recently appeared in his journal, relating to Charles Dickens's nurse—the Mary Weller of his boyhood (and perhaps the Peggotty as well), but known to later generations as Mrs. Mary Gibson of Front Row, Ordnance Place, Chatham, who died in the spring of the year 1888, at the advanced age of eighty-four. Very touchingly, but unknowingly, did Dickens write from Gad's Hill, 24th September, 1857, being unaware that she was still living:—

"I feel much as I used to do when I was a small child, a few miles off, and somebody—*who*, I wonder, and which way did *she* go when she died?—hummed the evening hymn, and I cried on the pillow—either with the remorseful consciousness of having kicked somebody else, or because still somebody else had hurt my feelings in the course of the day."

Mrs. Gibson, when Mary Weller (what a host of pleasant recollections does the married name of the "pretty housemaid" bring up of the Pickwickian days!), lived with the family of Mr. John Dickens, at No. 11, Ordnance Terrace, Chatham, and afterwards when they moved to the House on the Brook. Her recollections were most vivid and interesting.

According to the testimony of her son, communicated to Mr. Wildish, Mrs. Gibson "used to be very fond of talking of the time she passed with the Dickens family, and one of her highest satisfactions in her later years was to hear Charles Dickens's works read by her son Robert; and while listening to the descriptions of characters read to her, his mother would detect likenesses unsuspected by other persons whom Dickens must have known when a boy; and she also agreed in thinking, with Dickens's biographer, that in Mr. Micawber's troubles were related some of the experiences of the elder Dickens, who is believed for a time to have occupied a debtor's prison. She, however, would never bring herself to believe that her hero was himself ever reduced to such great hardships as the blacking-bottle period in *David Copperfield* would suggest if taken literally. She used to speak of the future author as always fond of reading, and said he was wont to retire to the top room of the House on the Brook, and spend what should have been his play-hours in poring over his books, or in acting to the furniture of the room the creatures that he had read about."

Mr. Langton, who had a personal interview with Mrs. Gibson herself, has recorded the fact that she well remembered singing the Evening Hymn to the children of John Dickens, and seemed very much surprised at being asked such a question. She lived with the family when Dickens's little sister, Harriet Ellen, died—a circumstance that no doubt in after years inspired the *Child's Dream of a Star* already referred to. When the family removed to London, Mary Weller was pressed to accompany them, but was not in a position to accept the offer, in consequence of her promise to marry Mr. Thomas Gibson, a shipwright of the Chatham

Dockyard, with whom she lived happily until his death, in 1886, at the age of eighty-two.

Mrs. Gibson modestly declined, on her son Robert's suggestion, to seek an introduction to Charles Dickens, when he read some of his works at the old Mechanics' Institute at Chatham, fearing that he had forgotten her. It is certain, however, that, from the reproduction of her name as the pretty housemaid at Mr. Nupkins's at Ipswich, and from the extract from the letter above referred to, she had a kindly place in his recollections.

Poor David Copperfield, on his way to his aunt's at Dover, stopped at Chatham—"footsore and tired," he says, "and eating bread that I had bought for supper." He is afraid "because of the vicious looks of the trampers;" and even if he could have spared the few pence he possessed for a bed at the "one or two little houses" with the notice "lodgings for travellers," he would have hardly cared to go in, on account of the company he would have been thrown into. And so he says, "I sought no shelter, therefore, but the sky; and toiling into Chatham—which, in that night's aspect, is a mere dream of chalk, and draw-bridges, and mastless ships in a muddy river, roofed like Noah's arks,—crept, at last, upon a sort of grass-grown battery overhanging a lane, where a sentry was walking to and fro. Here" [he continues] "I lay down near a cannon; and, happy in the society of the sentry's footsteps, . . . slept soundly until morning." Of course it is not possible for us to identify this spot. "Very stiff and sore of foot," he says, "I was in the morning, and quite dazed by the beating of drums and marching of troops, which seemed to hem me in on every side when I went down towards the long narrow street." However, he has to reserve his strength for getting to his journey's end, and to this effect he resolves upon selling his jacket.

There are plenty of marine-store dealers at Chatham, whom we notice on our tramp, but none of them would, we believe, now answer to the description of "an ugly old man, with the lower part of his face all covered with a stubbly grey beard, in a filthy flannel waistcoat, and smelling terribly of rum," such as he who assailed little David, in reply to his offer to sell the jacket, with, "Oh, what do you want? Oh, my eyes and limbs, what do you want? Oh, my lungs and liver, what do you want? Oh—goroo, goroo!" After losing his time, and being rated at and frightened by this "dreadful old man to look at," who in every way tries to avoid giving him the money asked for,—half-a-crown,—offering him in exchange such useless things to a hungry boy as "a fishing-rod, a fiddle, a cocked hat, and a flute," the poor lad is obliged to close with the offer of a few pence, "with which [he says] I soon refreshed myself completely; and, being in better spirits then, limped seven miles upon my road."

The Convict Prison at Chatham is said to have been built on a piece of ground which, in the middle of the last century, belonged to one Thomas Clark, a singular character, who lived on the spot for many years by himself in a small cottage, and who used every night, as he went home, to sing or shout, "Tom's all alone! Tom's all alone!" This, according to the opinion of some, may have given rise to the "Tom all alone's" of *Bleak House*, more especially considering the fact that military operations were frequently going on at Chatham, which Dickens would notice in his early days. The circumstance is thus referred to in the novel:—"Twice lately there has been a crash, and a crowd of dust, like the springing of a mine, in Tom all alone's, and each time a house has fallen."

Mr. George Robinson of Strood directs our attention to the fact that a "child's caul," such as that described in the first chapter of *David Copperfield*, which he was born with, and which was advertised "at the low price of fifteen guineas," would be a likely object to be sought after in a sea-faring town like Chatham, in Dickens's early days, when the schoolmaster was less abroad than he is now.

In after years, memories of Chatham Dockyard appear in many of the sketches in the *Uncommercial Traveller* and other stories. "One man in a Dockyard" describes it as having "a gravity upon its red brick offices and houses, a staid pretence of having nothing to do, an avoidance of display, which I never saw out of England." "Nurse's Stories" says that "nails and copper are shipwrights' sweethearts, and shipwrights will run away with them whenever they can." In *Great Expectations* the refrain, "Beat it out, beat it out—old Clem! with a clink for the stout—old Clem!" which Pip and his friends sang, is from a song which the blacksmiths in the dockyard used to sing in procession on St. Clement's Day.

By accident we make the acquaintance of Mr. William James Budden of Chatham, who informs us that Charles Dickens was better known there in his latter years for his efforts, by readings and otherwise, to place the Mechanics' Institute on a sound basis and free from debt.

Dickens, as the *Uncommercial Traveller*, thus describes the Mechanics' Institute and its early efforts to succeed:—

"As the town was placarded with references to the Dullborough Mechanics' Institution, I thought I would go and look at that establishment next. There had been no such thing in the town in my young days, and it occurred to me that its extreme prosperity might have brought adversity upon the Drama. I found the Institution with some difficulty, and should scarcely have known that I had found it if I had judged from its external appearance only; but this was attributable to its never having been finished, and having no front: consequently, it led a modest and retired existence up a stable-yard. It was (as I learnt, on enquiry) a most flourishing Institution, and of the highest benefit to the town: two triumphs which I was glad to understand were not at all impaired by the seeming drawbacks that no mechanics belonged to it, and that it was steeped in debt to the chimney-pots. It had a large room, which was approached by an infirm step-ladder: the builder having declined to construct the intended staircase, without a present payment in cash, which Dullborough (though profoundly appreciative of the Institution) seemed unaccountably bashful about subscribing."

Mr. Budden is of opinion that the origin of the "fat boy" in *Pickwick* was Mr. James Budden, late of the Red Lion Inn in Military Road, who afterwards acquired a competence, and who had the honour of entertaining Dickens at a subsequent period of his life. Mr. Budden is under the impression, from local hearsay, that Dingley Dell formerly existed somewhere in the neighbourhood of Burham.

* * * * * *

We are obligingly favoured with an interview by Mr. John Baird of New Brompton, Chairman of the Chatham Waterworks Company, although he is suffering from serious indisposition at the time of our visit. This gentleman was born in 1810 (two years before Charles Dickens), and recollects reading with delight the famous *Sketches by Boz*, as they appeared in the *Morning Chronicle*. The most curious coincidence about Mr. Baird is, that in stature and facial appearance he is the very counterpart of the late Charles Dickens in the flesh—his double, so to speak. This remarkable resemblance, our informant says, is "something to be proud of, to be mistaken for so great a man, but it was very inconvenient at times."

On one occasion, as Mr. Baird was hastening to catch a rain at Rochester Bridge Station, a stout elderly lady, andsomely dressed, supposed to be Dean Scott's wife,—but o whom he was unknown,—bowed very politely to him, and n slackening his pace to return the compliment, which he aturally did not understand, he very nearly missed his train.

Sir Arthur Otway told Mr. Baird that the Rev. Mr. Vebster, late Vicar of Chatham, had always mistaken him or Charles Dickens.

At one of the Readings given by Dickens on behalf of the Iechanics' Institute at Chatham, Mr. Charles Collins, his son-1-law, and his wife and her sister being present in the reserved eats in the gallery, Mr. Baird noticed that they looked very agerly at him, and this pointed notice naturally made him el very uncomfortable. Dickens himself, accompanied by is son and daughter, once passed our friend in the street, nd scanned him very closely, and he fancies that Dickens alled attention to the resemblance.

At the last reading which the novelist gave at Chatham, Ir. Baird being present as one of the audience, the policeman the door mistook him for Dickens, and shouted to those attendance outside, "Mr. Dickens's carriage!" It is teresting to add, that after the reading a cordial vote of anks to Dickens was proposed by Mr. H. G. Adams, the aturalist, at one time editor of *The Kentish Coronal*, who counted the well-known story of the novelist's father taking m, when a little boy, to see Gad's Hill Place, and of the rong impression it made upon his mind.

Our informant had the honour of meeting Dickens at dinner at Mr. James Budden's, and states that he was standing against the mantel-piece in the drawing-room when the novelist arrived, and that he walked up to him and shook hands cordially, without the usual ceremony of introduction. Dickens was no doubt too polite to refer to the curious resemblance.

But the most remarkable case remains to be told, illustrating the converse of the old proverb—"It is a wise father that knows his own child." This is given in Mr. Baird's own words:—

"My daughter, when a little girl about six years old, was with her mother and some friends in a railway carriage at Strood station (next Rochester), and one of them called the child's attention to a gentleman standing on the platform, asking if she knew who he was. With surprised delight she at once exclaimed, 'That's my papa!' That same gentleman was Mr. Charles Dickens!"

Mr. Baird speaks of the great appreciation which the people of Chatham had of Dickens's services at the readings, and says it was very good and kind of him to give those services gratuitously. He confirms the general opinion as to the origin of the "fat boy," and the "very fussy little man" at Fort Pitt, who was the prototype of Dr. Slammer.

It struck us both forcibly that Mr. Baird's appearance at the time of our visit was very like the last American photograph of Dickens, taken by Gurney in 1867.

* * * * * *

Mr. J. E. Littlewood[5] of High Street, Chatham, knew

[5] Since this was written, Mr. Littlewood has passed over to the great majority. He was found drowned near Chatham Pier in March, 1890.

Charles Dickens about the year 1845 or 1846 at the Royalty (Miss Kelly's) Theatre in Dean Street, Soho, our informant having been in times past a bit of an amateur actor, and played Bob Acres in *The Rivals*. He subsequently heard Dickens read at the Chatham Mechanics' Institute about 1861, and said that the facial display in the trial scene from *Pickwick* (one of the pieces read) was wonderful. He had the honour of dining at the late Mr. Budden's in High Street, opposite Military Road, to meet Dickens. There was a large company present. In acknowledging the toast of his health, which had been proposed at the dinner—either by Sir Arthur Otway or Captain Fanshawe—Dickens said he was very pleased to read "in memory of the old place," meaning Chatham, but that he might be reading "all the year round" for charities.

Mr. Littlewood also heard Dickens say, that "he had passed many happy hours in the House on the Brook" looking at "the Lines" opposite. "At that time" (said our informant) 'the place was more rural—considered a decent spot—not so crowded up as now—nor so vulgar—many respectable people lived there in Dickens's boyhood. The place has sadly changed since for the worse."

* * * * * *

Mr. Humphrey Wood, Solicitor, of Chatham, was, about the year 1867, local Hon. Secretary to the Royal Society for the Prevention of Cruelty to Animals, and, having applied to Charles Dickens to give a Reading on behalf of the Society, received the following polite answer to his application. If only a few words had to be said, they were well said and to the purpose.

"GAD'S HILL PLACE,
"HIGHAM BY ROCHESTER, KENT.
"*Thursday*, 5*th September*, 1867.

"SIR,

"In reply to your letter, I beg to express my regret that my compliance with the request it communicates to me, is removed from within the bounds of reasonable possibility by the nature of my engagements, present and prospective.

"Your faithful servant,
"CHARLES DICKENS.

"HUMPHREY WOOD, ESQ."

Like other towns in Kent, Chatham contains many names which are suggestive of some of Dickens's characters, *viz.* Dowler, Whiffen, Kimmins, Wyles, Arkcoll, Perse, Winch, Wildish, Hockaday, Mowatt, Hunnisett, and others.

It is, of course, scarcely necessary to mention, in passing, that Chatham is one of the most important centres of ship-building for the Royal Navy; the dockyards—often referred to in Dickens's minor works—cover more than seventy acres, and are most interesting. Here, at the Navy Pay-Office, the elder Dickens was employed during his residence at Chatham.

Fort Pitt next claims our attention. It stands on the high ground above the Railway Station at Chatham, just beyond Ordnance Terrace. In Charles Dickens's early days, and indeed long after, until the establishment of the magnificent Institution at Netley, Fort Pitt was the principal military Hospital in England, and was visited by Her Majesty during the Crimean War. It is still used as a hospital, and contains about two hundred and fifty beds. The interesting museum which previously existed there has been removed to Netley.

From Fort Pitt we see the famous "Chatham lines," which constitute the elaborate and almost impregnable fortifications of this important military and ship-building town. The "lines" were commenced as far back as 1758, and stretch from Gillingham to Brompton, a distance of several miles, enclosing the peninsula formed by the bend of the river Medway. Forster says:—

Navy Pay-Office, Chatham.

"By Rochester and the Medway to the Chatham lines was favourite walk with Charles Dickens. He would turn out f Rochester High Street through the Vines, . . . would pass und by Fort Pitt, and coming back by Frindsbury would ring himself by some cross-fields again into the high-road."

The Chatham lines are locally understood as referring to a ece of ground about three or four hundred yards square, near ort Pitt, used as an exercising-ground for the military.

Chapter IV. of *Pickwick*, "describing a field day and bivouac," refers to the Chatham lines as the place where the review was held, on the third day of the visit of the Pickwickians to this neighbourhood, and which (having been relieved of the company of their quondam friend, Mr. Jingle, who had caused at least one of the party so much anxiety) they all attended, possibly at Mr. Pickwick's suggestion, as he is stated to have been "an enthusiastic admirer of the army." The programme is thus referred to:—

> "The whole population of Rochester and the adjoining towns, rose from their beds at an early hour of the following morning, in a state of the utmost bustle and excitement. A grand review was to take place upon the lines. The manœuvres of half a dozen regiments were to be inspected by the eagle eye of the commander-in-chief; temporary fortifications had been erected, the citadel was to be attacked and taken, and a mine was to be sprung."

The evolutions of this "ceremony of the utmost grandeur and importance" proceed. Mr. Pickwick and his two friends (Mr. Tupman "had suddenly disappeared, and was nowhere to be found"), who are told to keep back, get hustled and pushed by the crowd, and the unoffending Mr. Snodgrass, who is in "the very extreme of human torture," is derided and asked "vere he vos a shovin' to." Subsequently they ge hemmed in by the crowd, "are exposed to a galling fire o blank cartridges, and harassed by the operations of th military." Mr. Pickwick loses his hat, and not only regain that useful article of dress, but finds the lost Mr. Tupman and the Pickwickians make the acquaintance of old Wardl and his hospitable family from Dingley Dell, by whom the are heartily entertained, and from whom they receive a warn invitation to visit Manor Farm on the morrow.

There is a fine view of Chatham and Rochester from the fields round Fort Pitt, and on a bright sunny morning the air coming over from the Kentish Hills is most refreshing, very different indeed to what it was on a certain evening in Mr. Winkle's life, when "a melancholy wind sounded through the deserted fields like a giant whistling for his house-dog." We ramble about for an hour or more, and in imagination call up the pleasant times which Charles Dickens, as a boy, spent here.

Fort Pitt, Chatham.

Almost every inch of the ground must have been gone over by him. What a delightful "playing-field" this and the neighbouring meadows must have been to him and his young companions, before the railway and the builder took possession of some of the lower portions of the hill which forms the base of Fort Pitt. "Here," says Mr. Langton, "is the place where the schools of Rochester and Chatham used to meet to settle their differences, and to contend in the more friendly rivalry of cricket," and no doubt Dickens frequently played when "Joe Specks" in Dullborough "kept wicket."

In after life the memory of the past came back to Dickens with all its freshness, when he again visited the neighbourhood as the *Uncommercial Traveller* in "Dullborough":—

"With this tender remembrance upon me" [that of leaving Chatham as a boy], "I was cavalierly shunted back into Dullborough the other day, by train. My ticket had been previously collected, like my taxes, and my shining new portmanteau had had a great plaster stuck upon it, and I had been defied by Act of Parliament to offer an objection to anything that was done to it, or me, under a penalty of not less than forty shillings or more than five pounds, compoundable for a term of imprisonment. When I had sent my disfigured property on to the hotel, I began to look about me; and the first discovery I made, was, that the Station had swallowed up the playing-field.

"It was gone. The two beautiful hawthorn-trees, the hedge, the turf, and all those buttercups and daisies, had given place to the stoniest of jolting roads; while, beyond the Station, an ugly dark monster of a tunnel kept its jaws open, as if it had swallowed them and were ravenous for more destruction. The coach that had carried me away, was melodiously called Timpson's Blue-eyed Maid, and belonged to Timpson, at the coach-office up street; the locomotive engine that had brought me back was called severely No. 97, and belonged to S.E.R., and was spitting ashes and hot-water over the blighted ground.

"When I had been let out at the platform-door, like a prisoner whom his turnkey grudgingly released, I looked in again over the low wall, at the scene of departed glories. Here, in the haymaking time, had I been delivered from the dungeons of Seringapatam, an immense pile (of haycock), by my countrymen, the victorious British (boy next door and his two cousins), and had been recognized with ecstasy by my affianced one (Miss Green), who had come all the way from England (second house in the terrace) to ransom me, and marry me."

Fort Pitt must have had considerable attractions in Mr. Pickwick's time, as it would appear that it was visited by him and his friends on the first day of their arrival at Rochester. Lieutenant Tappleton (Dr. Slammer's second), when presenting the challenge for the duel, thus speaks to Mr. Winkle in the second chapter of *Pickwick* :—

"'You know Fort Pitt?'

"'Yes; I saw it yesterday.'

"'If you will take the trouble to turn into the field which borders the trench, take the foot-path to the left, when you arrive at an angle of the fortification; and keep straight on till you see me; I will precede you to a secluded place, where the affair can be conducted without fear of interruption.'

"'*Fear* of interruption!' thought Mr. Winkle."

Everybody remembers how the meeting took place on Fort Pitt. Mr. Winkle, attended by his friend Mr. Snodgrass, as second, is punctuality itself.

"'We are in excellent time,' said Mr. Snodgrass, as they climbed the fence of the first field; 'the sun is just going down.' Mr. Winkle looked up at the declining orb, and painfully thought of the probability of his 'going down' himself, before long."

Presently the officer appears, "the gentleman in the blue cloak," and "slightly beckoning with his hand to the two friends, they follow him for a little distance," and after climbing a paling and scaling a hedge, enter a secluded field.

Dr. Slammer is already there with his friend Dr. Payne,—Dr. Payne of the 43rd, "the man with the camp-stool."

The arrangements proceed, when suddenly a check is experienced.

"'What's all this?' said Dr. Slammer, as his friend and Mr. Snodgrass came running up.—'That's not the man.'

"'Not the man!' said Dr. Slammer's second.

"'Not the man!' said Mr. Snodgrass.

"'Not the man!' said the gentleman with the camp-stool in his hand.

"'Certainly not,' replied the little doctor. 'That's not the person who insulted me last night.'

"'Very extraordinary!' exclaimed the officer.

"'Very,' said the gentleman with the camp-stool."

Mutual explanations follow, and, notwithstanding the temporary dissatisfaction of Dr. Payne, Mr. Winkle comes out like a trump—defends the honour of the Pickwick Club and its uniform, and wins the admiration of Dr. Slammer.

"'My dear sir,' said the good-humoured little doctor, advancing with extended hand, 'I honour your gallantry. Permit me to say, Sir, that I highly admire your conduct, and extremely regret having caused you the inconvenience of this meeting, to no purpose.'

"'I beg you won't mention it, Sir,' said Mr. Winkle.

"'I shall feel proud of your acquaintance, Sir,' said the little doctor.

"'It will afford me the greatest pleasure to know you, Sir,' replied Mr. Winkle.

"Thereupon the doctor and Mr. Winkle shook hands, and then Mr. Winkle and Lieutenant Tappleton (the doctor's second), and then Mr. Winkle and the man with the camp-stool, and finally Mr. Winkle and Mr. Snodgrass: the last-named gentleman in an excess of admiration at the noble conduct of his heroic friend.

"'I think we may adjourn,' said Lieutenant Tappleton.

"'Certainly,' added the doctor."

We ourselves also adjourn, taking with us many pleasant memories of Chatham and Fort Pitt, and of the period relating to "the childhood and youth of Charles Dickens."

* * * * * *

No tramp in "Dickens-Land" can possibly be complete without a visit to the birthplace of the great novelist, and on another occasion we therefore devote a day to Portsea, Hants. A fast train from Victoria by the London, Brighton, and South Coast Railway takes us to Portsmouth Town, the nearest station, which is about half a mile from Commercial Road,

BIRTHPLACE OF CHARLES DICKENS,
387 Mile End Terrace, Commercial Road, Landport.

and a tram-car puts us down at the door. We immediately recognize the house from the picture in Mr. Langton's book, but the first impression is that the illustration scarcely does justice to it. From the picture it appears to us to be a very ordinary house in a row, and to be situated rather low in a crowded and not over respectable neighbourhood. Nothing of the kind. The house, No. 387, Mile End Terrace, Commercial Road, Landport, where the parents of Charles Dickens resided before they removed to another part of Portsea, and subsequently went to live at Chatham, and where the future genius first saw light, was eighty years ago quite in a rural neighbourhood ; and in those days must have been considered rather a genteel residence for a family of moderate means in the middle class. Even now, with the pressure which always attends the development of large towns, and their extension on the border-land of green country by the frequent conversion of dwelling-houses into shops, or the intrusion of shops where dwelling-houses are, this residence has escaped and remains unchanged to this day.

There is another point of real importance to notice. Mr. Langton, referring to this house, says:—"The engraving shows the little fore-court or front garden, with the low kitchen window of the house, whence the movements of Charles [who is presumably represented in the engraving by the figure of a boy about two or three years old, with curly locks, dressed in a smart frock, and having a large ball in his right hand], attended by his dear little sister Fanny, could be overlooked."[6] Very pretty indeed, but alas! I am afraid, purely imaginary, considering, as will hereafter appear, that Charles was a baby in arms, aged about four months and sixteen days, when his parents quitted the house in which he was born.

[6] This was taken from the first edition of Mr. Langton's book, published in 1883. In the new edition, 1891—a beautiful volume—this passage has been eliminated, but the engraving is untouched.

The house is now, and has been for many years, occupied by Miss Sarah Pearce, the surviving daughter of Mr. John Dickens's landlord, her sisters, who formerly lived with her, being all dead. It stands high on the west side of a good broad road, opposite an old-fashioned villa called Angus House, in the midst of well-trimmed grounds, and the situation is very open, pleasant, and cheerful. It is red-brick built, has a railing in front, and is approached by a little entrance-gate opening on to a lawn, whereon there are a few flower-beds; a hedge divides the fore-court from the next house,[7] and a few steps guarded by a handrail lead to the front door. It is a single-fronted, eight-roomed house, having two under-ground kitchens, two floors above, and a single dormer window high up in the sloping red-tiled roof. As is usual with old-fashioned houses of this type, the shutters to the lower windows are outside. Both the front and back parlours on the ground floor are very cheerful, cosy little rooms (in one of them we are glad to see a portrait of the novelist), and the view from the back parlour looking down into the well-kept garden, which abuts on other gardens, is very pretty, marred only by a large gasometer in the distance, which could hardly have been erected in young Charles Dickens's earliest days. In the garden we notice a lovely specimen of the *Lavatera arborea*, or tree-mallow, covered with hundreds of white and purple blossoms. It is a rarity to see such a handsome, well-grown tree, standing nearly eight feet high, and it is not unlikely, from the luxuriance of its growth, that

[7] This house is appropriately named "Highland House," and was also the property of John Dickens's landlord, in which the family then and for many years after resided. At the time referred to Mr. Pearce owned not only the above-mentioned houses, but all the surrounding property.

it existed in Charles Dickens's infancy. From the pleasant surroundings of the place generally, and from the fact that flowers are much grown in the neighbourhood (especially roses), it is more than probable that Dickens's love for flowers was early developed by these associations. The road leads to Cosham, and to the picturesque old ruin of Porchester Castle, a nice walk from the town of Portsmouth, and probably often traversed by Dickens, his sister, and his nurse.

Mr. Langton states that "it is said in after years Charles Dickens could remember places and things at Portsmouth that he had not seen since he was an infant of little more than two years old (he left Portsmouth when he was only four or five), and there is no doubt whatever that many of the earliest reminiscences of *David Copperfield* were also tender childish memories of his own infancy at this place."

Mr. William Pearce, solicitor of Portsea, son of the former landlord, and brother of Miss Sarah Pearce, the present occupant, has been kind enough to supply the following interesting information respecting No. 387, Mile End Terrace:—

"The celebrated novelist was born in the front bedroom of the above house, which my sisters many years ago converted into a drawing-room, and it is still used as such.

"Mr. John Dickens, the father of the novelist, and his wife came to reside in the house directly after they were married. Mr. John Dickens rented the house of my father at £35 a-year, from the 24th June, 1808, until the 24th June, 1812, when he quitted, and moved into Hawke Street, in the town of Portsea. Miss Fanny Dickens, the novelist's sister, was the first child born in the house, and then the novelist.

"I was born on the 22nd February, 1814, and have often heard my mother say that Mr. Gardner, the surgeon, and Mrs. Purkis, the monthly nurse (both of whom attended my mother with me and her six other children), attended Mrs. Dickens with her two children, Fanny and Charles, who were both born in the above house; besides this, Mrs. Purkis has often called on my sisters at the house in question, and alluded to the above circumstances.

St. Mary's Church, Portsea.

"Mr. Cobb (whom I recollect), a fellow-clerk of Mr. John Dickens in the pay-office in the Portsmouth Dockyard, rented the same house of my father after Mr. John Dickens left, and often alluded to the many happy hours he spent in it while Mr. Dickens resided there."

We next visit the site of old Kingston Parish Church,—St. Mary's, Portsea—where Charles Dickens was baptized on 4th March, 1812. A very handsome and large new church, costing nearly forty thousand pounds, and capable of seating over two thousand persons, has been erected, and occupies the place of the old church, where the ceremony took place. Mr. Langton has given a very pretty little drawing of the old church in his book, so that its associations are preserved to lovers of Dickens. The old church itself was the second edifice erected on the same spot, and thus the present one is the third parish church which has been built here. There is a large and crowded burial-ground attached to it; but a cursory examination does not disclose any names on the gravestones to indicate characters in the novels.

It is right to note here, that the kind people of Portsmouth were desirous of inserting a stained-glass window in their beautiful new church to the memory of one of their most famous sons (the eminent novelist, Mr. Walter Besant, was born at Portsmouth, as also were Isambard K. Brunel, the engineer, and Messrs. George and Vicat Cole, Royal Academicians), but they were debarred by the conditions of Dickens's will, which expressly interdicted anything of the kind. It states:—

"I conjure my friends on no account to make me the subject of any monument, memorial, or testimonial whatever. I rest my claim to the remembrance of my country upon my published works, and to the remembrance of my friends upon their experience of me in addition thereto."

Before leaving Portsmouth, we just take a hasty glance at the Theatre Royal, which remains much as it was during the days of Mr. Vincent Crummles and his company, as graphically described in the twenty-second and following chapters of *Nicholas Nickleby*. Of that genial manager, Mr. T. Edgar Pemberton, in his *Charles Dickens and the Stage*, observes:—

"Every line that is written about Mr. Crummles and his followers is instinct with good-natured humour, and from the moment when, in the road-side inn 'yet twelve miles short of Portsmouth,' the reader comes into contact with the kindly old circuit manager, he finds himself in the best of good company."

Mr. Rimmer, in his *About England with Dickens*, referring to the "Common Hard" at Portsmouth, says that the "people there point out in a narrow lane leading to the wharf, the house where Nicholas is supposed to have sojourned."

CHAPTER X.

AYLESFORD, TOWN MALLING, AND MAIDSTONE.

"Its river winding down from the mist on the horizon, as though that were its source, and already heaving with a restless knowledge of its approach towards the sea."—*Edwin Drood.*

"Oh, the solemn woods over which the light and shadow travelled swiftly, as if Heavenly wings were sweeping on benignant errands through the summer air; the smooth green slopes, the glittering water, the garden where the flowers were symmetrically arranged in clusters of the richest colours, how beautiful they looked!"—*Bleak House.*

ANOTHER delightful morning, fine but overcast, favours our tramp in this neighbourhood. We are up betimes on Monday and take the train by the South-Eastern Railway from Strood station to Aylesford. It is a distance of nearly eight miles between these places; and the intermediate stations of any note which we pass on the way are Cuxton (about three miles) and Snodland (about two miles further on), which are two large villages. As the railway winds, we obtain excellent views of the chalk escarpments on the series of hills opposite these being the result of centuries of quarrying. The land on either side of the river is marshy and intersected by numerous water-courses. These grounds are locally termed "saltings," caused by the overflow of the Medway at certain times, and are used as sanitaria for horses which require bracing.

Cuxton is at the entrance of the valley between the two chalk ranges of hills which form the water-parting of the

river Medway. As Mr. Phillips Bevan rightly observes—"this valley is utilized for quarrying and lime-burning to such an extent, that it has almost the appearance of a northern manufacturing district but it is a consolation, on the authority of Sir A. C. Ramsay, to know that "man cannot permanently disfigure nature!"

At Snodland the river becomes narrower, and the scenery of the valley is more picturesque. Early British and Roman remains have been found in the district, and according to the authority previously quoted—"In one of the quarries, which are abundant, Dr. Mantell discovered some of the most interesting and rarest chalk fossils with which we are acquainted, including the fossil Turtle (*Chelonia Benstedi*)."

Alighting from the train at Aylesford station, we have but a few minutes to ramble by the river, the banks of which are brightened by the handsome flowers of the purple loose-strife. We notice the charming position of the Norman church, which stands on an eminence on the right bank of the Medway, overlooking the main street, and is surrounded by fine old elm trees—the bells were chiming "Home, sweet home," a name very dear to Dickens. The Medway ceases to be a tidal river at Allington beyond Aylesford, and one or other of the weirs at Allington or Farleigh (further on may have suggested the idea of "Cloisterham Weir" in *Edwin Drood;* but they are too far distant (as shown in Chapter V.) to fit in with the story. The ancient stone bridge which spans the Medway at Aylesford is seven-arched; a large central one, and three smaller ones on either side. One or two of the arches on the left bank are filled up, as though the river had silted on that side. Mr. Roach Smith considers the bridge to be a very fine specimen of mediæval architecture. It is somewhat narrow, but there are large abutments which afford shelter to foot passengers.

We are much inclined to think that Aylesford Bridge was in the mind of Dickens when he makes the Pickwickian

Aylesford Bridge
F. G. Kitton

cross the Medway, only a wooden bridge is mentioned in the text for the purpose perhaps of concealing identity. The place is certainly worth visiting, and the approach to it by the river is exceedingly picturesque.

Aylesford is supposed to be the place where the great battle between Hengist and Vortigern took place. Near to it, at a place called Horsted, is the tomb of Horsa, who fell in the battle between the Britons and Saxons, A.D. 455. Names of Dickens's characters, Brooks, Joy, etc., occur at Aylesford. There is a very fine quarry here, from whence the famous Kentish rag-stone—"a concretionary limestone"—is obtained. It forms the base, and is overlaid by the Hassock sands and the river drift. In the distance is seen the bold series of chalk rocks constituting the ridge of the valley.

Just outside Aylesford we pass Preston Hall, a fine modern Tudor mansion standing in very pretty grounds, and belonging to Mr. H. Brassey.

We now resume our tramp towards the principal point of our destination, Town Malling,[1] or West Malling, as it is indifferently called (the "a" in Malling being pronounced long, as in "calling"). The walk from Aylesford lies through the village of Larkview, and is rather pretty, but there is nothing remarkable to notice until we approach Town Malling. Here it becomes beautifully wooded, especially in the neighbourhood of Clare House Park, the Spanish or edible chestnut, with its handsome dark green lanceolate serrate leaves, and clumps of Scotch firs, with their light red trunks and large cones, the result of healthy growth, which

[1] Lambarde says, "Malling, in Saxon Mealing, or Mealuing, that is, the Low place flourishing with Meal or Corne, for so it is everywhere accepted."

would have delighted the heart of Mr. Ruskin, being conspicuous. On the road we pass a field sown with maize, a novelty to one accustomed to the Midlands. The farmer to whom it belongs says that it is a poor crop this year, owing to the excess of wet and late summer, but in a good season it gives a fine yield. We are informed that it is used in the green state as food for cattle and chickens.

A pleasant tramp of about three miles brings us to Town Malling, which stands on the Kentish rag. The approach to Town Malling is by a waterfall, and there are the ruins of the old Nunnery, founded by Bishop Gundulph in 1090, in the place. East Malling is a smaller town, and lies nearer to Maidstone. Our object in visiting this pretty, old-fashioned Kentish country town, is to verify its identity with that of Muggleton of the *Pickwick Papers*. Great weight must be attached to the fact that the present Mr. Charles Dickens, in his annotated Jubilee Edition of the above work, introduces a very pretty woodcut of "High Street, Town Malling," with a note to the effect that—

"Muggleton, perhaps, is only to be taken as a fancy sketch of a small country town; but it is generally supposed, and probably with sufficient accuracy, that, if it is in any degree a portrait of any Kentish town, Town Malling, a great place for cricket in Mr. Pickwick's time, sat for it."

The reader will remember that when at the hospitable Mr. Wardle's residence at Manor Farm in Dingley Dell (by the bye, there is a veritable "Manor Farm" at Frindsbury, near Strood, with ponds adjacent, which may perhaps have suggested the episode of Mr. Pickwick on the ice), an excursion was determined on by the Pickwickians to witness a grand cricket match about to be played between the "All Muggleton" and the "Dingley Dellers," a conference first took place as to whether the invalid, Mr. Tupman, should remain or go with them.

"'Shall we be justified,' asked Mr. Pickwick, 'in leaving our wounded friend to the care of the ladies?'

"'You cannot leave me in better hands,' said Mr. Tupman.

"'Quite impossible,' said Mr. Snodgrass."

The result of the conference was satisfactory.

"It was therefore settled that Mr. Tupman should be left at home in charge of the females, and that the remainder of the guests under the guidance of Mr. Wardle should proceed to the spot, where was to be held that trial of skill, which had roused all Muggleton from its torpor, and inoculated Dingley Dell with a fever of excitement.

"As their walk, *which was not above two miles long*,[2] lay through

[2] The italics are interpolated.

shady lanes and sequestered footpaths, and as their conversation turned upon the delightful scenery by which they were on every side surrounded, Mr. Pickwick was almost inclined to regret the expedition they had used, when he found himself in the main street of the town of Muggleton."

The chronicle of *Pickwick* then proceeds to state that—

"Muggleton is a corporate town, with a mayor, burgesses, and freemen; . . . an ancient and loyal borough, mingling a zealous advocacy of Christian principles with a devoted attachment to commercial rights; in demonstration whereof, the mayor, corporation, and other inhabitants, have presented at divers times, no fewer than one thousand four hundred and twenty petitions, against the continuance of negro slavery abroad, and an equal number against any interference with the factory system at home; sixty-eight in favour of the sales of livings in the Church, and eighty-six for abolishing Sunday trading in the streets."

On the occasion of their second visit to Manor Farm to spend Christmas, the Pickwickians came by the "Muggleton Telegraph," which stopped at the "Blue Lion," and they walked over to Dingley Dell.

Assuming, as has been suggested by Mr. Frost in his *In Kent with Charles Dickens*, that Dingley Dell is somewhere on the eastern side of the river Medway, within fifteen miles of Rochester,—Mr. William James Budden (a gentleman whom we met at Chatham) gave as his opinion that it was near Burham,[3]—then it would require a much greater walk than that ("which was not above two miles long") to reach Town Malling (leaving out of the question the fact that Burham is only about six miles from Rochester instead of fifteen miles, as the waiter at the Bull told Mr. Pickwick in reply to his

[3] Burham, although now enshrouded in the smoke of lime-making, was probably sixty years ago a delightfully rural spot.

enquiry), whereby we reluctantly for the time arrive at the conclusion,—as Mr. Frost did before us—that Dingley Dell as such near Town Malling cannot be identified.

On another visit to "Dickens-Land" Mr. R. L. Cobb suggested that Cobtree Hall, near Aylesford, was the prototype of Dingley Dell. It may have been; but except one goes as the crow flies, it is more than two miles distant from Town Malling. But as Captain Cuttle would say—we "make a note of it."

After all, Dingley Dell is no doubt a type of an English yeoman's hospitable home. There are numbers of such in Kent, Warwickshire, Worcestershire, Devonshire, and other counties, and the one in question may have been seen by Dickens almost anywhere.

There is, at any rate, one objection to Muggleton being Town Malling—the latter is not, as mentioned in the text, "a corporate town." The neighbouring corporate towns which might be taken for it are Faversham, Tunbridge Wells, and Seven Oaks; but, as Mr. Rimmer, in his *About England with Dickens*, points out—"These have no feature in common with the enterprising borough which had so distinguished itself in the matter of petitions." On the other hand, there is *one* very strong reason in favour of Town Malling, and that is its devotion to the noble old English game of cricket. So far as we could make out, no town in Kent has done better service in this respect. But more of this presently.

* * * * * *

So many friends recommended us to see Cobtree Hall that, after the foregoing was written, we determined to follow their advice, and on a subsequent occasion we take the train to Aylesford and walk over, the distance being a pleasant stroll of about a mile. We were well repaid. The mansion, formerly called Coptray Friars, belonging to the Aylesford Friary, is an Elizabethan structure of red brick with stone facings prettily covered with creeping plants, standing on an elevated position in a beautifully wooded and undu-

lating country overlooking the Medway and surrounded by cherry orchards and hop gardens. Major Trousdell was so courteous as to show us over the building, which has been altered and much enlarged during the last half century. Internally there is something to favour the hypothesis of its being the type of Manor Farm, Dingley Dell. Such portions of the old building remaining, as the kitchen, are highly suggestive of the gathering described in that good-humoured Christmas chapter of *Pickwick* (xxviii.), and there is a veritable beam to correspond with Phiz's plate of "Christmas Eve at Mr. Wardle's." "The best sitting-room, [described as] a good long, dark-panelled room with a high chimney-piece, and a capacious chimney up which you could have driven one of the new patent cabs, wheels and all," may still be discerned in the handsome modern dining-room, with carved marble mantel-piece of massive size formerly supplied with old-fashioned "dogs." The views from the bay-window are very extensive and picturesque. The mansion divides the two parishes of Boxley and Allington, the initials of which are carved on the beam in the kitchen. Externally, there is much more to commend it to our acceptance. Remains of a triangular piece of ground, with a few elm-trees, still survive as "the rookery," where Mr. Tupman met with his mishap, and to our delight there is "the pond," not indeed covered with ice, as on Mr. Pickwick's memorable adventure, but crowded with water-lilies on its surface; its banks surrounded by the fragrant meadow-sweet and the brilliant rose-coloured willow herb. Furthermore we were informed, by Mr. Franklin of Maidstone, that the "Red Lion," which formerly stood on the spot now occupied by Mercer's Stables, is locally considered to be the original of "a little roadside public-house, with two elm-trees, a horse-trough, and a sign-post in front;" where the Pickwickians sought assistance after the break-down of the "four-wheeled chaise" which "separated the wheels from the body and the bin from the perch," but were inhospitably repulsed by the "red-headed man and the tall bony woman," who suggested that they had stolen the "immense horse" which had recently played Mr. Winkle such pranks. Finally, in a pleasant chat with the Rev. Cyril Grant, Vicar of Aylesford, and his curate, the Rev. H. B. Boyd (a son of A. K. H. B.), we elicited the fact that Cobtree Hall is locally recognized as the original of Manor Farm. Nay more, in Aylesford churchyard a tomb was pointed out on the west side with the inscription:—"Also to the memory of Mr. W. Spong, late of Cobtree, in the Parish of Boxley, who died Nov. 15th, 1839," who is said to have been the prototype of the genial and hospitable "old Wardle."

True, neither the distance to Rochester nor to Town Malling fits in with the narrative, but this is not material. Dickens, with the usual "novelist's licence," found it convenient often-times to take a nucleus of fact, and surround it with a halo of fiction, and this may have been one of many similar instances. His wonderfully-gifted and ever-facile imagination was never at fault.

So on our return journey we console ourselves by reading the following description, in chapter vi. of *Pickwick*, of the first gathering of the Pickwickians at their host's, one of the most delightful bits in the whole book, and "make-believe," as the Marchioness would say, that we have actually seen Manor Farm, Dingley Dell.

"Several guests who were assembled in the old parlour, rose to greet Mr. Pickwick and his friends upon their entrance; and during the performance of the ceremony of introduction, with all due formalities, Mr. Pickwick had leisure to observe the appearance, and speculate upon the characters and pursuits, of the persons by whom he was surrounded—a habit in which he in common with many other great men delighted to indulge.

"A very old lady, in a lofty cap and faded silk gown,—no less a personage than Mr. Wardle's mother,—occupied the post of honour on the right-hand corner of the chimney-piece; and various certificates of her having been brought up in the way she should go when young, and of her not having departed from it when old, ornamented the walls, in the form of samplers of ancient date, worsted landscapes of equal antiquity, and crimson silk tea-kettle holders of a more modern period. The aunt, the two young ladies, and Mr. Wardle, each vying with the other in paying zealous and unremitting attentions to the old lady, crowded round her easy-chair, one holding her ear-trumpet, another an orange, and a third a smelling-bottle, while a fourth was busily engaged in patting and punching the pillows, which were arranged for her support. On the opposite side sat a bald-headed old gentleman, with a good-humoured benevolent face, —the clergyman of Dingley Dell; and next him sat his wife, a stout, blooming old lady, who looked as if she were well skilled, not only in the art and mystery of manufacturing home-made cordials, greatly to other people's satisfaction, but of tasting them occasionally, very much to her own. A little hard-headed, Ripstone pippin-faced man, was conversing with a fat old gentleman in one corner; and two or three more old gentlemen, and two or three more old ladies, sat bolt upright and motionless on their chairs, staring very hard at Mr. Pickwick and his fellow-voyagers.

"'Mr. Pickwick, mother,' said Mr. Wardle, at the very top of his voice.

"'Ah!' said the old lady, shaking her head; 'I can't hear you.'

"'Mr. Pickwick, grandma!' screamed both the young ladies together.

"'Ah!' exclaimed the old lady. 'Well; it don't much matter. He don't care for an old 'ooman like me, I dare say.'

"'I assure you, madam,' said Mr. Pickwick, grasping the old lady's hand, and speaking so loud that the exertion imparted a crimson hue to his benevolent countenance; 'I assure you, ma'am, that nothing delights me more, than to see a lady of your time of life heading so fine a family, and looking so young and well.'

"'Ah!' said the old lady, after a short pause; 'it's all very fine, I dare say; but I can't hear him.'

"'Grandma's rather put out now,' said Miss Isabella Wardle, in a low tone; 'but she'll talk to you presently.'

"Mr. Pickwick nodded his readiness to humour the infirmities of age, and entered into a general conversation with the other members of the circle.

"'Delightful situation this,' said Mr. Pickwick.

"'Delightful!' echoed Messrs. Snodgrass, Tupman, and Winkle.

"'Well, I think it is,' said Mr. Wardle.

"'There ain't a better spot o' ground in all Kent, sir,' said the hard-headed man with the pippin-face; 'there ain't indeed, sir—I'm sure there ain't, sir,' and the hard-headed man looked triumphantly round, as if he had been very much contradicted by somebody, but had got the better of him at last. 'There ain't a better spot o' ground in all Kent,' said the hard-headed man again after a pause.

"''Cept Mullins' meadows!' observed the fat man, solemnly.

"'Mullins' meadows!' ejaculated the other, with profound contempt.

"'Ah, Mullins' meadows,' repeated the fat man.

"'Reg'lar good land that,' interposed another fat man.

"'And so it is, sure-ly,' said a third fat man.

"'Everybody knows that,' said the corpulent host.

"The hard-headed man looked dubiously round, but finding himself in a minority, assumed a compassionate air, and said no more.

"'What are they talking about?' inquired the old lady of one of her grand-daughters, in a very audible voice; for, like many deaf people, she never seemed to calculate on the possibility of other persons hearing what she said herself.

"'About the land, grandma.'

"'What about the land? Nothing the matter, is there?'

"'No, no. Mr. Miller was saying our land was better than Mullins' meadows.'

"'How should he know anything about it?' inquired the old lady indignantly. 'Miller's a conceited coxcomb, and you may tell him I said so.' Saying which, the old lady, quite unconscious that she had spoken above a whisper, drew herself up, and looked carving-knives at the hard-headed delinquent."

* * * * * *

In the course of our tramp we fall in with "a very queer small boy," rejoicing in the Christian names of "Spencer Ray," upon which we congratulate him, and express a hope that he will do honour to the noble names which he bears, one being that of the great English philosopher, and the other that of the famous English naturalist. This boy, who is just such a bright intelligent lad as Dickens himself would have been at his age (twelve and a half years), gives us some interesting particulars respecting Town Malling and its proclivities for cricket, upon which he is very eloquent. It appears that in the year 1887 the cricketers of Town Malling won eleven matches out of twelve; but during this year they have not been so successful. He directed us to the cricket-

ground, which we visit, and find to be but a few minutes' walk from the centre of the town, bearing to the westward. It is a very fine field, nearly seven acres in extent, in splendid order, as level as a die, and as green as an emerald. It lies well open, and is flanked by the western range of hills of the Medway valley.

The marquee into which Mr. Pickwick and his friends were invited, first by "one very stout gentleman, whose body and legs looked like half a gigantic roll of flannel, elevated on a couple of inflated pillow-cases," and then by the irrepressible Jingle with—"This way—this way—capital fun—lots of beer—hogsheads; rounds of beef—bullocks; mustard—cart-loads; glorious day—down with you—make yourself at home—glad to see you—very," has been replaced by a handsome pavilion.

There is no cricket-playing going on at the time, but there are several cricketers in the field, and from them we learn confirmatory evidence of the long existence of the ground in its present condition, and the enthusiasm of the inhabitants for the old English game.

Another proof of the long-established love of the people of Town Malling for cricket we subsequently find in the fact that the parlour of the Swan Hotel, which is an old cricketing house, and probably represents the "Blue Lion of Muggleton," has in it many very fine lithographic portraits of all the great cricketers of the middle of the nineteenth century, including:—Pilch, Lillywhite, Box, Cobbett, Hillyer (a native of Town Malling), A. Mynn, Taylor, Langdon, Kynaston, Felix (*Felix on the Bat*), Ward, Kingscote, and others. Several of these names will be recognized as those of eminent Kentish cricketers. About a quarter of a century ago—my friend and colleague Mr. E. Orford Smith (himself a Kentish man and a cricketer) informs me that—the Kentish eleven stood against all England, and retained their position for some years.

As we stand on the warm day in the centre of the ground, and admire the lights and shadows passing over the surrounding scenery, we can almost conjure up the scene of the famous contest, when, on the occasion of the first innings of the All-Muggleton Club, "Mr. Dumkins and Mr. Podder, two of the most renowned members of that most distinguished club, walked, bat in hand, to their respective wickets. Mr.

Luffey, the highest ornament of Dingley Dell, was pitched to bowl against the redoubtable Dumkins, and Mr. Struggles was selected to do the same kind office for the hitherto unconquered Podder."

Everybody remembers how the game proceeded under circumstances of the greatest excitement, in which batters, bowlers, scouts, and umpires, all did their best under the encouraging shouts of the members:—"Run—run—another. —Now, then, throw her up—up with her—stop there—another —no—yes—no—throw her up! throw her up!" Mr. Jingle himself being as usual very profuse in his remarks, as—"'Ah, ah!—stupid'—'Now, butter-fingers'—'Muff'—'Humbug'—and so forth." "In short, when Dumkins was caught out, and Podder stumped out, All-Muggleton had notched some fifty-four, while the score of the Dingley Dellers was as blank as their faces." So "Dingley Dell gave in, and allowed the superior prowess of All-Muggleton," Mr. Jingle again expressing his views of the winners:—"'Capital game—well played —some strokes admirable,' as both sides crowded into the tent at the conclusion of the game."

Yes! We are convinced that Muggleton and Town Malling (except for the mayor and corporation) are one. At any rate we feel quite safe in assuming that Town Malling was the type from which Muggleton was taken; and we confidently recommend all admirers of *Pickwick* to include that pleasant Kentish country-town in their pilgrimage.

Having exhausted, so far as our examination is concerned, the cricket-ground, by the kindness of our young friend who acts as guide, we see a little more of the town. It consists of a long wide street, with a few lateral approaches. The houses are well built, and the church, which is partly

Norman, and, like most of the village churches in Kent, is but a little way from the village, stands on an eminence from whence a good view may be obtained. We observe, as indicative of the fine air and mild climate of the place, many beautiful specimens of magnolia, and wistaria (in second flower) in front of the better class of houses. One of these is named "Boley House," and as we are told that Sir Joseph Hawley resided near, our memories immediately revert to the cognomen of a well-known character in *The Chimes*. Other names in the place are suggestive of Dickens's worthies, *e.g.* Rudge, Styles, Briggs, Saunders, Brooker, and John Harm*a*n. The last-mentioned is the second instance in which Dickens has varied a local name by the alteration of a single letter. There is also the not uncommon name of "Brown," who, it will be remembered, was the maker of the shoes of the spinster aunt when she eloped with the faithless Jingle; "in a po-chay from the 'Blue Lion' at Muggleton," as one of Mr. Wardle's men said; and the discovery of the said shoes led to the identification of the errant pair at the "White Hart" in the Borough. After Sam Weller had described nearly all the visitors staying in the hotel from an examination of their boots:—

"'Stop a bit,' replied Sam, suddenly recollecting himself. 'Yes; there's a pair of Vellingtons a good deal vorn, and a pair o' lady's shoes, in number five.' 'Country make.'

"'Any maker's name?'

"'Brown.'

"'Where of?'

"'Muggleton.'

"'It *is* them,' exclaimed Wardle. 'By heavens, we've found them.'"

What happened afterwards every reader of *Pickwick* very well knows.

Near Town Malling there is a curious monument erected to the memory of Beadsman, the horse, belonging to Sir Joseph Hawley, which won the Derby in 1859, and which was bred in the place. The monument (an exceedingly practical one) consists of a useful pump for the supply of water.

After some luncheon at the Boar Inn, we are sorry to terminate our visit to this pleasant place; but time flies, and trains, like tides, "wait for no man." So we hurry to the railway station, passing on our way a fine hop-garden, and take tickets by the London, Chatham, and Dover Railway for Maidstone. We have a few minutes to spare, and our notice is attracted to a curious group in the waiting-room. It consists of a rural policeman, and what afterwards turned out to be his prisoner, a slouching but good-humoured-looking labourer, with a "fur cap" like Rogue Riderhood. The officer leans against the mantelpiece, pleasantly chatting with his charge, who is seated on the bench, leisurely eating some bread and cheese with a large clasp-knife, in the intervals of which proceeding he recounts some experiences for the edification of the officer and bystanders. These are occasionally received with roars of laughter. One of his stories relates to a house-breaker who, being "caught in the act" by a policeman, and being asked what he was doing, coolly replied, "Attending to my business, of course!" (This must surely be taken "in a Pickwickian sense.") After finishing his bread and cheese, the charge eats an apple, and then regales himself with something from a large bottle. The unconcernedness of the man, whatever his offence may be (poaching perhaps), is in painful contrast to the careworn and anxious faces of his wife and little daughter (both decently dressed), the latter about seven years old, and

made too familiar with crime at such an age. After we arrive at Maidstone (only a few minutes' run by railway), it is a wretched sight to witness the leave-taking at the gaol. First the man shakes hands with his wife, all his forced humour having left him, and then affectionately kisses the little girl, draws a cuff over his eyes, and walks heavily into the gaol after the officer. We are glad to notice that he is not degraded as a wild beast by being handcuffed. It was an episode that Dickens himself perhaps would have witnessed with interest, and possibly stored up for future use. What particularly strikes us is the difference in the relations between these people and what would be the case under similar circumstances in a large town. There is not that feature of hardness, that familiarity with crime which breeds contempt, in the rural incident. Poor man! let us hope his punishment will soon be finished, and that he may return to his family, and not become an old offender; but for the present, as Mr. Bagnet says, "discipline must be maintained."

Maidstone, the county and assize town of Kent, appears to be a thriving and solid-looking place, as there are several paper-mills, saw-mills, stone quarries, and other indications of prosperity. There are but few historical associations connected with it, as Maidstone "has lived a quiet life." Sir Thomas Wyatt's rebellion, and the attack on the town by Fairfax in 1648, are among the principal incidents. Dickens frequently walked or drove over to this town from Gad's Hill. Many of the names which we notice over the shops in the principal street are very suggestive of, if not actually used for, some of the characters in his novels, *e.g.* Pell, Boozer, Hibling, Fowle, Stuffins, Bunyard, Edmed, Gregsbey, Dunmill, and Pobgee.

It has been said that Maidstone possesses a gaol; it also has large barracks, and, what is better still, a Museum, Free Library, and Public Gardens. Chillington Manor House,—a highly picturesque and well-preserved Elizabethan structure, formerly the residence of the Cobhams,—contains the Museum and Library. Standing in a quiet nook in the Brenchley Gardens, the lines of George Macdonald, quoted in the local *Guide Book*, well describe its beauties:—

> "Its windows were aërial and latticed,
> Lovely and wide and fair,
> And its chimneys like clustered pillars
> Stood up in the thin blue air."

The Museum—the new wing of which was built as a memorial of his brother, by Mr. Samuel Bentlif—is the property of the Corporation, and owes much of its contents to the liberality of Mr. Pretty, the first curator, and to the naturalist and traveller, Mr. J. L. Brenchley. It contains excellent fine art, archæological, ethnological, natural history, and geological collections. Among the last-named, in addition to other interesting local specimens, are some fossil remains of the mammoth (*Elephas primigenius*) from the drift at Aylesford, obtained by its present able curator, Mr. Edward Bartlett, to whom we are indebted for a most pleasant ramble through the various rooms. We notice an original "Dickens-item" in the shape of a very good carved head of the novelist, forming the right top panel of an oak fire-place, the opposite side being one of Tennyson, by a local carver named W. Hughes, who was formerly employed at Gad's Hill Place. No pilgrim in "Dickens-Land" should omit visiting Maidstone and its treasures in Chillington Manor House; nor of seeing the splendid view of the Medway from the churchyard, looking towards Tovil.

We are particularly anxious to verify Dickens's experience

of the walk from Maidstone to Rochester. In a letter to Forster, written soon after he came to reside at Gad's Hill Place, he says:—"I have discovered that the seven miles between Maidstone and Rochester is one of the most beautiful walks in England," and so indeed we find it to be. It is, however, a rather long seven miles; so, cheerfully leaving the

gloomy-looking gaol to our right and proceeding along the raised terrace by the side of the turn-pike road, we pass through the little village of Sandling, and soon after commence the ascent of the great chalk range of hills which form the eastern water-parting of the Medway. The most noticeable object before we reach "Upper Bell" is "Kit's Coty (or Coity)

House," about one and a half miles north-east from Aylesford, and not very far from the Bell Inn. According to Mr. Phillips Bevan, the peculiar name is derived from the Celtic "Ked," and "Coity" or "Coed" (Welsh), and means the Tomb in the Wood. Seymour considers the words a corruption of "Catigern's House." Below Kit's Coty House, Mr. Wright, the archæologist, found the remains of a Roman villa, with quantities of Samian ware, coins, and other articles.

There are many excavations in the chalk above Kit's Coty House, apparently for interments; and the whole district appears in remote ages to have been a huge cemetery. Tradition states that "the hero Catigern was buried here, after the battle fought at Aylesford between Hengist and Vortigern."

The Cromlech, which is now included in the provisions of the Ancient Monuments Protection Act, 1882, lies under the hillside, a few yards from the main road, and is fenced in with iron railings, and beautifully surrounded by woods, the yew,[4] said to have been one of the sacred trees of the Druids, being conspicuous here and there. That somewhat rare plant the juniper is also found in this neighbourhood. The "dolmens" which have been "set on end by a vanished people" are four in number, and consist of sandstone, three of them, measuring about eight feet each, forming the uprights, and the fourth, which is much larger, serving as the covering stone.

In a field which we visit, not very far from Kit's Coty House, is another group of stones, called the "countless stones." As we pass some boys are trying to solve the arithmetical

[4] Mr. Roach Smith reminded us that the yew was in times past planted for its wood to be used as bows.

problem, which cannot be readily accomplished, as the stones lie intermingled in a very strange and irregular manner, and are overgrown with brushwood. The belief that these stones cannot be counted is one constantly found connected with similar remains, *e.g.* Stonehenge, Avebury, etc. We heard a

KIT'S COTY HOUSE

local story of a baker, who once tried to effect the operation by placing a loaf on the top of each stone as a kind of check or tally; but a dog running away with one of his loaves, upset his calculations.

Both the "Coty House" and the "countless stones" consist of a silicious sandstone of the Eocene period, overlying the chalk, and are identical with the "Sarsens," or "Grey Wethers," which occur at the pre-historic town of Avebury, and at

Stonehenge; the smaller stones of the latter are, however, of igneous origin, and "are believed by Mr. Fergusson to have been votive offerings." These masses, of what Sir A. C. Ramsay calls "tough and intractable silicious stone," have been, he says, "left on the ground, after the removal by denudation of other and softer parts of the Eocene strata." We subsequently saw several of these "grey wethers" in the grounds of Cobham Hall, and we noticed small masses of the same stone *in situ* in Pear Tree Lane, near Gad's Hill Place.

Speaking of Kit's Coty House in his *Short History of the English People*, the late Mr. J. R. Green, in describing the English Conquest and referring to this neighbourhood, says:—"It was from a steep knoll on which the grey weather-beaten stones of this monument are reared that the view of their first battle-field would break on the English warriors; and a lane which still leads down from it through peaceful homesteads would guide them across the ford which has left its name in the little village of Aylesford. The Chronicle of the conquering people tells nothing of the rush that may have carried the ford, or of the fight that went struggling up through the village. It only tells that Horsa fell in the moment of victory, and the flint heap of Horsted, which has long preserved his name, and was held in after-time to mark his grave, is thus the earliest of those monuments of English valour of which Westminster is the last and noblest shrine. The victory of Aylesford did more than give East Kent to the English; it struck the keynote of the whole English conquest of Britain."

Dickens's visits to this locality in his early days may

have suggested the discovery of the stone with the inscription:—

+
B I L S T
U M
P S H I
S. M.
A R K

In later life he was fond of bringing his friends here "by a couple of postilions in the old red jackets of the old red royal Dover road" to enjoy a picnic. Describing a visit here with Longfellow he says:—"It was like a holiday ride in England fifty years ago."

Returning to the main road, we reach the high land of Blue Bell—"Upper Bell," as it is marked on the Ordnance Map. We are not quite on the highest range, but sufficiently high (about three hundred feet) to enable us to appreciate the splendid view that presents itself. In the valley below winds the Medway, broadening as it approaches Rochester.[5] The opposite heights consist of the western range of hills, the width of the valley from point to point being about ten miles. The "sky-line" of hills running from north to south cannot

[5] Professor Huxley, in his *Physiography*, has estimated that "at the present rate of wear and tear, denudation can have lowered the surface of the Thames Basin by hardly more than an inch since the Norman Conquest; and nearly a million years must elapse before the whole basin of the Thames will be worn down to the sea-level"; and Dr. A. Geikie, after a series of elaborate calculations, has postulated "as probably a fair average, a valley of 1000 feet deep may be excavated in 1,200,000 years." Taking these estimates as a basis, and allowing for an average height of three hundred feet, we roughly arrive at a period of about four hundred thousand years as the possible length of time which it has taken to form this beautiful valley. Professor Huxley may well say that "the geologist has thoughts of time and space to which the ordinary mind is a stranger."

From the Painting by Gegan

Kit's Coty House and 'Blue Bell'.

be less than sixty miles, extending to the famous Weald of Kent (weald, wald, or wolde, being literally "a wooded region, an open country"); all the intervening space of undulating slope and valley (river excepted) is filled up by hamlets, grass, root, and cornfields, hop-gardens, orchards and woodlands, the whole forming a picture of matchless beauty. No wonder Dickens was very fond of this delightful walk; it must be gone over to be appreciated.[6]

We tramp on through Boxley and Bridge Woods, down the hill, and pass Borstal Convict Prison and Fort Clarence, where there are guns which we were informed would carry a ball from this elevated ground right over the Thames into the county of Essex (a distance of seven miles); and so we get back again to Rochester.

[6] Mr. Kitton's illustration (from the painting by Gegan, a local artist, executed many years since) gives a good idea of the scenery of this beautiful district. It also reproduces the profile of a huge chalk cliff not now visible, but which existed about half a century ago, having a curious resemblance to the head of a lion, and forming at the time a conspicuous landmark to travellers.

CHAPTER XI.

BROADSTAIRS, MARGATE, AND CANTERBURY.

"We have a fine sea, wholesome for all people; profitable for the body, profitable for the mind."—*Our English Watering-Place.*

"All is going on as it was wont. The waves are hoarse with repetition of their mystery; the dust lies piled upon the shore; the sea-birds soar and hover; the winds and clouds go forth upon their trackless flight; the white arms beckon in the moonlight to the invisible country far away."—*Dombey and Son.*

"A moment, and I occupy my place in the Cathedral, where we all went together every Sunday morning, assembling first at school for that purpose. The earthy smell, the sunless air, the sensation of the world being shut out, the resounding of the organ through the black and white arched galleries and aisles, are wings that take me back and hold me hovering above those days in a half-sleeping and half-waking dream."—*David Copperfield.*

TAKING advantage of an excursion train (for tramps usually go on the cheap), we start early on Wednesday by the South-Eastern Railway from Chatham station for Broadstairs. As usual the weather favours us—it is a glorious day. Passing the stations of New Brompton, Rainham, Newington, and Sittingbourne, we soon get into open country, in the midst of hop gardens with their verdant aisles of the fragrant and tonic, tendril-like plants reaching in some instances perhaps to several hundred yards, and crowned with yellowish-green fruit-masses, which have a special charm for those unaccustomed to such scenery. The odd-looking "oast-houses,"[1] or drying-houses for the hops, are a noticeable feature of the neighbourhood, dotting it about here and there in pairs. They are mostly red-brick and cone-shaped, somewhat smaller than the familiar glass-houses of the Midland districts, and have a wooden cowl, painted white, at the apex for ventilation. We are rather too early for the hop-picking, and thus—but for a time only—miss an interesting sight. Dickens, in one of his letters to Forster, gives a dreary picture of this annual harvest:—

"Hop-picking is going on, and people sleep in the garden, and breathe in at the key-hole of the house door. I have been amazed, before this year, by the number of miserable lean wretches, hardly able to crawl, who come hop-picking. I find it is a superstition that the dust of the newly-picked hop, falling freshly into the throat, is a cure for consumption. So the poor creatures drag themselves along the roads, and sleep under wet hedges, and get cured soon and finally."

On the whole it is said to be a very indifferent season, but many plantations look promising. "If," as a grower remarks to us in the train, "we could have a little more of this fine weather! There has been too much rain, and too little sun this year." The apples also are a poor crop.

On a second visit to this pleasant neighbourhood, we see at Mear's Barr Farm, near Rainham, the whole process of hop-picking. True, it is not executed by that ragamuffinly crowd of strangers which Dickens had in his "mind's eye" when he wrote the words just quoted, and which usually

[1] According to a "Note" in the *Rochester and Chatham Journal*, the derivation of this curious term is from *uro* to burn (ustus).

Hop-picking in Kent

takes possession of most of the hop-growing districts of Kent during the picking season, but by an assemblage of native villagers, mostly women, girls, and boys,—neat, clean, and homely,—together with a few men who do the heavier part of the work. They are of all ages, from the tottering old grandmother, careworn wife, and buxom maiden, to the child in perambulator and baby in arms; and in the bright sun-light, amid the groves of festooning green columns, form a most orderly, varied, and picturesque gathering—a regular picnic in fact, judging from the cheerful look on most of the faces, and the merry laugh that is occasionally heard.

Mr. Fred Scott, tenant of the farm, of which Lord Hothfield is owner, is kind enough to go over the hop-garden with us, and describe all the details. When the hops are ripe (*i.e.* when the seeds are hard) and ready to be gathered, the pickers swarm on the ground, and a man divides the "bine" at the bottom of the "pole" by means of a bill-hook—not cutting it too close for fear of bleeding—leaving the root to sprout next year, and then draws out the pole, to which is attached the long, creeping bine, trailing over at top. If the pole sticks too fast in the ground, he eases it by means of a lever, or "hop-dog" (a long, stout wooden implement, having a toothed iron projection). "Mind my dog don't bite you, sir," says one of the men facetiously, as we step over this rough-looking tool. Women then carry the poles to, and lay them across, the "bin," a receptacle formed by four upright poles stuck in the ground and placed at an angle, supporting a framework from which depends the "bin-cloth," made of jute or hemp, holding from ten to twenty bushels of green hops, weighing about 1¼ lbs. per bushel when dry.

The picking then commences, and nimble fingers of all

sizes very soon strip the poles of the aromatically-smelling ripe hops, the poles being cast aside in heaps, to be afterwards cleared of the old bines and put into "stacks" of three hundred each, and used again next season.

The bins, which vary in number according to the size of the hop-garden, are placed in rows on the margin of the plantation, and usually have ten "hop-hills" (*i. e.* plants) on each side, and are moved inside the plantation as the poles are pulled up. Each bin belongs to a "sett" (*i. e.* family or companionship), consisting of from five to seven persons, and is taken charge of by a "binman." When the bin is full, a "measurer" (either the farmer himself or his deputy) takes account of the quantity of hops picked, and records it in a book to the credit of each working family. Then the green hops are carted off in "pokes" or sacks to the "oast-houses" to be dried. For this purpose, anthracite coal and charcoal are used in the kiln, a shovelful or two of sulphur being added to the fire when the hops are put on. The process of drying takes eleven hours, and afterwards the dried hops are packed in pockets which, when full, weigh about a hundredweight and a half each, the packing being effected by hydraulic pressure. They are then sent to market, the earliest arrivals fetching very high prices. As much as £50 per cwt. was paid in 1882, but the ordinary price averages from £4 to £8 per cwt.

Humulus Lupulus, the hop, belongs to the natural order *Urticaceæ*—a plant of rather wide distribution, but said to be absent in Scotland—and is a herbaceous, diœcious perennial, usually propagated by removal of the young shoots or by cuttings. According to Sowerby, the genus is derived from *humus*, the ground, as, unless supported or trained, the plant falls to the earth; and the common name "hop" from the Saxon *hoppan*, to climb. William King, in his *Art of Cookery*, says that "heresy and hops came in together"; while an old popular rhyme records that:—

> "Hops, carp, pickerel, and beer,
> Came into England all in one year."

Tusser in his *Hondreth Good Points of Husbandrie*, published in 1557, gives sundry directions for the cultivation of hops, and quaintly advocates their use as follows:—

> "The hop for his profit I thus do exalt,
> It strengtheneth drink, and it savoureth malt;
> And being well brewed, long kept it will last,
> And drawing abide—if you draw not too fast."

The hop has many varieties—thirty or more—among which may be mentioned prolifics, bramblings, goldings, common goldings, old goldings, Canterbury goldings, Meopham goldings, etc. When once planted they last for a hundred years, but some growers replace them every ten years or sooner.

The principal enemies of the hop are "mould" caused by the fungus *Sphærotheca Castagnei*, and several kinds of insects, especially the "green fly," *Aphis humuli*, but the high wind is most to be dreaded. It tears the hop-bines from the poles and throws the poles down, which in falling crush other bines, and thus bruise the hops and prevent their growth, besides obstructing the passage of air and sunlight, and causing the development of mould or mildew. The remedy for mould is dusting with sulphur, and for the green fly, syringing with tobacco or quassia water and soap, "Hop-wash," as it is called. Sometimes the lady-bird (*Coccinella septempunctata*) is present in sufficient numbers to consume the green fly. Very little can be done to obviate the effects of the wind, but a protective fence of the wild hop—called a "lee" or "loo"—is sometimes put up round very choice plantations.

The hop-poles, the preparation of which constitutes a distinct industry, are either of larch, Spanish chestnut, ash, willow, birch, or beech—larch or chestnut being preferred. Women clear the poles of the bark, and men sharpen them at one end, which is dipped in creosote before being used. The ground is cleared, and the poles are stuck in against the old plants in February or March.

We are informed that the hop-picking is much looked forward to by the villagers with pleasure as the means of supplying them with a little purse for clothing, etc., against winter-time. Each family or companionship earns from thirty shillings to two pounds per week during the season.

We proceed on our excursion, and pass Faversham, which stands in a rather picturesque bit of country some way up Faversham Creek, and is sheltered on the west by a ridge of wooded hills where the hop country ceases, as the railway bends north-easterly for Margate and Ramsgate. Whitstable, the next station passed, is famous for the most delicate oysters in the market, the fishery of which is regulated by an nnual court; and it is said that one grower alone sends fifty housand barrels a year to London from this district. We peculate whether these delicious molluscs were supplied at hat famous supper described in the thirty-ninth chapter of *he Old Curiosity Shop*, at which were present Kit, his other, the baby, little Jacob, and Barbara, after the night the play, when Kit told the waiter "to bring three dozen his largest-sized oysters, and to look sharp about it," and fulfilled his promise "to let little Jacob know what oysters meant." All along, as the railway winds from Whitstable to Margate, glimpses of the sea are visible, and vary our excursion pleasantly.

The next noteworthy place we pass is Reculver—the ancient Regulbium—which, according to Mr. Phillips Bevan, is "mentioned in the Itinerary of Antoninus as being garrisoned by the first cohort of Brabantois Belgians. After the Romans, it was occupied by the Saxon Ethelbert, who is said to have occupied it as a palace, and to have been buried there." "The two picturesque towers" (quoting Bevan again), "which form so conspicuous a land and sea mark, are called 'The Sisters,' and are in reality modern-built by the Trinity Board in place of two erected traditionally by an Abbess of Faversham, who was wrecked here with her sister on their way to Broadstairs." The sea is fast encroaching on the land here, notwithstanding the erection of a large sea-wall and piles.

Passing Margate, we reach Broadstairs, about thirty-seven miles from Chatham. Broadstairs, immortalized in *Our English Watering Place* (which paper, says Forster, "appeared while I was there, and great was the local excitement") is so inseparably associated with the earlier years of Charles Dickens's holiday-life, that it becomes most interesting to his admirers. Forster also says, "His later seaside holiday September 1837, was passed at Broadstairs, as were those of many subsequent years; and the little watering-place has been made memorable by his pleasant sketch of it." At the time of his first visit (1837) he was writing a portion of *Pickwick* (Part 18); in 1838 part of *Nicholas Nickleby;* and in 1839 part of *The Old Curiosity Shop.* He was also there in 1840, 1841, and 1842, when writing the *American Notes;* in

1845 and 1847, when writing *Dombey and Son;* in 1848 and 1850, when engaged on *David Copperfield;* and in 1851, when he was drafting the outlines of *Bleak House.* At the end of November of that year, when he had settled himself in his new London abode (Tavistock House), the book was begun, "and, as so generally happened with the more important incidents of his life, but always accidentally, begun on a Friday." After 1851, he returned not again to Broadstairs until 1859, when he paid his last visit to the place, and stayed a week there. The reason for his forsaking it was that it had become too noisy for him.

Broadstairs stands midway between the North Foreland and Ramsgate, and owes its name to the breadth of the sea-gate or "stair," which was originally defended by a gate or archway. An archway still survives on the road to the sea, and bears on it two inscriptions, (1) "Built by George Culenier about 1540"; (2) "Repaired by Sir John Henniker, Bart., 1795."

Broadstairs has good sands, precipitous chalk cliffs, and a very fine sea-view. The railway station is about a mile from the pier, and the town is approached by a well-kept road ("the main street of our watering-place. . . . You may know it by its being always stopped up with donkey chaises. Whenever you come here and see the harnessed donkeys eating clover out of barrows drawn completely across a narrow thoroughfare, you may be quite sure you are in our High Street"), with villas standing in their own gardens, most of which are brightened by summer flowers, notably the blue clematis (*Clematis Jackmani*) and by those charming seaside evergreens the *Escallonia* and the *Euonymus.* As we near the sea, the shops become more numerous, and, on the right-hand side, we have no difficulty in finding (although we heard it had been altered considerably) the house "No. 12, High Street," in which Dickens lived when he first visited Broadstairs. It is a plain little dwelling of single front, with a small parlour looking into the street, and has one story over—just the place that seems suited to the financial position of the novelist when he was commencing life. The house is now occupied by Mr. Bean, plumber and glazier, whose wife courteously shows us over it, and into the back yard and little garden, kindly giving us some pears from an old tree growing there, whereon we speculate as to whether Dickens himself had ever enjoyed the fruit from the same old tree. He appears to have lived in this house during his visits in 1837 and 1838. We ask the good lady if she is aware that Charles Dickens had formerly stayed in her house, and she replies in the negative, so we recommend her to get her husband to put up a tablet outside to the effect "Charles Dickens lived here, 1837," in imitation of the example of the Society of Arts in Furnival's Inn. There can be no doubt as to the identity of the house, for we take the precaution of ascertaining that the numbers have not been altered.

Our efforts to discover "Lawn House," where Dickens stayed on his visits from 1838 to 1848, are attended with some difficulty. First we are told it lay this way, then that, and then the other; a smart villa in a new road is pointed out to us as the object of our search, which we at once reject, as being too recent. But we are patient and persevering, feeling, with Mr. F.'s aunt, that "you can't make a head and brains out of a brass knob with nothing in it. You couldn't do it when your Uncle George was living; much less when he's dead!" Finally, we appeal to some one who looks like the "oldest inhabitant," and obtain something like a clue.

We are eventually directed to a veritable "Lawn House," which is the last house on the left as you approach "Fort House." It must have changed in respect of its surroundings since forty years have passed, and although there is nothing outside to indicate it as such, it seems fair to assume that this was the house described in the *Life* as "a small villa between the hill and the cornfield." The present occupier, who has no recollection of Dickens ever having been there, courteously allows us to see the hall and dining-room. The house is of course a great improvement upon "No 12, High Street."

A few steps from "Lawn House" lead us to the drive approaching "Fort House," pleasantly surrounded by a sloping lawn and shrubbery. John Forster, alluding to it in the *Life*, says:—

"The residence he most desired there, 'Fort House,' stood prominently at the top of a breezy hill on the road to Kingsgate, with a cornfield between it and the sea, and this in many subsequent years he always occupied."

Alas! the cornfield is no more, but "Fort House," or "Bleak House," as it is indifferently termed locally, remains intact. It is the most striking object of the place, standing on a cliff overlooking the sea, the harbour, and the town (made familiar by several photographs and engravings), with its curious verandahs and blinds, as seen in the vignette of J. C. Hotten's interesting book, *Charles Dickens: The Story of His Life.* An excellent photograph is published in the town, of which we are glad to secure a copy.

In the sixth chapter of *Bleak House* it is called "an old-fashioned house with three peaks in the roof in front, and a severe sweep leading to the porch." In the same chapter there is a minute account of the interior, too lengthy to be quoted;

but the description does not resemble Fort House. We are kindly permitted by the occupier to see the study in which the novelist worked, a privilege long to be remembered. This room is approached by "a little staircase of shallow steps" from the first floor, as described in *Bleak House;* but it will be borne in mind that the "Bleak House" of the novel is placed in Hertfordshire, near St. Albans, and *not* at Broadstairs,

although many persons still believe that Fort House is the original of the story. From the study we have a lovely view of the sea—the balmy breeze of a summer's day lightly fanning the waves, and just sufficing to move the delicate filamentous foliage of the tamarisk trees now standing in the place where the cornfield was. Even at the time we see it, changed as all its surroundings are, we can imagine the enjoyment which Dickens had in this healthy spot on the North Downs.

In that interesting "book for an idle hour" called *The Shuttlecock Papers*, Mr. J. Ashby-Sterry thus sympathetically alludes to "Bleak House":—"What a romantic place this is to write in, is it not? What a glorious study to work in! Indeed, both from situation and association, it would be impossible to find a better place for writing, were it not that one feels that so much superb work has been done on this very spot by so great an artist, that the mere craftsman is inclined to question whether it is worth while for him to write at all."

How well Dickens loved Broadstairs is told in his letter of the 1st September, 1843, addressed to Professor Felton, of Cambridge, U. S. A., as follows:—

"This is a little fishing-place; intensely quiet; built on a cliff, whereon—in the centre of a tiny semi-circular bay—our house stands; the sea rolling and dashing under the windows. Seven miles out are the Goodwin Sands (you've heard of the Goodwin Sands?), whence floating lights perpetually wink after dark, as if they were carrying on intrigues with the servants. Also there is a lighthouse called the North Foreland on a hill behind the village, a severe parsonic light, which reproves the young and giddy floaters, and stares grimly out upon the sea. Under the cliff are rare good sands, where all the children assemble every morning and throw up impossible fortifications, which the sea throws down again at high-water. Old gentlemen and ancient ladies flirt after their own manner in two reading-rooms, and on a great many scattered seats in the open air. Other old gentlemen look all day long through telescopes and never see anything.

"In a bay-window in a one-pair sits, from nine o'clock to one, a gentleman with rather long hair and no neckcloth, who writes and grins as if he thought he were very funny indeed.

His name is Boz. At one he disappears, and presently emerges from a bathing machine, and may be seen—a kind of salmon-coloured porpoise—splashing about in the ocean. After that he may be seen in another bay-window on the ground-floor, eating a strong lunch; after that, walking a dozen miles or so, or lying on his back in the sand reading a book. Nobody bothers him unless they know he is disposed to be talked to; and I am told he is very comfortable indeed. He's as brown as a berry, and they *do* say is a small fortune to the innkeeper who sells beer and cold punch. But this is mere rumour. Sometimes he goes up to London (eighty miles or so away), and then I'm told there is a sound in Lincoln's Inn Fields at night, as of men laughing, together with a clinking of knives and forks, and wine-glasses."

And further in a letter to another correspondent recently made public:—

"When you come to London, to assist at Miss Liston's sacrifice, don't forget to remind your uncle of our Broadstairs engagement to which I hold you bound. A good sea—fresh breezes—fine sands—and pleasant walks—with all manner of fishing-boats, lighthouses, piers, bathing-machines, are its only attractions, but it's one of the freshest little places in the world, consequently the proper place for you."

In the year 1851, in a letter dated 8th September, addressed to Mr. Henry Austin, he thus alludes to a wreck which took place at Broadstairs:—

"A great to-do here. A steamer lost on the Goodwins yesterday, and our men bringing in no end of dead cattle and sheep. I stood supper for them last night, to the unbounded gratification of Broadstairs. They came in from the wreck very wet and tired, and very much disconcerted by the nature of their prize—which, I suppose after all, will have to be recommitted to the sea, when the hides and tallow are secured. One lean-faced boatman murmured, when they were all ruminating over the bodies as they lay on the pier: 'Couldn't sassages be made on it?' but retired in confusion shortly afterwards, overwhelmed by the execrations of the bystanders."

Dickens got tired of Broadstairs in 1847, for reasons given in the following letter to Forster, though he did not forsake it till some years after:—

"Vagrant music is getting to that height here, and is so impossible to be escaped from, that I fear Broadstairs and I must part company in time to come. Unless it pours of rain, I cannot write half an hour without the most excruciating organs, fiddles, bells, or glee singers. There is a violin of the most torturing kind under the window now (time, ten in the morning), and an Italian box of music on the steps—both in full blast."

By good luck we fall in with an "old salt," formerly one of the boatmen of *Our English Watering Place* who are therein immortalized by much kindly mention, with whom we have a pleasant chat about Charles Dickens. Harry Ford (the name of our friend) well remembers the great novelist, when in early days he used to come on his annual excursions with his family to Broadstairs. "Bless your soul," he says, "I can see 'Old Charley,' as we used to call him among ourselves here, a-coming flying down from the cliff with a hop, step, and jump, with his hair all flying about. He used to sit sometimes on that rail" (pointing to the one surrounding the harbour), "with his legs lolling about, and sometimes on the seat that you're a-sitting on now" (adjoining the old Look-out House opposite the Tartar Frigate Inn), "and he was very fond of talking to us fellows and hearing our tales—he was very good-natured, and nobody was liked better. And if you'll read" (continues our informant) "that story that he wrote and printed about *Our Watering Place*, *I* was the man who's mentioned there as mending a little ship for a boy. *I* held that child between my knees. And what's more, sir, *I* took 'Old Charley,' on the very last

time that he came over to Broadstairs (he wasn't living here at the time), round the foreland to Margate, with a party of four friends. I took 'em in my boat, the *Irene*," pointing to a clinker-built strong boat lying in the harbour, capable of holding twenty people. "The wind was easterly —the weather was rather rough, and it took me three or four hours to get round. There was a good deal of chaffing going on, I can tell you."

Mrs. Long, of Zion Place, Broadstairs, the wife of an old coastguardman, who was stationed at the Preventive Station when Dickens lodged at Fort House, also remembered the novelist. The coastguard men are also immortalized in *Our English Watering Place*, as " a steady, trusty, well-conditioned, well-conducted set of men, with no misgiving about looking you full in the face, and with a quiet, thorough-going way of passing along to their duty at night, carrying huge sou'-wester clothing in reserve, that is fraught with all good pre-possession. They are handy fellows—neat about their houses, industrious at gardening, would get on with their wives, one thinks, in a desert island—and people it too soon."

Mrs. Long says "Mr. Dickens was a very nice sort of gentleman, but he didn't like a noise." The windows of Fort House, she reminds us, overlooked the coastguard station, and whenever the children playing about made more noise than usual, he used to tell her husband gently " to take the children away," or " to keep the people quiet." This little story fully confirms Dickens's often-expressed feeling of dislike, which subsequently grew intolerable, to Broadstairs as a watering-place.

After taking a turn or two on the lively Promenade,—made bright by the rich masses of flesh-coloured flowers of the valerian which fringe its margin,—to enjoy the sunshine and air, and watch the holiday folks, we bid adieu to Broadstairs, and proceed to Margate.

Of Margate there is not much to say. We reach it by an early afternoon train of the London, Chatham, and Dover Railway, to get the quickest service by the South-Eastern Railway on to Canterbury. Our stay at Margate is consequently very limited.

To some minds this popular Cockney watering-place has great attractions; its broad sands, its beautiful air, and its boisterous amusements, negro-melodies, merry-go-rounds, and the like; but it was a place seldom visited by Dickens, although he was so often near it. Only twice in the *Life* is it recorded that he came here; once being in 1844, when he wrote to Forster respecting the theatre as follows:—

"'*Nota Bene.*—The Margate Theatre is open every evening, and the four Patagonians (see Goldsmith's *Essays*) are performing thrice a week at Ranelagh.' A visit from me"—Forster goes on to say—"was at this time due, to which these were held out as inducements; and there followed what it was supposed I could not resist, a transformation into the broadest farce of a deep tragedy by a dear friend of ours. 'Now you really must come. Seeing only is believing, very often isn't that, and even Being the thing falls a long way short of believing it. Mrs. Nickleby herself once asked me, as you know, if I really believed there ever was such a woman; but there will be no more belief, either in me or my descriptions, after what I have to tell of our excellent friend's tragedy, if you don't come and have it played again for yourself, 'by particular desire.' 'We saw it last night, and oh! if you had but been with us! Young Betty, doing what the mind of man without my help never *can* conceive, with his legs like padded boot-trees wrapped up in faded yellow drawers, was the hero. The comic man of the company, enveloped in a white sheet, with his head tied with red tape like a brief, and greeted with yells of laughter whenever he appeared, was the venerable priest. A poor toothless old idiot, at whom the very gallery roared with contempt when he was called a tyrant, was the remorseless and aged Creon. And Ismene, being arrayed in spangled muslin trousers very loose in the legs and very tight in the ankles, such as Fatima would wear in *Blue Beard*, was at her appearance immediately called upon for a song! After this can you longer—?'"

He speaks in a letter to Forster, dated September, 1847, of "improvements in the Margate Theatre since his memorable first visit." It had been managed by a son of the great

comedian Dowton, and the piece which Dickens then saw was *As You Like It*, "really very well done, and a most excellent house." It was Mr. Dowton's benefit, and "he made a sensible and modest kind of speech," which impressed Dickens, who thus concludes his letter:—"He really seems a most respectable man, and he has cleaned out this dusthole of a theatre into something like decency."

There is also the following significant mention of Margate in chapter nineteen of *Bleak House*:—

"It is the hottest long vacation known for many years. All the young clerks are madly in love, and according to their various degrees, pant for bliss with the beloved object at Margate, Ramsgate, or Gravesend."

If Broadstairs was noisy, Margate must have been intensely so. We leave the crowded holiday-making place without much feeling of regret, and passing Ramsgate—of which there is but one mention in the *Life*—on our way, reach Canterbury in the afternoon.

We are delighted with this exquisitely beautiful old city, our only regret being that our time is very limited, and our means of ascertaining places situated in "Dickens-Land" more so.

Taking up our temporary quarters at the "Sir John Falstaff" Hotel, in remembrance of its namesake at Gad's Hill, after the refreshment of a meal, we commence our tramp through Canterbury, where David Copperfield passed some of his happiest days. Of the Falstaff here there is an excellent picture in Mr. Rimmer's *About England with Dickens*; a very quaint old inn with double front, and bay-windows top and bottom, possibly of the sixteenth century, and with a long swinging sign extending over the pavement, on which is painted a life-like presentment of the portly knight, the pretty ornamental ironwork supporting it reminding one of Washington Irving's description in *Bracebridge Hall*, "fancifully wrought at top into flourishes and flowers."

A few steps further on is the West Gate, "standing between two lofty and spacious round towers erected in the river," built by Archbishop Sudbury, who was barbarously murdered by Wat Tyler in the reign of Richard II., which is the sole remaining one of six gates formerly constituting the approaches to the city. From this gate, looking eastward, with the river Stour on either side, banked by neatly-trimmed private gardens, a beautiful view of the city is obtained. The High Street, crowded with gables of the sixteenth century and later timbered houses, slightly bends and rises as well, until the perspective seems to lose itself in a distant grove

of trees, locally called the "Dane John," a corruption of "Donjon." This view, especially when seen on a summer afternoon, is most picturesque. The present appearance of the quiet street is decidedly unlike that which it presented on that busy market-day when Miss Betsey Trotwood drove her nephew along it, for David says, "My aunt had a good opportunity of insinuating the grey pony among carts, baskets, vegetables, and hucksters' goods. The hair-breadth turns and twists we made drew down upon us a variety of speeches from the people standing about, which were not always complimentary; but my aunt drove on with perfect indifference."

, We notice in the windows and in many of the shops an abundance of brightly-coloured cut-flowers, a notable feature of the county of Kent; but we have little time to spare, and hasten on to the Cathedral precincts.

"What a magnificent edifice!" is our first thought on beholding the Cathedral, a noble pile so well befitting the Metropolitan See of England, from which the Christianity of the Kingdom first flowed. Dating from Ethelbert, at the close of the sixth century, three structures have successively occupied the site, culminating in the present one, which, according to Mr. Phillips Bevan, was erected at different times between 1070 and 1500; and he goes on to say:—"No wonder that it exhibits so many styles and peculiarities of detail, although the two most prominent architectural eras are those of 'Transition-Norman' and 'Perpendicular.'"

The appropriate stone figures in niches of distinguished Royal and Ecclesiastical personages associated with the Cathedral (which at the suggestion of Dean Alford in 1863 replaced those of the murderers of the martyr, Thomas à Becket), from King Ethelbert to Queen Victoria, and from Archbishop Lanfranc to Archbishop Longley; the lofty groined arches and stately towers, the beautiful carved screen, the noble monuments, the splendid choir (a hundred and eighty feet in length) approached by many steps, the rich stained-glass windows, all attract our admiring attention, and confirm our impression that a modern pilgrimage to Canterbury is a thing to be highly appreciated; and on no account would we have missed this part of our excursion. The murder of

Bell Harry Tower: Canterbury Cathedral:

Thomas à Becket (1170) took place between the nave and the choir in a transept or cross aisle called "The Martyrdom."

There is an interesting Sidney Cooper Gallery of Art, and also a Museum in the city, the latter containing some rare old Roman Mosaic pavement discovered in Burgate Street at a depth of ten feet.

But our object is to identify spots made memorable in *David Copperfield*, and we walk round the spacious Cathedral Close and "make an effort" (as Mrs. Chick said) in trying to find the simple-minded and good Dr. Strong's House. It is described as "a grave building in a courtyard, with a learned air about it that seemed very well suited to the stray rooks and jackdaws who came down from the Cathedral towers, and walked with a clerkly bearing on the grass-plat."

Alas! it is not here, although there are many such houses that correspond with it in some particulars. So we try several of the "dear old tranquil streets," but fail to discover the identical building.

The next object of our search is Mr. Wickfield's residence, "a very old house bulging out over the road; a house with low latticed windows, bulging out still further, and beams with carved heads on the ends, bulging out too." How strongly the description in many parts tallies with the houses in Rochester opposite "Eastgate House"; but here again we are baffled, as other modern pilgrims have been before, and we cannot associate any particular building with either of the two houses. The house in Burgate Street now occupied as offices by Messrs. Plummer and Fielding, Diocesan Registrars, who obligingly permit an examination of it, is suggested to us as being Mr. Wickfield's house, but, after

Scene of the Martyrdom
Canterbury Cathedral

an inspection, on several grounds we are obliged to reject this suggestion.

There was many a "low old-fashioned room, walked straight into from the street," which would have served for the "umble" dwelling of Uriah Heep and his mother, but none can be pointed out with absolute certainty as being the veritable one. By the kindness of Dr. Sheppard

"Bits" of Old Canterbury.

and Mr. T. B. Rosseter, F.R.M.S., we are, however, enabled

to identify two houses in Canterbury alluded to in *David Copperfield.* The "County Inn," where Mr. Dick slept on his visits to David "every alternate Wednesday," was no doubt The Royal Fountain Hotel in St. Margaret's Street (formerly the Watling Street), which is still recognized as such. A passage in the seventeenth chapter thus refers to these visits:—

"Mr. Dick was very partial to ginger-bread. To render his visits the more agreeable, my aunt had instructed me to open a credit for him at a cake-shop, which was hampered with the stipulation that he should not be served with more than one shilling's-worth in the course of any one day. This, and the reference of all his little bills at the County Inn, where he slept, to my aunt before they were paid, induced me to think that Mr. Dick was only allowed to rattle his money, and not to spend it."

The "little Inn" (as recorded in the same chapter) where Mr. Micawber "put up" on his first visit to Canterbury, and where he "occupied a little room in it partitioned off from the commercial, and strongly flavoured with tobacco smoke," is doubtless the "Sun Inn" in Sun Street, which is at the opposite corner of the square where the ancient "Chequers" in Mercery Lane—the Pilgrim's Inn of Chaucer—stood. It was a place of resort from afar, and was altered in the seventeenth century. Dr. Sheppard calls attention to the interesting fact that the omnibus from Herne Bay stopped at the Sun; and probably, in his visits to Broadstairs, Dickens would often run over for a day's trip to Canterbury.

On their first visit to the "little Inn," Mr. and Mrs. Micawber—notwithstanding their chronic impecuniosity—thus entertained David Copperfield:—

"We had a beautiful little dinner. Quite an elegant dish of fish; the kidney end of a loin of veal roasted; fried sausage-meat; a partridge and a pudding. There was wine, and there was strong ale; and after dinner Mrs. Micawber made us a bowl of hot punch with her own hands."

They spent a jolly evening, and ended with singing *Auld Lang Syne.*

The "little Inn" is again alluded to later in the story, where Mr. Micawber announces his full determination to abstain from everything until he has exposed the machinations of, and blown to pieces, "the—a—detestable serpent—HEEP;" and finally, where David Copperfield "assisted at an explosion," and Mr. Micawber is triumphant, and the "transcendent and immortal hypocrite and perjurer, HEEP," is forced to succumb.

Speaking of the "little Inn" for the last time, David says:—"I looked at the old house from the corner of the street. . . . The early sun was striking edgewise on its gables and lattice-windows, touching them with gold; and some beams of its old peace seemed to touch my heart."

Dr. Sheppard subsequently told us that, when he was beginning to turn his attention to the deciphering and utilizing of ancient MSS., he was much impressed, when perusing some articles in *Household Words*, or some other papers written by Dickens, relating to the neglected state of public records, more particularly at Canterbury; and when many years after the very records of which he wrote came under his (Dr. Sheppard's) care, he was surprised to find the names of Snodgrass, Sam Weller, and others therein. The records to which Dr. Sheppard referred were those in charge of the Archbishop's Registrar at Canterbury.

If time permits it would be pleasant to go on to Dover,[2] to see "Miss Betsey Trotwood's house," but this is impossible; and indeed, all that can be said about a tramp in search of "that very neat little cottage with cheerful bow windows in front of it, a small square gravelled court

The "Little Inn", Canterbury

or garden full of flowers carefully tended, and smelling deliciously," has been well said by Mr. Ashby-Sterry in his delightful little volume, *Cucumber Chronicles.*

[2] One of the "Five Cinque Ports, and two Ancient Towns" often referred to, but not always remembered—Hastings, Sandwich, Dover, New Romney, Hythe, Winchelsea and Rye.

After much perseverance, and in spite of almost as many dif-ficulties as beset poor little David Copperfield himself in his search for his aunt (who, as the Dover boatmen told him, "lived in the South Foreland Light, and had singed her whiskers by doing so"—"that she was made fast to the great buoy outside the harbour, and could only be visited at half-tide"—"that she was locked up in Maidstone Jail for child-stealing"—and that "she was seen to mount a broom in the last high wind and make direct for Calais"), Mr. Ashby-Sterry succeeded although his greatest embarrassment arose from that irre-pressible nuisance, "Buggins the Builder," who cannot be controlled even in the neighbourhood of Dover, so "hugely does he delight to mar those spots that have been hallowed by antiquity, seclusion, or the pen of the novelist. Hence the abode of Betsey Trotwood is not so pleasant as it must have been formerly, for other houses have clustered about the back and the front." But Mr. Ashby-Sterry quite satisfied himsel as to the identity on Dover Heights of the very neat little cottage, and assures us that "the house, however, still stands high, the fresh breezes from over the sea and across the Down smite it. It still has a view of the sea, though perhaps not so uninterrupted as it was in the days of David Copperfield." He further states that it is, perhaps, not quite so neat as i was in Miss Betsey Trotwood's time, though there are no donkeys about. Here are the bow windows, with the room above, where Mr. Dick alarmed poor David by nodding and laughing at him on his first arrival. The window on the right must have belonged to the neat room "with the drugget covered carpet," and the old-fashioned furniture brightly polished, where might be found "the cat, the kettle-holder the two canaries, the old china, the punch-bowl full of dried

tall press guarding all sorts of bottles and
·fully out of keeping with the rest." On the
lescription by an ardent lover of Dickens, we
ır minds to visit Dover at no distant date to
Trotwood's house for ourselves.

Miss Trotwood's domicile, we have been
, C. K. Worsfold, an old resident of Dover,
ntaining some interesting particulars, from
: the following :—

scription of the local habitation of Betsey
consistent with the surroundings. The hills
f the town belong to the War Department,
l as fortifications; on the eastern side is the
he western side barracks and forts. On the
there is a house somewhat answering to
ption, having a garden in front of it, and a
ass in front of the garden; and about forty
lived in this house a lady of rather masculine
ılways resented any intrusion of boys, and
s, on the grass in front of her house and
:lieve she was occasionally rather rough with
here the likeness to Betsey Trotwood ends.
ied lady living with her husband.

as a matter of conversation forty years ago
ust have found his original in the lady in
hink he was rather in the habit of selecting
thout reference to locality, and then adapting
irements.

; a frequent visitor to Dover, and he may
en a witness of some encounter between this
ys, and on that occasion donkeys may have

been present.[3] I do not know of any relative of the lady answering to Miss Trotwood's worthy nephew."

"A moderate stroke," as Mr. Datchery said, "is all I am justified in scoring up"; and we reluctantly leave the "sunny street of Canterbury, dozing, as it were, in the hot light," and take our places in the train for Chatham, distant about twenty-seven miles.

The only new parts of interest which we go over, on our return journey by rail, are the green fields surrounding the ancient city, wherein are numbers of those beautiful and quiet-feeding cattle, which the eminent artist, Mr. T. Sidney Cooper, R.A. (who resides in the neighbourhood), loves to paint, and paints so well; and in due time we pass the chalk-topped hills called Harbledown, overlooking Canterbury, from whence the best view of the city is obtained, and safely reach our headquarters at Rochester.

[3] Mr. Charles Dickens kindly writes to me:—"The lady who objected to the donkeys lived at Broadstairs. I knew her when I was a boy."

CHAPTER XII.

COOLING, CLIFFE, AND HIGHAM.

'And now the range of marshes lay clear before us, with the sails of the ships on the river growing out of it; and we went into the Churchyard . . . and the light wind strewed it with beautiful shadows of clouds and trees."

*   *   *   *   *   *   *

"What might have been your opinion of the place?"

"A most beastly place. Mudbank, mist, swamp and work; work, swamp, mist, and mudbank."—*Great Expectations.*

*   *   *   *   *   *   *

'They were now in the open country; the houses were very few and scattered at long intervals, often miles apart. Occasionally they came upon a cluster of poor cottages, some with a chair or low board put across the open door, to keep the scrambling children from the road; others shut up close, while all the family were working in the fields. These were often the commencement of a little village; and after an interval came a wheelwright's shed, or perhaps a blacksmith's forge; then a thriving farm, with sleepy cows lying about the yard, and horses peering over the low wall, and scampering away when harnessed horses passed upon the road, as though in triumph at their freedom."—*The Old Curiosity Shop.*

ow for a long tramp in the country of the Marshes—the mous "Meshes" of *Great Expectations.* The air is sultry n this Thursday afternoon, and there is thunder in the istance. The storm, however, does not pass over Rochester, ut further on we find traces of it where the roadways have een washed up. Afterwards the air becomes deliciously ool, and that hum of all Nature which succeeds the quiet receding the storm is distinctly perceptible. Crossing ochester Bridge, keeping to the right along Strood and

Frindsbury—the churchyard of which affords a splendid view of Rochester, Chatham, and the Medway—passing up Four Elms Hill and through the little village of Wainscot, nothing of interest calls for notice until we have travelled some miles from Strood. After crossing a tramway belonging to Government, and utilized by the Royal Engineers as a means of communication between the powder-magazine and Chatham Barracks, we observe that vegetation, which is so rich in other parts of Kent, here appears to be dwarfed and stunted. A hop-garden presents a very miserable contrast, in its struggle for existence, to others we have seen in the more central parts of the county, and even some of these were far from being luxuriant, owing to such a peculiarly wet and cold season. The hedges in places are diversified with the small gold and violet star-like flowers and the green and scarlet berries of the climbing woody nightshade, or bitter-sweet (*Solanum Dulcamara*), often mistaken for the deadly nightshade (*Atropa Belladonna*—a fine bushy herbaceous perennial, with large ovate-shaped leaves, and lurid, purple bell-shaped flowers), quite a different plant, and happily somewhat rare in England. The delicate light-blue flowers of the chicory are very abundant here.

A tramp of upwards of six miles from Rochester, by way of Hoo,[1] brings us to Lodge Hill, overlooking Perry Hill, which affords a magnificent view of the mouth of the Thames beyond the low-lying Marshes, and of Canvey Island, off the coast of Essex, on the opposite side. By the kindness of a farmer's wife we are allowed to take a short cut through

[1] Speaking of Hoo, Lambarde says (1570)—"Hoh in the old English signifieth sorrow or sickness, wherewith the Inhabitants of that unwholesome Hundred be very much exercised [!]."

the farm-garden and grounds, which leads direct to Cooling (or Cowling) Church, a cheerless, grey-stone structure, the tower standing out as a beacon long before we reach it.

Those unacquainted with this part of Kent may be interested in knowing that the Marshes, which stretch out over a considerable distance on either side of the Thames, on both the Kent and the Essex coasts, consist entirely of alluvial soil reclaimed at some time from the river. They are intersected by ditches and water-courses, and covered with rank vegetation, chiefly of grass, rushes, and flags, where not cultivated. Higher up the land is rich, and large tracts of it are planted with vegetables as market gardens. Sea-gulls, plovers, and herons are numerous; their call-notes in the still evening sounding shrill and uncanny over the long stretches of flat lands.

Dear old Michael Drayton, the Warwickshire poet, who touched upon almost everything, has not omitted to describe the Marshes in a somewhat similar locality, for in the *Polyolbion* (Song XVIII.) he gracefully compares them to a female enamoured of the beauties of the River Rother, thus:—

"Appearing to the flood, most bravely like a Queen,
Clad all from head to foot, in gaudy Summer's green,
Her mantle richly wrought with sundry flow'rs and weeds;
Her moistful temples bound with wreaths of quiv'ring reeds;
And on her loins a frock, with many a swelling plait,
Emboss'd with well-spread horse, large sheep, and full-fed neat;
With villages amongst, oft powthered here and there;
And (that the same more like to landscape should appear)
With lakes and lesser fords, to mitigate the heat
In summer, when the fly doth prick the gadding neat."

Readers of *Great Expectations* will remember that the

scene in the first chapter between Pip and the convict, Magwitch, is laid in Cooling churchyard, and on reaching this spot we are instantly reminded of what doubtless gave origin to the idea of the five dead little brothers of poor Philip Pirrip, for there, on the left of the principal pathway, are indeed, not five stone lozenges, but *ten* in one row and three more at the back of them, such peculiarly-shaped and curiously-arranged little monuments as we never before beheld. They consist of a grey stone (Kentish-rag, probably, but lichen-encrusted by time) of cylindrical shape, widening at the shoulders, coffin-like, and about a yard in length, the diameter being about eight inches, including the portion buried in the earth. Four little foot-stones are placed in front, and separating the ten little memorials from the three at the back is a large head-stone, bearing the name—"Comport of Cowling Court, 1771." Cooling Church, which has the date 1615 on one of the bells, has an example of a Hagioscope, a curious, small, square, angular, tunnel-like opening through the wall, which divides the nave from the chancel. It is said to have been the place through which those members of the church, who were unworthy or unable to receive the sacred elements, might get a look at their more acceptable companions during the administration of the sacrament. The Rev. W. H. A. Leaver, the Rector, who kindly shows us over his church, in reply to our question as to whether he could give any information about Charles Dickens, said that he was a new-comer in the district, and that all he remembers is, that when his sister was a little baby in arms, her mother happened once to be travelling in the same train with the great novelist, who, with his usual kindness, gave the child an orange, which she acknowledged very ungratefully by scratching his face!

The following is a picture of the neighbourhood, given in the opening sentences of the story :—

"Ours was the marsh country, down by the river, within, as the river wound, twenty miles of the sea. My first most vivid and broad impression of the identity of things, seems to me to have been gained on a memorable raw afternoon towards evening. At such a time, I found out for certain, that this bleak place overgrown with nettles was

the churchyard; and that Philip Pirrip, late of this parish, and also Georgiana, wife of above, were dead and buried; and that Alexander, Bartholomew, Abraham, Tobias, and Roger, infant children of the aforesaid, were also dead and buried; and that the dark flat wilderness beyond the churchyard, intersected with dykes, and mounds, and gates, with scattered cattle feeding on it, was the marshes; and that the low leaden line beyond was the river; and that the distant savage lair, from which the wind was rushing, was the sea; and that the small bundle of shivers growing afraid of it all, and beginning to cry, was Pip."

Here follows the appearance of the awful convict, and the

terrible threats by which he induces Pip to bring him "that file and them wittles" on the morrow; to enforce obedience the convict tilts Pip two or three times, "and then" [says Pip] "he gave me a most tremendous dip and roll, so that the church jumped over its own weathercock." Then he held him by the arms in an upright position on the top of the stone, finally threatening him "with having his heart and liver torn out," in case of non-compliance.

All the characters described in *Great Expectations*, and all the scenes wherein they played their parts—Pip, with and without his "great expectations"; his sister Mrs. Joe Gargery, "on the rampage with Tickler;" Joe Gargery, "ever the best of friends, dear Pip;" Mr. and Mrs. Hubble, the former fond of "a bit of savoury pork pie as would lay atop of anything you could mention and do no harm;" the stage-struck Wopsle, *alias* "Mr. Waldengarver"; "the servile Pumblechook;" the two convicts, "Pip's convict," Magwitch, with "the great iron on his leg," and the "other convict," Compeyson, also ironed; "slouching old" Orlick; Biddy, simple-hearted and loving; "the Serjeant" and "party of soldiers"; Mr. Jaggers, "the Old Bailey lawyer"; Estella, Miss Havisham, Herbert Pocket, and Bentley Drummle at "the market town"; Joe's Forge (now converted into a dwelling-house); "The Three Jolly Bargemen" (obviously taken from "The Three Horse-shoes," the present village inn); the "old Battery," "the little sluice-house by the lime-kiln;"—all centre round Cooling churchyard, and appear before us as though traced on a map.

Forster says in the *Life*:—"It is strange as I transcribe the words, with what wonderful vividness they bring back the very spot on which we stood when he said he meant to make it the

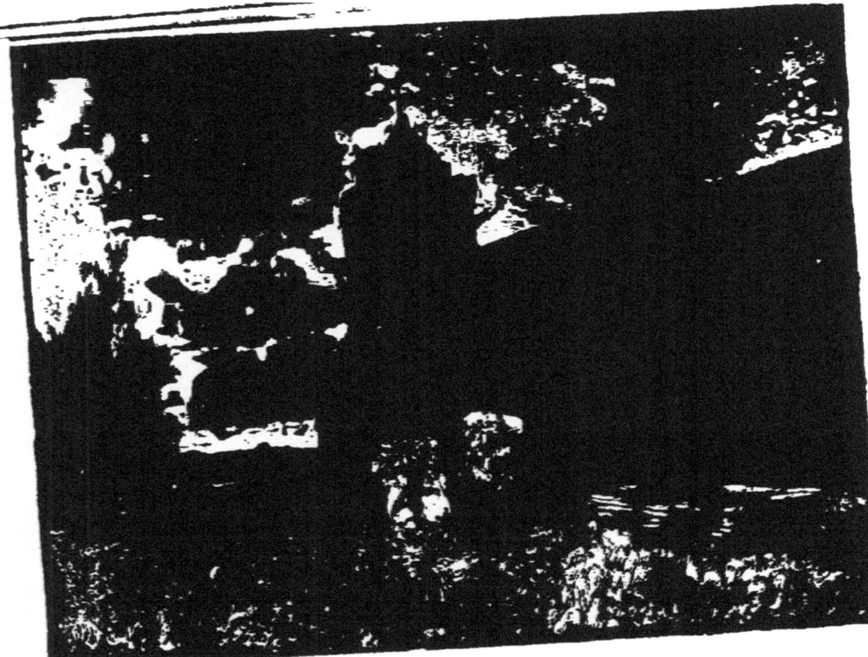

Cooling Church.

scene of the opening of this story—Cooling Castle ruins and the desolate Church, lying out among the marshes seven miles from Gad's Hill!"

Beyond where the river runs to the sea, we conjure up the chase and recapture of Pip's convict, while poor Pip himself assisted by his friend Herbert Pocket, is straining every nerve to get him away. As illustrative of the wonderfully careful way in which Dickens did all his work, we also read in Forster's *Life*:—

"To make himself sure of the actual course of a boat in such circumstances, and what possible incidents the adventure might have, Dickens hired a steamer for the day from Blackwall to Southend. Eight or nine friends, and three or four members of his family, were on board, and he seemed to have no care, the whole of that summer day (22nd of May, 1861) except to enjoy their enjoyment and entertain them with his own in shape of a thousand whims and fancies; but his sleepless observation was at work all the time, and nothing had escaped his keen vision on either side of the river. The fifteenth chapter of the third volume is a masterpiece."

Speaking generally of this fascinating story, which possesses a thousand-fold greater interest to us now we visit the country there described (not formerly very accessible, but now readily approached by the railway from Gravesend to Sheerness, alighting at Cliffe, the nearest station to Cooling), Forster says:—

"It may be doubted if Dickens could better have established his right to the front rank among novelists claimed for him, than by the ease and mastery with which, in these two books of *Copperfield* and *Great Expectations*, he kept perfectly distinct the two stories of a boy's childhood, both told in the form of autobiography."

The marshes are also alluded to twice in *Bleak House*—first, in chapter one—"Fog on the Essex marshes, fog on the Kentish heights;" and secondly, in the twenty-sixth chapter, in the dialogue between Trooper George and his odd but kind-hearted attendant Phil Squod, the original of which, by the bye, was a Chatham character.

"'And so, Phil,' says George of the shooting gallery, after several urns in silence; 'you were dreaming of the country last night.'

"Phil, by the bye, said as much, in a tone of surprise, as he scrambled out of bed.

"'Yes, guv'ner.'

"'What was it like?'

"'I hardly know what it was like, guv'ner,' said Phil, considering.

"'How did you know it was the country?'

"'On accounts of the grass, I think. And the swans upon it,' says Phil, after further consideration.

"'What were the swans doing on the grass?'

"'They was a eating of it, I expect,' says Phil. . . .

"'The country,' says Mr. George, applying his knife and fork, why I suppose you never clapped your eyes on the country, Phil?'

"'I see the marshes once,' says Phil, contentedly eating his reakfast.

"'What marshes?'

"'*The* marshes, commander,' returns Phil.

"'Where are they?'

"'I don't know where they are,' says Phil, 'but I see 'em, guv'ner. hey was flat. And miste.'"

Forster says:—"About the whole of this Cooling church-ard, indeed, and the neighbouring castle ruins, there was a eird strangeness that made it one of his [Dickens's] attractive alks in the late year or winter, when from Higham he could et to it across country, over the stubble fields; and, for a orter summer walk, he was not less fond of going round the village of Shorne, and sitting on a hot afternoon in its pretty shady churchyard."

Altogether, the place has a dreary and lonesome appearance in the close of the summer evening, and we can picture with wonderful vividness the remarkable scenes described in *Great Expectations*, as the lurid purple reflection from the setting sun spreads over the Thames valley, and lights up the marshes; the tall pollards standing out like spectres contribute to the weirdness and beauty of the scene.

Dickens was not the only admirer of the Marshes. Turner also visited them, and painted some of his most famous pictures from observation there, namely "Stangate Creek," "Shrimping Sands," and "Off Sheerness."

A few paces from the church brings us to Cooling Castle built by Sir John de Cobham, the third Baron Cobham, in the reign of Richard II., whose arms appear on the gatehouse, together with a very curious motto in early English characters. We extract the following interesting account of the tower from the *Archæologia Cantiana* (vol. xi.):—

"On the south face of the eastern Outer Gate Tower, we see the well-known inscription, which takes the form of a Charter, with Lord Cobham's seal appended to it. This is formed of fourteen copper plates exquisitely enamelled. The writing is in black, while the ground is of white enamel; the seal and silk cords are of the proper colours. The whole work is an exquisite example of enamel, which after five hundred years' exposure to the weather remains nearly as good as when it was put up. The inscription states very clearly why Lord Cobham erected a castle here, viz. for the safety of the country. The French invasion had shewn the need, and the inscription was perhaps intended to disarm the suspicions and

Gateway
Cooling Castle

hostility of the serfs by reminding them of that need. It runs thus, in four lines, each enamelled upon three plates of copper:—

"'Knoweth that beth and schul be
That i am mad in help of the cuntre
In knowyng of whyche thyng
Thys is chartre and witnessyng.'"

"(Seal, 'gules', on a chevron 'or' three lions rampant 'sable'.)

"Inscriptions are rare on Gothic buildings, especially on castles. This at Coulyng is remarkable from being in English, at a time when Latin was employed in all charters; it contains that early form of the plural 'beth' instead of 'are.' The inscription measures thirty-two inches by fourteen, and the diameter of the seal is no less than seven and a quarter inches long."

After stopping a short time to admire the imposing entrance gate and the remains of the ancient moat, we wend our way for two or three miles, by lanes and "over the stubble-fields," to the straggling village of Cliffe,[2] the houses of which are very old and mostly weather-boarded. The approach to the church is by a rare example of a lich-gate, having a room over it for muniments, and the church itself (which is very large, and seems to be out of proportion to the size of the village) stands in a commanding position on a ridge of chalk, overlooking the marshes, from whence the views of the river

[2] Lambarde says, "The Town [of Cliffe at Hoo] is large, and hath hitherto a great Parish Church: and (as I have been told) many of the houses were casually burned (about the same time that the Emperor *Charles* came into this Realme to visite King *Henry* the eight), of which hurt it was never thorowly cured."

in the distance are very fine. It is supposed to be the place where the Saxon Church held its councils, and there is a local tradition of a ferry having once existed near here. Evidence of this seems to survive in the fact that all the roads both on the Kent and Essex shores appear to converge to this point.

The church has some interesting *miserere* stalls and brasses to the Faunce family (17th century). On the walls we find specimens of that somewhat rare fern, the scaly spleenwort (*Ceterach officinarum*).

Time does not permit us to go on to Gravesend, which like

this place was one of Dickens's favourite spots ("We come, you see" [says Mr. Peggotty, speaking of himself and Ham to David Copperfield, when they visited him at Salem House], "the wind and tide making in our favor, in one of our Yarmouth lugs to Gravesen'"), so we defer our visit to that popular resort until another occasion.

We notice in places where the harvest has been cleared (which, alas! owing to excess of wet and absence of sun, has not been an abundant one), preparations for cultivation next year, exhibiting that peculiar effect from ploughing which that gifted writer and born naturalist, the late Richard Jeffreys, described in his book *Wild Life in a Southern County*, with that love for common things which was so characteristic of him :—

"The ploughmen usually take special care with their work near public roads, so that the furrows end on to the base of the highway shall be mathematically straight. They often succeed so well that the furrows look as if traced with a ruler, and exhibit curious effects of vanishing perspective. Along the furrow, just as it is turned, there runs a shimmering light as the eye traces it up. The ploughshare, heavy and drawn with great force, smooths the earth as it cleaves it, giving it for a time a 'face,' as it were, the moisture on which reflects the light. If you watch the farmers driving to market, you will see that they glance up the furrows to note the workmanship and look for game; you may tell from a distance if they espy a hare, by the check of the rein and the extended hand pointing."

Our destination is now Higham—"Higham by Rochester, Kent,"—Dickens's nearest village, in which, from his first coming to Gad's Hill, he took the deepest interest, and after a further long tramp of nearly four miles steadily maintained, we reach Lower Higham towards dusk; and in a lane we ask an old labourer (who looks as though he would be all the better for "Three Acres and a Cow") if we are on the right road to Higham Station. Curtly but civilly the man answers, "Keep straight on," when an incident occurs which brightens up matters considerably. The questioner says to the labourer, "Do you remember the late Charles Dickens?" (We always spoke, when in the district, of "the *late* Charles Dickens," to distinguish him from his eldest son, who lived at Gad's Hill for some years after his father's death. Frequently the great novelist was spoken of by residents as "old Mr. Dickens!")

"Do I remember Muster Dickens?" responds the venerable rustic, and his eyes sparkle, and his face beams with such animation that he becomes a different being. "Of course I do; he used to have games—running, jumping, and such-like—for us working people, and I've often won a prize. He used to come among us and give us refreshments, and make himself very pleasant."

"How long have you lived in this parish?" says the questioner.

"Sixty-seven year," is the answer.

Time prevents further inquiries, so we bid our friend "good-evening."

In referring to the sports at Gad's Hill, Mr. Langton has recorded how a friend sent him a broadside of a portion of one day's amusements, which from its amateurish appearance was probably printed by Dickens's sons at the private printing-press before alluded to. The occasion was the 26th December, 1866, and the Christmas sports were held in a field at the back of Gad's Hill Place. Mr. Trood, a former landlord of the "Sir John Falstaff" (whose name has been previously mentioned), had, by permission of Charles Dickens, a booth erected for the refreshment of persons contesting. The attendance was between two and three thousand, and there was not a single case of misconduct or damage. Mr. A. H. Layard, M.P. (afterwards Sir Austin Layard), was present, and took great interest in the proceedings, Dickens having appointed him "chief commissioner of the domestic police." Sir Austin Layard said of the sports, "Dickens seemed to have bound every creature present upon what honour the creature had to keep order. What was the special means used, or the art employed, it might have been difficult to say, but that was the result." We made every effort to obtain one of the bills of these sports, but without success, and therefore take the liberty of quoting from Mr. Langton's copy:—

Christmas Sports.

The All-Comers' Race.
Distance—Once round the field.
First Prize 10*s.*; Second, 5*s.*; Third, 2*s.* 6*d.*
Entries to be made in MR. TROOD'S tent before 12 o'clock.
To start at 2.45.
Starter—M. STONE, ESQ.
Judge and Referee—C. DICKENS, ESQ.
Clerk of the Course—C. DICKENS, JUNR., ESQ.
Stewards and Keepers of the Course—MESSRS. A. H. LAYARD, M.P., H. CHORLEY, J. HULKES, and H. DICKENS.

In a letter written to Mr. Forster next day, Dickens said, "The road between this and Chatham was like a fair all day, and surely it is a fine thing to get such perfect behaviour out of a reckless sea-port town."

We presently meet with another representative of the class of village labourer at Upper Higham, a cheery old man, although, as is sadly too often the case in his class, he was suffering from "the Rheumatiz." "Those are nice chrysanthemums in your garden," we observe. "Yes, they are, sir," he replies; "but if they had been better attended to when they was young, they'd have been nicer." "Well, I suppose both of us would," is the rejoinder. We are in touch on the instant. Our new acquaintance laughs, and so a question or two is put to him, and the following is the substance of his answers, rendered *à la* Jingle but very feelingly:—

"Mr. Dickens was a nice sort of man—very much liked—missed a great deal when he died—poor people and the like felt the miss of him. He was a man as shifted a good deal of money in the place. You see, he had a lot of friends—kept a good many horses,—and then there was the men to attend to 'em, and the corn-chandler, the blacksmith, the wheelwright, and others to be paid—the poor—and such-like—felt the miss of him when he died."

"How long have you lived here?"

"Well, I come in '45, eleven years before Mr. Dickens."

"And I suppose you are over sixty."

"Well, sir, I shall never see seventy again."

Wishing our friend "good-night," we continue our tramp. On another occasion we met, in the same place, a third specimen of village labourer, "a mender of roads," who knew Charles Dickens, and so we walked and chatted pleasantly with him for some distance. Said our informant, "You see, Mr. Dickens was a very liberal man; he held his head high up when he walked, and went at great strides." The "mender of roads" was some years ago a candidate for a vacant place as under-gardener at Gad's Hill, but the situation was filled up just an hour before he applied for it. He said Mr. Dickens gave him half-a-crown, and afterwards always recognized him when he met him with a pleasant nod, or cheerfully "passed the time of day." We heard in many places that Dickens was "always kindly" in this way to his own domestics, and to the villagers in a like station of life to our intelligent friend "the mender of roads." A fourth villager, a groom, who had been in his present situation for twenty years, said:—"Both the old gentleman and young Mr. Charles were very much liked in Higham. There wasn't a single person in the place, I believe, but what had a good word for them."

It may be interesting to mention that Higham—the old name of which was Lillechurch—is an extensive parish divided into several hamlets. In a useful little book published in 1882, called *A Handbook of Higham*, the Rev. C. H. Fielding, M.A., the author, says:—"There are few parishes more interesting than Higham, as it provides food for the antiquarian and the student of Nature; while its position near the 'Medway smooth, and the Royal-masted Thame,' affords to the artist many an opportunity for a picture, while the idler has the privilege of lovely views." Mr. Roach Smith was of opinion that Higham was the seat of "a great Roman pottery." A Monastery of importance existed here for several centuries, Mary, daughter of King Stephen, being one of the Prioresses; but it was dissolved by Henry VIII. The list of flowering plants given in Mr. Fielding's book is extensive and interesting, and contains many rarities.

A "Cheap Jack," a veritable Doctor Marigold, had taken up

his quarters at Higham, and we loiter among the bystanders to hear his patter. We feel quite sure that had Dickens been present he would have listened and been as amused with him as ourselves. We heard a few days previously the public crier going round in his cart, announcing the arrival of this worthy by ringing his bell and proclaiming in a stentorian voice something to this effect:—

"The public is respectfully informed that the Cheap Jack has arrived, bringing with him a large assortment of London, Birmingham, and Sheffield goods, together with a choice collection of glass and earthenware, which he will sell every evening at the most reasonable prices."

On our arrival here we find him on his rostrum surrounded by some flaring naphtha lamps, and thus disposing of some penny books of songs: "Now, ladies and gentlemen, what shall we have the pleasure of saying for this handsome book, containing over a hundred songs sung by all the great singers of the day—Macdermott, Madam Langtry, Sims Reeves, and other eminent vocalists—besides numerous toasts and readings. Well, I won't ask sixpence, and I won't take fivepence, fourpence, threepence, twopence—no, I only ask a penny. Sold again, and got the money. Take care of the ha'pence" (to his assistant), "for we gives them to the blind when they can see to pick 'em up." We of course bought a copy of the famous collection as a "Dickens-item."

Before returning to Rochester we are anxious to identify the blacksmith's shop where the *feu de joie* was fired from "two smuggled cannons," in honour of the marriage of Miss Kate Dickens to Mr. Charles Collins. Alterations have taken place which render identification impossible; but a local blacksmith, who has established himself here, gives us some interesting particulars of the games in which he took part. He mentions also a circumstance relating to Dickens's favourite horse, Toby. It appears that it was an express wish of the novelist that when he died this horse should be shot; and according to our informant the horse was shod on the Tuesday before the 9th of June (the day of Dickens's death), and shot on the following Monday. The gun was loaded with small shot, and poor Toby died immediately it was fired. The blacksmith thoroughly confirms the opinion of the old labourers as to the kindness of Charles Dickens to his poorer neighbours. A curious episode occurs in our conference with this man: he seems under the impression, which no amount of assertion on our part can overcome, that my friend and fellow tramp, Mr. Kitton, is Mr. Henry Fielding Dickens. Whether there was any facial resemblance or likeness of manner did not transpire, but again and again he kept saying, "Now ain't you Harry Dickens?" Among the names at Higham we notice that of a well-remembered Dickens character—Mr. Stiggins!

On arriving at Higham Railway Station, we chat a bit with the station-master and porter there, but both are comparatively fresh comers and knew not Charles Dickens. After an enjoyable but somewhat fatiguing tramp, we are glad to take a late evening train from Higham to Strood, and thus ends our inspection of the land of "the Meshes."

* * * * * *

By the kindness of Mr. Henry Smetham (locally famed as the "Laureate of Strood"), we subsequently had an introduction to Mrs. Taylor, formerly school-mistress at Higham, who came there in 1860, and remained until some years after the death of Charles Dickens. She knew the novelist well, and used to see him almost every day when he was at home. She said, "If I had met him and did not know who he was, I should have set him down as a good-hearted English gentleman." He was very popular and much liked in the neighbourhood. On his return from America, in the first week of May, 1868, garlands of flowers were put by the villagers across the road from the railway station to Gad's Hill. There was a flag at Gad's (a Union Jack, she thinks), which was always hoisted when Dickens was at home. He never read at Higham, and never came to the school; but he always allowed the use of the meadow at the back of Gad's Hill Place for the school treats, either of church or chapel, and contributed to such treats sweets and what not.

Mrs. Taylor remembers that the carriage was sent down from Gad's Hill Place to the Higham railway station nearly every night at ten o'clock to meet either Charles Dickens or his friends. It passed the school, and she well recollects the pleasant sound made by the bells. She heard Dickens read *Sairey Gamp* in London once, and did not like the dress he wore, but thought the reading very wonderful.

This lady says she was in London at the time of the death of Charles Dickens, the announcement of which she saw on a newspaper placard, and was ill the whole of the day afterwards. It was a sorrowful day for her.

* * * * * *

We are much indebted to Mrs. Budden of Gad's Hill Place for the following interesting particulars which she obtained from Mrs. Easedown, of Higham, "who was parlour-maid to Mr. Dickens, and left to be married on the 8th of June, the day he was seized with the fit. She says it was her duty to hoist the flag on the top of the house directly Mr. Dickens arrived at Gad's Hill. It was a small flag, not more than fourteen inches square, and was kept in the billiard-room. She says he was the dearest and best gentleman that ever lived, and the kindest of masters. He asked her to stay and wait at table the night he was taken ill; she said if he wished it she would, and then he said, 'Never mind; I don't feel well.' She saw him after he was dead, laid out in the dining-room, when his coffin was covered with scarlet geraniums—his favourite flower. The flower-beds on the lawns at Gad's Hill in his time were always filled with scarlet geraniums; they have since been done away with. Over the head of the coffin was the oil painting of himself as a young man (probably Maclise's portrait)—on one side a picture of 'Dolly Varden,' and on the other 'Kate Nickleby.' He gave Mrs. Easedown, on the day she left his service, a photograph of himself with his name written on the back. Each of the other servants at Gad's Hill Place was presented with a similar photograph. She said he was unusually busy at the time of his death, as on the Monday morning he ordered breakfast to be ready during the week at 7.30 ('Sharp, mind') instead of his usual time, 9 o'clock, as he said 'he had so much to do before Friday.' But—'Such a thing was never to be,' for on the Thursday he breathed his last!"

* * * * * *

Mrs. Wright, the wife of Mr. Henry Wright, surveyor of Higham, lived four years at Gad's Hill Place as parlour-maid. She is the proud possessor of some interesting relics of her late master. These include his soup-plate, a meerschaum pipe (presented to him, but he chiefly smoked cigars—he was not a great smoker), a wool-worked kettle-holder (which he constantly used), and a pair of small bellows. When she was married Mr. Dickens presented her with a China tea service, "not a single piece of which," said Mrs. Wright proudly, "has been broken."

She remembers, at the time of her engagement as parlour-maid, that the servants told her to let a gentleman in at the front door who was approaching. She didn't know who it was, as she had never seen Mr. Dickens before. She opened the door, and the gentleman entered in a very upright manner, and after thanking her, looked hard at her, and then walked up-stairs. On returning to the kitchen the servants asked who it was that had just come in. She replied, "I don't know, but I think it was the master." "Did he speak?" they asked. "No," said she, "but he looked at me in a very determined way." Said they, "He was reading your character, and he now knows you thoroughly," or words to that effect.

As parlour-maid, it was part of her duty to carve and wait on her master specially. The dinner serviettes were wrapped up in a peculiar manner, and Mrs. Wright remembers that Lord Darnley's servants were always anxious to learn how the folding was done, but they never discovered the secret. At dinner-parties, it was the custom to place a little "button-hole" for each guest. This was mostly made up of scarlet geranium (Dickens's favourite flower), with a bit of the leaf and a frond of maidenhair fern. On one occasion in her early days, the dinner-lift (to the use of which she was unaccustomed) broke and ran down quickly, smashing the crockery and bruising her arm. Mr. Dickens jumped up quickly and said, "Never mind the breakage; is your arm hurt?" As it was painful, he immediately applied arnica to the bruise, and gave her a glass of port wine, "treating me," Mrs. Wright remarked, "more like a child of his own than a servant."

When she was married, and left Gad's Hill, she brought her first child to show her former master. He took notice of it, and asked her what he could buy as a present. She thanked him, and said she did not want anything. On leaving he gently put a sovereign into the baby's little hand, and said, "Buy something with that."

Mrs. Wright spoke of the great interest which Dickens took in the children's treats at Higham, lending his meadow for them, providing sweets and cakes for the little ones, and apples to be scrambled for. He took great delight in seeing the scrambles.

She also referred to the cricket club, and said that when the matches were going on it was a regular holiday at Higham. Dickens used to take the scores, and at the end of the game he gave prizes and made little speeches. Her husband, Mr. Henry Wright, acted as secretary to the club, and is the possessor of a letter written by Mr. Dickens, in reply to an address which had been presented to him, of which letter the following is a copy:—

"GAD'S HILL PLACE,
"HIGHAM BY ROCHESTER, KENT.
"*Tuesday*, 29*th July*, 1862.

"DEAR SIR,

"As your name is the first on the list of signatures to the little address I have had the pleasure of receiving—on my return from a short absence—from the greater part of the players in the match the other day, I address my reply to you.

"I beg you to assure the rest that it will always give me great pleasure to lend my meadow for any such good purpose, and that I feel a sincere desire to be a good friend to the working men in this neighbourhood. I am always interested in their welfare, and am always heartily glad to see them enjoying rational and healthful recreation.

"It did not escape my notice that some expressions were used the other day which would have been better avoided, but I dismiss them from my mind as being probably unintentional, and certainly opposed to the general good feeling and good sense.

"Faithfully yours,

"CHARLES DICKENS.

"MR. H. WRIGHT."

Both Mrs. Easedown and Mrs. Wright informed us (through Mrs. Budden) that "Mr. Dickens was the best of masters, and a dear good man; that he gave a great deal away in the parish, and was very much missed; that he frequently went to church and sat in the chancel. . . . When he lived in Higham there used to be a great deal of ague, and he gave away an immense quantity of port wine and quinine. Since the Cement Works have been at Cliffe there has been very little ague at Higham."

* * * * * *

Mr. Robert Lake Cobb, of Mockbeggar House, Higham, a land agent of high position and a County Councillor, told us that he took in the *Pickwick Papers* as they appeared in numbers, and he recollected how eagerly he read them, and how tiresome it was to have to wait month by month until the story was finished. The book made a tremendous sensation at the time. Many years afterwards Charles Dickens came to reside at Gad's Hill Place, and the families became intimate. "Mr. Dickens," observed our informant, "was a very pleasant neighbour, and had always got something nice to say. He was a dreadful man to walk—very few could keep up with him."

Mr. Cobb had one son, Herbert, who was a playfellow of Dickens's boys; and as illustrative of the interest he took in his neighbours, on one occasion the novelist and our informant were talking over matters, when the former said, "What are you going to bring your boy up to?" "A land agent," replied Mr. Cobb. "Ah," said the novelist, "whatever you do, make him self-reliant." He thought that of all the sons Mr. Henry Fielding Dickens most resembled his father.

Among the notable people Mr. Cobb met at Gad's Hill Place were Mr. Forster, Mr. Wilkie Collins, Mr. Fechter the actor, and others. When Hans Christian Andersen was visiting there, Dickens took him to Higham Church. Mr. Cobb spoke of the pleasant picnic parties which Dickens gave on Blue Bell Hill. He was of opinion that Cob-Tree Hall in that neighbourhood, about one and a half miles from Aylesford, nearly parallel with the river, suggested the original of Manor Farm, Dingley Dell. It formerly belonged to Mr. Franklin, and is now occupied by Major Trousdell. Mr. Cobb believed that Dickens took the title of *No Thoroughfare*—which he and Wilkie Collins contributed to the 1867 number of *All the Year Round*, and in the dramatizing of which Dickens subsequently was so interested—from the notice-boards which were put up by Lord Darnley in many parts of Cobham Park.

On one occasion our informant remembers a stoppage of

the train in Higham tunnel, which caused some consternation to the passengers, as no explanation of the delay was forthcoming from any of the railway officials. The station-master coming up at the time, Dickens remarked—" Ah! an unwilling witness, Mr. Wood."

Mr. Cobb mentioned that Miss Hogarth, Dickens's sister-in-law, was a great favourite in the neighbourhood, from her kindness and thoughtfulness for all with whom she came in contact, and especially the poor of Higham.

CHAPTER XIII.

COBHAM PARK AND HALL, THE LEATHER BOTTLE, SHORNE, CHALK, AND THE DOVER ROAD.

"It's a place you may well be fond of and attached to, for it's the prettiest spot in all the country round."—*The Village Coquettes.*

"The last soft light of the setting sun had fallen on the earth, casting a rich glow on the yellow corn sheaves, and lengthening the shadows of the orchard trees."—*The Pickwick Papers.*

WE reserve this, our last long tramp in "Dickens-Land," for the Friday before our departure. Mrs. Perugini, the novelist's second daughter, had recently told us that this was the most beautiful of all the beautiful parts of Kent, and so indeed it proves to be. Its sylvan scenery is truly unique.

Mr. Charles Dickens the younger, in his valuable annotated Jubilee edition of *Pickwick*, has included this note relating to Cobham:—

"As all the world knows, the neighbourhood of Rochester was dear to Charles Dickens. There it is that Gad's Hill Place stands, the house to which, as 'a queer, small boy,' he looked forward as the possible reward of an industrious career, and in which he passed the later years of his life; and near Rochester, still approached by the 'delightful walk' here described, is Cobham, one of the most charming villages in that part of Kent. Down the lanes, and through the park to Cobham, was always a favourite walk with Charles Dickens; and he never wearied of acting as *cicerone* to his guests to its fine church and the quaint almshouses with the disused refectory behind it."

Happily the weather again favours us on this delightful excursion. It is just such a day as that on which we made our visit to Gad's Hill. As we have had much tramping about Rochester during the morning, we prudently take an early afternoon train to Higham, to save our legs. The short distance of about four miles consists almost entirely of tunnels cut through the chalk.

Alighting at Higham Station, we make our way for the Dover Road and reach Pear Tree Lane, which turns out of it for Cobham. We notice in passing through Higham by daylight that the lanes are much closed in by banks, in fact, the tertiary and chalk systems have been cut through to form the roads; but here and there one gets glimpses of the Thames, its course being marked by the white or brown wings of sailing-boats.

The lane above alluded to, a little above Gad's Hill, is the direct road to Cobham, and on entering it we are immediately struck with the different scene presented, as compared with any part of the county we have previously gone over. It is cut through the Thanet Sands, which at first are of ashy gray colour, but after some distance are of a bright red hue, probably owing to infiltration, and the road rises gently until the woods are reached. The vegetation growing on the high banks consists of oak, hazel, beech, sycamore, and Spanish chestnut, in many places intermingled with wild clematis. The branches of the trees are not allowed to grow over into the road, but are kept well cut back so as practically to form a wall on either side, extending in some places to twelve feet high. The effect is to present an almost unbroken surface of various shades of green, deliciously cool and shady in the heat of summer, and brightened here and there in autumn by the rich orange-coloured fruit of the arum, the scarlet berries of the white bryony, and—deeper in the woods—by the pinky-waxen berries of the spindle-tree, described by Lord Tennyson as "the fruit which in our winter woodland looks a flower."

As the road continually winds in its upward progress, and as no part within view extends beyond a few hundred yards before it turns again, the limit of perspective is frequently arrested by a number of evergreen arches. It was a Devonshire lane, so to speak, in a state of cultivation. Of course in the early spring, the delicacy of the fresh green foliage would give another picture; and again the autumnal tints would present a totally different effect under the influence of the rich colouring of decaying vegetation.

No wonder Dickens and his friends had such admiration for this walk, the last, by the way, that he ever enjoyed, on Tuesday, 7th June, 1870, with his sister-in-law, Miss Hogarth, the day before the fatal seizure. In a letter written from Lausanne, so far back as the year 1846, he says:—

"Green woods and green shades about here are more like Cobham, in Kent, than anything we dream of at the foot of Alpine passes."

When we reach an elevation and are able to get an extended view of the country we have traversed, a magnificent prospect of the Thames valley on the west side, and of the

Medway valley on the east, discloses itself. On a bank in this lane we find a rather rare plant, the long-stalked crane's-bill (*Geranium columbinum*), its rose-pink flowers standing out like rubies among the green foliage. *Pteris aquilina*, the common brake or bracken, is very luxuriant here; but we have met with few ferns in the part of Kent which we visited. We were afterwards informed that *asplenium*, *lastrea*, *scolopendrium*, and others are to be found in the neighbourhood. We pass at Shorne Ridgway a village inn with a curious sign, "Ye Olde See Ho Taverne." On inquiry, we learn that "See Ho" is the sportsman's cry in coursing, when a hare appears in sight.

The woods surrounding the entrance to the park are presently reached, and here the vegetation, which in the lanes had been kept under, is allowed to grow unchecked. At intervals walks (or "rides," as they are called in some counties) are cut through the woods, the grass being well mown underneath, and each of these walks is a shaded grove, losing itself in the distance. The deep silence of the place is only broken by the cooing of the wood-pigeon, and the occasional piercing note of the green woodpecker. It is said that the nightingales appear here about the 13th of April and continue singing until June, and that the best time for seeing this neighbourhood is during the blossoming season in May.

The temptation to quote Dickens's own description of Cobham Park from *Pickwick* cannot be resisted:—

"A delightful walk it was; for it was a pleasant afternoon in June, and their way lay through a deep and shady wood, cooled by the light wind which gently rustled the thick foliage, and enlivened by the songs of the birds that perched upon the boughs. The ivy and the moss crept in thick clusters over the old trees, and the soft green turf overspread the ground like a silken mat. They emerged upon an open park, with an ancient hall, displaying the quaint and picturesque architecture of Elizabeth's time. Long vistas of stately oaks and elm trees appeared on every side: large herds of deer were cropping the fresh grass; and occasionally a startled hare scoured along the ground with the speed of the shadows thrown by the light clouds, which swept across a sunny landscape like a passing breath of summer."

Another description of Cobham at another time of the year is found in the *Seven Poor Travellers*:—

"As for me, I was going to walk, by Cobham Woods, as far upon my way to London as I fancied. . . . And now the mists began to rise in the most beautiful manner, and the sun to shine; and as I went on through the bracing air, seeing the hoar-frost sparkle everywhere, I felt as if all Nature shared in the joy of the great Birthday. . . . By Cobham Hall I came to the village, and the churchyard where the dead had been quietly buried 'in the sure and certain hope' which Christmastide inspired."

We notice in our quiet tramp here a peculiarity in the foliage of the oaks which is worth recording. It will be remembered that in the late spring of 1888, anxiety was expressed by certain newspaper correspondents that the English oak would suffer extermination in consequence of caterpillars denuding it of its leaves. But naturalists who had studied the question knew better. The caterpillar, which is no doubt the larva of the green Tortrix moth (*Tortrix viridana*), spins its cocoon at the end of June or the beginning of July, and the effect of the heavy rains and warm sunny days since that time was to encourage the energy of the tree in putting forth its second growth of leaves. This second growth of delicate green almost covered the oaks in Cobham Park, and

Cobham Hall.

effectually concealed the devastation of the caterpillars on the old leaves. The effect was quite spring-like. Truly, as George Eliot says, "Nature repairs her ravages."

Cobham Park is nearly seven miles round, and its exquisitely varied scenery of wood and glade is conspicuous at the spot where the chestnut tree called "The Four Sisters" is placed. There is a lovely walk from Cobham Hall to Rochester through the "Long Avenue," so named in contradistinction to the "Grand Avenue," which opens into Cobham village. This walk, which slopes all the way down from the Mausoleum, leads to a seat placed midway in an open spot where charming views of the Medway valley are obtained. For rich sylvan scenery in the county of Kent, this is surely unrivalled.

Admission to Cobham Hall, the seat of the Earl of Darnley (whose ancestors have resided here since the time of King John), is on Fridays only, and such admission is obtained by ticket, procurable from Mr. Wildish, bookseller, of Rochester. A nominal charge is made, the proceeds being devoted towards maintaining Cobham schools.

The Hall is a red-brick edifice (temp. Elizabeth, 1587), consisting of two Tudor wings, connected by a central block designed by Inigo Jones. The most noticeable objects in the entrance corridor are a fine pair of columns of Cornish serpentine, nearly ten feet high, tapering from a base some two feet square. The white veining of the steatite (soapstone) is in beautiful contrast to the rich red and black colours of the marble. These columns were purchased at the great Exhibition of 1851. An enormous bath, hewn out of a solid block of granite said to have been brought from Egypt, is also a very noticeable object in this corridor.

The housekeeper—a chatty, intelligent, and portly personage

—shows visitors over the rooms and picture-galleries. There is a superb collection of pictures by the Old Masters, about which Dickens had always something facetious to say to his friends. They illustrate the schools of Venice, Florence, Rome, Netherlands, Spain, France, and England, and were formed mainly by purchases from the Orleans Gallery, and the Vetturi Gallery from Florence, and include Titian's 'Rape of Europa,' Rubens's 'Queen Tomyris dipping Cyrus's head into blood,' Salvator Rosa's 'Death of Regulus,' Vandyck's 'Duke of Lennox,' Sir Joshua Reynolds's 'The Call of Samuel,' and others. But the pictures in which we are most interested are the portraits of literary, scientific, and other worthies—an excellent collection, including Shakespeare, John Locke, Hobbes, Sir Richard Steele, Sir William Temple, Dean Swift, Dryden, Betterton, Pope, Gay, Thomson, Sir Hugh Middleton, Martin Luther, and the ill-fated Lord George Gordon.

There is also an ornithological museum, with some very fine specimens of the order of grallatores (or waders). In reply to a letter of inquiry, the Earl of Darnley kindly informs us that the examples of ostrich (*Struthio camelus*), cassowary (*Casuarius galeatus*), and common emu (*Dromaius ater*), were once alive in the menagerie attached to the hall, which was broken up about fifty years ago.

We are shown the music-room (which, by the bye, his late majesty King George IV., is said to have remarked was the finest room in England), a very handsome apartment facing the west, with a large organ, and capable of containing several hundred persons. The decorations are very chaste, being in white and gold; and, as the brilliant sun was setting in the summer evening, a delicate rose-coloured hue was diffused over everything in the room through the medium of the tinted blinds attached to the windows. It had a most peculiar and pretty effect, strongly recalling Mrs. Skewton and her "rose-coloured curtains for doctors."

By the special permission of his lordship, we see the famous

Dickens's Châlet, now in Cobham Park.

Swiss châlet, which is now erected in the terrace flower-garden at the back of Cobham Hall, having been removed to its present position some years ago from another part of the grounds. It stands on an elevated open space surrounded by beautiful trees—the rare Salisburia, tulip, cedar, chestnut and others—and makes a handsome addition to the garden, irrespective of its historical associations. The châlet is of dark wood varnished, and has in the centre a large carving of Dickens's crest, which in heraldic terms is described as: "a lion couchant 'or,' holding in the gamb a cross patonce 'sable.'"

There are two rooms in the châlet, each about sixteen feet square, the one below having four windows and a door, and the one above (approached in the usual Swiss fashion by an external staircase), which is much the prettier, having six windows and a door. There are shutters outside, and the overhanging roof at first sight gives the building somewhat of a top-heavy appearance, but this impression wears off after a time, and it is found to be effective and well-proportioned. "The five mirrors" which Dickens placed in the châlet have been removed from the upper room, but they are scarcely necessary, the views of rich and varied foliage and flowers seen from the open windows, through which the balmy air passes, forming a series of pictures in the bright sunlight of the August afternoon delightfully fresh and beautiful. We sit down quietly for a few minutes and enjoy the privilege; we ponder on the many happy and industrious hours spent by its late owner in this now classic building; and we leave it sadly, with the recollection that here were penned the last lines which the "vanished hand" was destined to give to the world.

The Earl of Darnley generously allows his neighbours to have a key of his park, and Dickens had one of such keys, a privilege greatly appreciated by him and his friends. Recently his lordship has erected a staircase round one of the highest trees in the park, called the "crow's nest," from whence a very pretty peep at the surrounding country is obtained.

During our visit we venture to ask the portly housekeeper if she remembers Charles Dickens? The ray of delight that illumines her good-natured countenance is simply magical.

"Oh," she says, "I liked Mr. Dickens very much. He was always so full of fun. Oh! oh! oh!" the recollection of which causes a fit of suppressed laughter, which "communicates a blancmange-like motion to her fat cheeks," and she adds: "He used to dine here, and was always very popular with the family, and in the neighbourhood."

We cannot help thinking that such delightful places as Cobham Hall were in Dickens's mind when, in *Bleak House* (*à propos* of Chesney Wold), he makes the volatile Harold Skimpole say to Sir Leicester Dedlock—"The owners of such places are public benefactors. They are good enough to maintain a number of delightful objects for the admiration and pleasure of us poor men, and not to reap all the admiration and pleasure that they yield, is to be ungrateful to our benefactors."

Leaving the park by a pretty undulating walk, and passing on our way a large herd of deer, their brown and fawn-coloured coats contrasting prettily with the green-sward, we come upon the picturesque village of Cobham, where Mr. Tupman sought consolation after his little affair with the amatory spinster aunt. Of course the principal object of interest is the Leather Bottle, or "Dickens's old Pickwick Leather Bottle," as the sign of the present landlord now calls it, wherein Dickens slept a night in 1841, and visited it many times subsequently. There is a coloured portrait of the President of the Pickwick Club on the sign, as he appeared addressing the members. A fire occurred at the Leather Bottle a few years ago, but it was confined to a back portion of the building; unfortunately its restoration and so-called "improvements" have destroyed many of the picturesque features which characterized this quiet old inn when Dickens wrote the famous Papers. Here is his description of it after Mr. Pickwick, Mr. Snodgrass, and Mr. Winkle had walked through Cobham Park to seek their lost friend:—

"'If this,' said Mr. Pickwick, looking about him; 'if this were the place to which all who are troubled with our friend's complaint came, I fancy their old attachment to this world would very soon return.'

"'I think so too,' said Mr. Winkle.

"'And really,' added Mr. Pickwick, after half an hour's walking had brought them to the village, 'really for a misanthrope's choice, this is one of the prettiest and most desirable places of residence I ever met with.'

"In this opinion also, both Mr. Winkle and Mr. Snodgrass expressed their concurrence; and having been directed to the Leather Bottle, a clean and commodious village ale-house, the three travellers entered, and at once inquired for a gentleman of the name of Tupman.

"'Show the gentlemen into the parlour, Tom,' said the landlady.

"A stout country lad opened a door at the end of the passage, and the three friends entered a long, low-roofed room, furnished with a large number of high-backed leather-cushioned chairs, of fantastic shapes, and embellished with a great variety of old portraits, and roughly-coloured prints of some antiquity. At the upper end of the room was a table, with a white cloth upon it, well covered with a roast fowl, bacon, ale, and etceteras; and at the table sat Mr. Tupman, looking as unlike a man who had taken his leave of the world, as possible.

"On the entrance of his friends, that gentleman laid down his knife and fork, and with a mournful air advanced to meet them.

"'I did not expect to see you here,' he said, as he grasped Mr. Pickwick's hand. 'It's very kind.'

"'Ah!' said Mr. Pickwick, sitting down, and wiping from his forehead the perspiration which the walk had engendered. 'Finish your dinner, and walk out with me. I wish to speak to you alone.'

"Mr. Tupman did as he was desired; and Mr. Pickwick having refreshed himself with a copious draught of ale, waited his friend's leisure. The dinner was quickly despatched, and they walked out together.

"For half an hour, their forms might have been seen pacing the churchyard to and fro, while Mr. Pickwick was engaged in combating his companion's resolution. Any repetition of his arguments would be useless; for what language could convey to them that energy and force which their great originator's manner communicated? Whether Mr. Tupman was already tired of retirement, or whether he was wholly unable to resist the eloquent appeal which was made to him, matters not; he did *not* resist it at last.

"'It mattered little to him,' he said, 'where he dragged out the miserable remainder of his days: and since his friend laid so much stress upon his humble companionship, he was willing to share his adventures.'

"Mr. Pickwick smiled; they shook hands; and walked back to rejoin their companions."

The Old Parlour of the "Leather Bottle."

In order to preserve the historical associations of the place, the landlord of the Leather Bottle has added to the art collection in the fine old parlour (that still contains "the high-

backed leather-cushioned chairs of fantastic shapes") many portraits of Dickens and illustrations from his works, including a copy of the life-like coloured Watkins photograph previously referred to. It has been already suggested that the neighbourhood of Kit's Coty House probably gave rise to the famous archæological episode of the stone with the inscription—"Bill Stumps, his mark," in *Pickwick*, which occurred near here, rivalling the "A. D. L. L." discovery of the sage Monkbarns in Scott's *Antiquary*.

Time presses with us, so, after a refreshing cup of tea, we just have a hasty glance at the beautiful old church, which contains some splendid examples of monumental brasses, which for number and preservation are said to be unique. They are erected to the memory of John Cobham, Constable of Rochester, 1354, his ancestors and others.[1] There are also some fine old almshouses which accommodate twenty pensioners. These almshouses are a survival of the ancient college. We then take our departure, returning through Cobham woods.

Turning off at some distance on the left, and passing through the little village of Shorne, with its pretty churchyard, a very favourite spot of Charles Dickens, and probably described by him in *Pickwick* as "one of the most peaceful and secluded churchyards in Kent, where wild flowers mingle with the grass, and the soft landscape around, forms the fairest spot in the garden of England"—we make for Chalk church. It will be remembered, that the first number of *Pickwick* appeared on the 31st March, 1836, and on the 2nd of April following Charles Dickens was married, and came to spend

[1] "Cobham Church [says a writer in the *Archæologia Cantiana*, 1877] is distinguished above all others as possessing the finest and most complete series of brasses in the kingdom. It contains some of the earliest and some of the latest, as well as some of the most beautiful in design. The inscriptions are also remarkable, and the heraldry for its intelligence is in itself a study. There is an interest also in the fact that for the most part they refer to one great family—the Lords of Cobham."

Shorne Church

his honeymoon at Chalk, and he visited it again in 1837, when doubtless the descriptions of Cobham and its vicinity were written. To this neighbourhood, "at all times of his life, he returned, with a strange recurring fondness."

Mr. Kitton has favoured me with permission to quote the following extract from his Supplement to *Charles Dickens by Pen and Pencil*, being the late Mr. E. Laman Blanchard's recollections of this pleasant neighbourhood :—

"In the year Charles Dickens came to reside at Gad's Hill, I took possession of a country house at Rosherville, which I occupied for some seventeen years. During that period a favourite morning walk was along the high road, of many memories, leading from Gravesend to Rochester, and on repeated occasions I had the good fortune to encounter the great novelist making one of his pedestrian excursions towards the Gravesend or Greenhithe railway station, where he would take the train to travel up to town. Generally, by a curious coincidence, we passed each other, with an interchange of salutations, at about the same spot. This was on the outskirts of the village of Chalk, where a picturesque lane branched off towards Shorne and Cobham. Here the brisk walk of Charles Dickens was always slackened, and he never failed to glance meditatively for a few moments at the windows of a corner house on the southern side of the road, advantageously situated for commanding views of the river and the far-stretching landscape beyond. It was in that house he had lived immediately after his marriage, and there many of the earlier chapters of *Pickwick* were written."

It is a long walk from Cobham to Chalk church,—the church, by the bye, being about a mile from the village, as is usual in many places in Kent,—and as the shades of evening are coming upon us, and as we are desirous of having a sketch of the curious stone-carved figure over the entrance porch, we hurry on, and succeed in effecting our object, though under the difficulty of approaching darkness.

This figure represents an old priest in a stooping position, with an upturned vessel (probably a jug), about which we

Curious Old Figure over the Porch, Chalk Church.

were informed there is probably a legend. Dickens used to be a great admirer of this quaint carving, and it is said that whenever he passed it, he always took off his hat to it, or gave it a friendly nod, as to an old acquaintance. [We regretfully record the fact that since our visit, both porch and figure have been demolished.]

Amid the many strange sounds peculiar to summer night

in the country, a very weird and startling effect is produced in this lonely spot, in the dusk of the evening, by the shrill whistle of the common redshank (*Totanus calidris*), so called from the colour of its legs, which are of a crimson-red. This bird, as monotonous in its call-note as the corn-crake, to which it is closely allied, doubtless has its home in the marshes hereabout, in which, and in fen countries, it greatly delights. The peculiar whistle is almost ventriloquial in its ubiquity, and must be heard to be properly appreciated.

We retrace our steps to the Dover road, and by the light of a match applied to our pipes, see that our pedometer marks upwards of fifteen miles for this tramp—"a rather busy afternoon," as Mr. Datchery once said.

Since these lines were written, the third volume of the *Autobiography and Reminiscences* of W. P. Frith, R.A., has been published, in which there is a most interesting reminiscence of Dickens; indeed, there are many scattered throughout the three volumes, but the one in question refers to "a stroll" which Dickens took with Mr. Frith and other friends in July 1868. Mr. Cartwright, the celebrated dentist, was one of the party, and the "stroll" was in reality, as the genial R. A. describes it, "a fearfully long walk" such as he shall never forget; nor the night he passed, without once closing his eyes in sleep, after it. "Dickens," continues Mr. Frith, "was a great pedestrian. His strolling was at the rate of perhaps a little under four miles an hour. He was used to the place, —I was not, and suffered accordingly."

Having a shrewd suspicion that this referred to one of the long walks taken in our tramp, the present writer communicated with Mr. Frith on the subject, and he was favoured with the following reply:—

"The stroll I mentioned in my third volume was through Lord Darnley's park, but after that I remember nothing. As the time spent in walking was four hours at least, we must have covered ground far beyond the length of the park.

"On another occasion,—Dickens, Miss Hogarth, and I went to Rochester to see the Castle, and the famous Pickwickian inn. On another day we went to the Leather Bottle at Cobham, where Dickens was eloquent on the subject of the Dadd parricide, showing us the place where the body was found, with many startling and interesting details of the discovery."

The subject of the Dadd parricide alluded to by Mr. Frith was a very horrible case; the son—an artist—was a lunatic, and was subsequently confined in Bethlehem Hospital, London. There are two curious pictures by him in the Dyce and Forster collection at South Kensington; one is inscribed "Sketches to Illustrate the Passions—Patriotism. By Richard Dadd, Bethlehem Hospital, London, May 30, 1857, St. George's-in-the-Fields." It has much minute writing on it. The other is "Leonidas with the Wood-cutters," and illustrates Glover's poem, *Leonidas*. It is inscribed, "Rd. Dadd, 1873." He died in Bethlehem Hospital in 1887.

The Dover Road! What a magic influence it has over us, as we tramp along it in the quiet summer evening, and recall an incident that happened nearly a hundred years ago, what time the Dover mail struggled up Shooter's Hill on that memorable Friday night, and Jerry Cruncher, who had temporarily suspended his "fishing" operations, and being free from the annoyances of the "Aggerawayter," caused consternation to the minds of coachman, guard, and passengers of the said mail, by riding abruptly up, *à la* highwayman, and demanding to speak to a passenger named Mr. Jarvis Lorry, then on his way to Paris,—as faithfully chronicled in *A Tale of Two Cities.* Again, in the early part of the present century, when a certain friendless but dear and artless boy, named David Copperfield,—who having been first robbed by a "long-legged young man with a very little empty donkey-cart, which was nothing but a large wooden-tray on wheels," of "half a guinea and his box," under pretence of "driving him to the pollis," and subsequently defrauded by an unscrupulous tailor named one Mr. Dolloby ("Dolloby was the name over the shop-door at least") of the proper price of "a little weskit," for which he, Dolloby, gave poor David only ninepence,—trudged along that same Dover road footsore and hungry, "and got through twenty-three miles on the straight road" to Rochester and Chatham on a certain Sunday; all of which is duly recorded in *The Personal History of David Copperfield.*

In after years, when happier times came to him, David made many journeys over the Dover road, between Canterbury and London, on the Canterbury Coach. Respecting the earliest of these (readers will remember Phiz's illustration, "My first fall in life"), he says:—

"The main object on my mind, I remember, when we got fairly on the road, was to appear as old as possible to the coachman, and to speak extremely gruff. The latter point I achieved at great personal inconvenience; but I stuck to it, because I felt it was a grown-up sort of thing."

In spite of this assumption, he is impudently chaffed by "William the coachman" on his "shooting"—on his "county" (Suffolk), its "dumplings," and its "Punches," and finally, at William's suggestion, actually resigns his box-seat in favour of his (William's) friend, "the gentleman with a very unpromising squint and a prominent chin, who had a tall white hat on with a narrow flat brim, and whose close-fitting drab trousers seemed to button all the way up outside his legs from his boots to his hips." In reply to a remark of the coachman this worthy says:—"There ain't no sort of 'orse that I 'ain't bred, and no sort of dorg. 'Orses and dorgs is some men's fancy. They're wittles and drink to me—lodging, wife, and children—reading, writing, and 'rithmetic—snuff, tobacker, and sleep."

"That ain't a sort of man to see sitting behind a coach-box, is it, though?" says William in David's ear. David construes this remark into an indication of a wish that "the gentleman" should have his place, so he blushingly offers to resign it.

"Well, if you don't mind," says William, "I think it would be more correct."

Poor David, "so very young!" gives up his box-seat, and thus moralizes on his action:—

"I have always considered this as the first fall I had in life. When I booked my place at the coach-office, I had had 'Box Seat' written against the entry, and had given the book-keeper half-a-crown. I was got up in a special great coat and shawl, expressly to do honour to that distinguished eminence; had glorified myself upon it a good deal; and had felt that I was a credit to the coach. And here, in the very first stage, I was supplanted by a shabby man with a squint, who had no other merit than smelling like a livery-stables, and being able to walk across me, more like a fly than a human being, while the horses were at a canter."

Pip, in *Great Expectations*, also made very many journeys to and from London, along the Dover road (the London road it is called in the novel), but the two most notable were, firstly, the occasion of his ride outside the coach with the two convicts as fellow-passengers on the back-seat—"bringing with them that curious flavour of bread-poultice, baize, rope-yarn, and hearth-stone, which attends the convict presence;" and secondly, that in which he walked all the way to London, after the sad interview at Miss Havisham's house, where he learns that Estella is to become the wife of Bentley Drummle:—

"All done, all gone! So much was done and gone, that when I went out at the gate the light of day seemed of a darker colour than when I went in. For awhile I hid myself among some lanes and by-paths, and then started off to walk all the way to London. . . . It was past midnight when I crossed London Bridge."

One more reference is made to the Dover road in *Bleak House*, where that most lovable of the many lovable characters in Dickens's novels, Esther Summerson, makes her journey, with her faithful little maid Charley, to Deal, in order to comfort Richard Carstone:—

"It was a night's journey in those coach times; but we had the mail to ourselves, and did not find the night very tedious. It passed with me as I suppose it would with most people under such circumstances. At one while, my journey looked hopeful, and at another hopeless. Now, I thought that I should do some good, and now I wondered how I could ever have supposed so."

When speaking of Dickens's characters, some critics have said that "he never drew a gentleman." One ventures to ask, Where is there a more chivalrous, honourable, or kind-hearted gentleman than Mr. John Jarndyce? Sir Leicester Dedlock in the same novel too, with some few peculiarities, is a thoroughly high-minded and noble gentleman of the old school. This by the way.

After walking some distance, we are able to verify one of those sage experiences of Mr. F.'s aunt:—"There's milestones on the Dover road!" for, by the light of another match, the darkness closing in, and there being no moon, we read "4 miles to Rochester." However, we tramp merrily on, with "the town lights right afore us," our minds being full of pleasant reminiscences of the scenes we have passed through,

and this expedition, like many a weightier matter, "comes to an end for the time."

* * * * * *

We had on another occasion the pleasure of a long chat with Mrs. Latter of Shorne, one of the daughters of Mr. W. S. Trood, for many years landlord of the Sir John Falstaff. She said her family came from Somersetshire to reside at Gad's Hill in the year 1849, and left in 1872. The Falstaff was then a little homely place, but it has been much altered since. She knew Charles Dickens very well, and saw him constantly during his residence at Gad's Hill Place. Mrs. Latter lost two sisters while she lived at the Falstaff—one died at the age of eleven, and the other at nineteen. The last-mentioned was named Jane, and died in 1862 of brain fever. Dickens was very kind to the family at the time, took great interest in the poor girl, and offered help of "anything that his house could afford." She remembers her mother asking Dickens if it would be well to have the windows of the bedroom open. At those times people were fond of keeping invalids closed up from the air. Dickens said—"Certainly: give her plenty of air." He liked fresh air himself. Mrs. Latter said in proof of this that the curtains were always blowing about the open windows at Gad's Hill Place.

When her sister Jane died, the funeral took place at Higham Church, and was very quiet, there being no show, only a little black pall trimmed with white placed over the coffin, which was carried by young men to the grave. Dickens afterwards commended what had been done, saying: "It showed good sense," and adding—"Not like an army of black beetles."

It will be remembered that in *Great Expectations* and elsewhere the ostentation, mummery, and extravagance of the "undertaking ceremony" are severely criticised. The same feeling, and a desire for funeral reform, no doubt prompted Dickens to insert the following clause in his Will:—

"I emphatically direct that I be buried in an inexpensive, unostentatious, and strictly private manner; that no public announcement be made of the time or place of my burial; that at the utmost not more than three plain mourning-coaches be employed; and that those who attend my funeral wear no scarf, cloak, black bow, long hatband, or other such revolting absurdity."

Mrs. Latter then told us the story of the two men with performing bears:—

It appears that soon after Dickens came to Gad's Hill a lot of labourers from Strood—some thirty or forty in number—had been for an outing in breaks to Cobham to a "bean-feast," or something of the kind, and some of them had got "rather fresh." On the return journey they stopped at the Falstaff, and at the time two men, who were foreigners, were there with performing bears, a very large one and a smaller one. The labourers began to lark with the bears, teased them, and made them savage, "becalled" the two men to whom they belonged, and a regular row followed. The owners of the bears became exasperated, and were proceeding to unmuzzle the animals, when Dickens (hearing the noise) came out of his gate holding one of his St. Bernard dogs by a chain. He told Mrs. Latter's father to take the bears up a back lane, said a few words to the crowd, and remonstrated with the Strood men on their conduct. The effect was magical; the whole affair was stilled in a minute or two.

* * * * * *

On a subsequent occasion we called upon the Rev. John Joseph Marsham of Overblow, near Shorne. This venerable clergyman, a bachelor, and in his eighty-fifth year, is totally blind, but in other respects is in the full possession of all his faculties, and remarked that he was much interested to hear anybody talk about old friends and times. He was inducted as Vicar of Shorne in the year 1837, came to live there in 1845, and resigned his cure in 1888, after completing his jubilee. He is a "Kentish man," having been born at Rochester. In our tramp the question of "Kentish man," or "man of Kent," often cropped up, and we had an opportunity of having the difference explained to us. A "Kentish man" is one born on the east side of the river Medway, and a "man of Kent" is one born on the west side.

The position of the residence "Overblow" is delightful. It stands on a little hill, the front having a fine view of the Thames valley and the marshes, the side looking on to the pretty hollow, in the centre of which stands Shorne Church, and the back being flanked in the distance by the beautiful Cobham Woods.

The reverend gentleman told us that he was a schoolfellow of the Right Honourable W. E. Gladstone and Sir Thomas Gladstone, his brother, at Eton, and had dined with the former at Hawarden on the occasion of his being thrice Premier, although he helped to turn his old friend out at Oxford in 1865, when he was succeeded by the Right Honourable Gathorne Hardy, now Lord Cranbrook.

Mr. Marsham was a neighbour of Charles Dickens, occasionally dined with him at Gad's Hill, and also met him at dinner sometimes at Mr. Hulkes's at the Little Hermitage. He spoke of him as a nice neighbour and a charming host, but he rarely talked except to his old friends. He frequently met Dickens in his walks, and had many a stroll with him, and always found him very interesting and amusing in his conversation. Once they were coming down from London together in a saloon carriage which contained about twelve or fourteen people. Dickens was sitting quietly in a corner. It was at the time that one of his serial novels was appearing, and most of the passengers were reading the current monthly number. No one noticed Dickens, and when the train stopped at Strood, he said—"We did not have much talk." "No," said Mr. Marsham, "the people were much better engaged," at which Dickens laughed. Charles Dickens did Mr. Marsham the kindness to send him early proofs of his Christmas stories before they were published.

After Dickens's death (which he heard of in London, and never felt so grieved in his life) Mr. Charles Dickens the younger, and Mr. Charles Collins, his brother-in-law, came to select a piece of ground on the east side of Shorne churchyard, which was one of Dickens's favourite spots, but in consequence of the arrangements for the burial in Westminster Abbey this was of course given up.

Mr. Marsham was staying in London, at Lord Penrhyn's, at the time of Dickens's death, and Lady Louisa Penrhyn told him that by accident she was in Westminster Abbey at about ten o'clock on the morning of 14th June, the day of the funeral, and noticing some persons standing round an open grave, her ladyship went to see it, and was greatly impressed on looking in to read the name of Charles Dickens on the coffin, on which were numerous wreaths of flowers.

Our venerable friend possesses a souvenir of the novelist in the two exquisite plaster statuettes, about eighteen inches high, of "Night" and "Morning," which he purchased at the Gad's Hill sale.

The reverend gentleman spoke of the great improvements in travelling as compared with times within his recollection. He said that before the railways were constructed he went to London by boat from Gravesend, and the river was so bad that he had to keep his handkerchief to his nose all the way to avoid the stench. This was long before the days of Thames Embankments and other improvements in travelling by river and road.

CHAPTER XIV.

A FINAL TRAMP IN ROCHESTER AND LONDON.

"You have been in every line I have ever read, since I first came here, . . you have been in every prospect I have ever seen since—on the river, on the sails of the ships, on the marshes, in the clouds, in the light, in the darkness, in the wind, in the woods, in the sea, in the streets." —*Great Expectations*.

"The magic reel, which, rolling on before, has led the Chronicler thus far, now slackens in its pace, and stops. It lies before the goal; the pursuit is at an end. . . . Good-night, and heaven send our journey may have a prosperous ending."—*The Old Curiosity Shop*.

IT is the morning of Saturday, the first of September, 1888, when our wonderfully pleasant week's tramp in "Dickens-Land" comes to an end. We have carried out every detail of our programme, without a single *contretemps* to mar the enjoyment of our delightful holiday; we have visited not only the spots where the childhood and youth of Charles Dickens were passed, and where the influence of the environment is specially traceable in the tone of both his earlier and later writings, but we have gone over and identified (as we proposed to do) a number of places in which he delighted, and often described in those writings, peopling them with airy characters (but to us most real), in whose footsteps we have walked. We have seen the place where he was born; we have seen nearly all the houses in which he lived in after life; and we have been over the charming home occupied by him for fourteen years, where his last moments passed away under the affectionate and reverential solicitude of his sons and daughters, and of Miss Hogarth, his sister-in-law, "the ever-useful, self-denying, and devoted friend."

And now we linger lovingly about a few of the streets and places in "the ancient city," and especially in the precincts of the venerable Cathedral, all sanctified by the memory of the mighty dead. We fain would prolong our visit, but the "stern mandate of duty," as Immanuel Kant called it, prevails, and we bow to the inevitable; or as Mr. Herbert Spencer better puts it, "our duty is our pleasure, and our greatest happiness consists in achieving the happiness of others." We feel our departure to-day the more keenly, as everything tempts us to stay. Listening for a moment at the open door—the beautiful west door—of the Cathedral, in this glorious morning in early autumn, we hear the harmonies of the organ and choir softly wafted to us from within; we feel the delicious morning air, which comes over the old Castle and burial-ground from the Kentish hills; we see the bright and beautiful flowers and foliage of the lovely catalpa tree, through which the sunlight glints; a solemn calm pervades the spot as the hum of the city is hushed; and, although we have read them over and over again, now, for the first time, do we adequately realize the exquisitely touching lines on the last page of *Edwin Drood,* written by the master-hand that was so soon to be stilled for ever:—

"A brilliant morning shines on the old City. Its antiquities and ruins are surpassingly beautiful, with the lusty ivy gleaming in the sun, and the rich trees waving in the balmy air. Changes of glorious light from moving boughs, songs of birds, scents from gardens, woods

Doorway
Rochester Cathedral

and fields—or, rather, from the one great garden of the whole of the cultivated island in its yielding time—penetrate into the Cathedral, subdue its earthy odour, and preach the Resurrection and the Life. The cold stone tombs of centuries ago grow warm; and flecks of brightness dart into the sternest marble corners of the building, fluttering there like wings."

Having time to reflect on our experiences, we are able to understand how greatly our feelings and ideas have been influenced for good, both regarding the personality of the novelist and his writings.

In the course of our rambles we have interviewed many people in various walks of life who knew Dickens well, and their interesting replies, mostly given in their own words, vividly bring before our mental vision the *man* as he actually lived and moved among his neighbours, apart from any glamour with which we, as hero-worshippers, naturally invest him. We see him in his home, beloved by his family, taking kindly interest, as a country gentleman, in the poor of the district, entering into and personally encouraging their sports, and helping them in their distress. To his dependents and tradesmen he was kind, just, and honourable; to his friends genial, hospitable, and true; in himself eager, enthusiastic, and thorough. No man of his day had more friends, and he kept them as long as he lived. His favourite motto, "courage—persevere," comes before us constantly. All that we heard on the other side was contained in the expression —"rather masterful!" Rather masterful? Of course he was rather masterful—otherwise he would never have been Charles Dickens. What does he say in that unconscious description of himself, which he puts into the mouth of Boots at *The Holly-Tree Inn*, when referring to the father of Master Harry Walmers, Junior?

"He was a gentleman of spirit, and good-looking, and held his head up when he walked, and had what you may call Fire about him. He wrote poetry, and he rode, and he ran, and he cricketed, and he danced, and he acted, and he done it all equally beautiful. . . . He was a gentleman that had a will of his own and a eye of his own, and that would be minded."

Perfectly true do we find the summing up of his character, in his home at Gad's Hill, as given by Professor Minto in the last edition of the *Encyclopædia Britannica* (one of the most faithful, just, and appreciative articles ever written about Dickens):—"Here he worked, and walked, and saw his friends, and was loved and almost worshipped by his poorer neighbours, for miles around."

Although tolerably familiar with most of the writings of Dickens from our youth, and, like many readers, having our favourites which may have absorbed our attention to the exclusion of others, we are bound to say that our little visit to Rochester and its neighbourhood—our "Dickens-Land" —rendered famous all the world over in the novels and minor works, gives a freshness, a brightness, and a reality to our conceptions scarcely expected, and never before experienced. The faithful descriptions of scenery witnessed by us for the first time in and about the "quaint city" of Rochester, the delightful neighbourhood of Cobham, the glorious old city of Canterbury, the dreary marshes and other localities: the more detailed pictures of particular places, like the Castle, the Cathedral, its crypt and tower, the Bull Inn, the Vines, Richard Watts's Charity, and others—the point of the situation in many of these cannot be realized without personal inspection and verification.

And further, as by a sort of reflex action, another feeling

comes uppermost in our minds, apart from the mere amusement and enjoyment of Dickens's works: we mean the actual benefits to humanity which, directly or indirectly, arise out of his writings; and we endorse the noble lines of dedication which his friend, Walter Savage Landor, addressed to him in his *Imaginary Conversations of Greeks and Romans* (1853):—

"Friends as we are, have long been, and ever shall be, I doubt whether I should have prefaced these pages with your name, were it not to register my judgment that, in breaking up and cultivating the unreclaimed wastes of Humanity, no labours have been so strenuous, so continuous, or half so successful, as yours. While the world admires in you an unlimited knowledge of mankind, deep thought, vivid imagination, and bursts of eloquence from unclouded heights, no less am I delighted when I see you at the school-room you have liberated from cruelty, and at the cottage you have purified from disease."

We have before us—its edges browned by age—a reprint of a letter largely circulated at the time, addressed by Dickens to *The Times*, dated "Devonshire Terrace, 13th Novr., 1849," in which he describes, in graphic and powerful language, the ribald and disgusting scenes which he witnessed at Horsemonger Lane Gaol on the occasion of the execution of the Mannings. The letter is too long to quote in its entirety, but the following extract will suffice:—"I have seen habitually some of the worst sources of general contamination and corruption in this country, and I think there are not many phases of London life that could surprise me. I am solemnly convinced that nothing that ingenuity could devise to be done in this city in the same compass of time could work such ruin as one public execution, and I stand astounded and appalled by the wickedness it exhibits." The letter contains an urgent appeal to the then Home Secretary, Sir George Grey, "as a solemn duty which he owes to society, and a responsibility which he cannot for ever put away," to originate an immediate legislative change in this respect. Forster says in allusion to the above-mentioned letter:—"There began an active agitation against public executions, which never ceased until the salutary change was effected which has worked so well." Dickens happily lived to see the fruition of his labours, for the Private Execution Act was passed in 1868, and the last public execution took place at Newgate on 26th May of that year. As indicative of the new state of feeling at that time, it may be mentioned that the number of spectators was not large, and they were observed to conduct themselves with unusual decorum.

It is valuable to record this as one of many public reforms which Dickens by his writings and influence certainly helped to accomplish. In his standard work on *Popular Government* (1885), Sir Henry Sumner Maine says:—"Dickens, who spent his early manhood among the politicians of 1832, trained in Bentham's school, [Bentham, by the bye, being quoted in *Edwin Drood*,] hardly ever wrote a novel without attacking an abuse. The procedure of the Court of Chancery and of the Ecclesiastical Courts, the delays of the Public Offices, the costliness of divorce, the state of the dwellings of the poor, and the condition of the cheap schools in the North of England, furnished him with what he seemed to consider, in all sincerity, the true moral of a series of fictions."

* * * * * *

We bid a kindly adieu to the "dear old City" where so many genial friends have been made, so many happy hours have been passed, so many pleasant memories have been stored, and for the time leave

> "the pensive glory,
> That fills the Kentish hills,"

to take our seats in the train for London, with the intention of paying a brief visit to South Kensington, where, in the Forster Collection of the Museum, are treasured the greater portion of the manuscripts which constitute the principal works of Charles Dickens. It will be remembered that the Will of the great novelist contained the following simple but important clause:—"I also give to the said John Forster (whom he previously referred to as 'my dear and trusty friend') such manuscripts of my published works as may be in my possession at the time of my decease;" and that Mr. Forster by his Will bequeathed these priceless treasures to his wife for her life, in trust to pass over to the Nation at her decease. Mrs. Forster, who survives her husband, generously relinquished her life interest, in order to give immediate effect to his wishes; and thus in 1876, soon after Mr. Forster's death, they came into the undisturbed possession of the Nation for ever.

Besides the manuscripts there are numbers of holograph letters, original sketches (including "The Apotheosis of Grip the Raven") by D. Maclise, R.A., and other interesting memorials relating to Charles Dickens. The *Handbook to the Dyce and Forster Collections* rightly says that:—"This is a gift which will ever have the highest value, and be regarded with the deepest interest by people of every English-speaking nation, as long as the English language exists. Not only our own countrymen, but travellers from every country and colony into which Englishmen have spread, may here examine the original manuscripts of books which have been more widely read than any other uninspired writings throughout the world. Thousands, it cannot be doubted, who have been indebted for many an hour of pleasurable enjoyment when in health, for many an hour of solace when in weariness and pain, to these novels, will be glad to look upon them as each sheet was sent last to the printer, full of innumerable corrections from the hand of Charles Dickens."

The manuscripts are fifteen in number, bound up into large quarto volumes, and comprise :—

1. *Oliver Twist*—two Volumes, with Preface to the *Pickwick Papers*, and matter relating to *Master Humphrey's Clock.*

2. *Sketches of Young Couples.*

3. *The Lamplighter*, a Farce. This MS. is not in the handwriting of Dickens.

4. *The Old Curiosity Shop*—two Volumes, with Letter to Mr. Forster of 17th January, 1841, and hints for some chapters.

5. *Barnaby Rudge*—two Volumes.

6. *American Notes.*

7. *Martin Chuzzlewit*—two Volumes, with various title-pages, notes as to the names, &c., and dedication to Miss Burdett Coutts.

8. *The Chimes.*

9. *Dombey and Son*—two Volumes, with title-pages, headings of chapters, and memoranda.

10. *David Copperfield*—two Volumes, with various title-pages, and memoranda as to names.

11. *Bleak House*—two Volumes, with suggestions for title-pages and other memoranda.

12. *Hard Times*—with memoranda.

13. *Little Dorrit*—two Volumes, with memoranda, Dedication to Clarkson Stanfield, and Preface.

14. *A Tale of Two Cities*—with Dedication to Lord John Russell, and Preface.

15. *Edwin Drood*—unfinished, with memoranda, and headings for chapters.

John Forster says:—"The last page of *Edwin Drood* was written in the châlet in the afternoon of his last day of consciousness."

Of the above-mentioned, the caligraphy of Nos. 1, 2, 3 and 4, is seen at a glance to be larger, bolder, and to have fewer corrections. In Nos. 5 to 15 it is smaller, and more confused by numerous alterations. According to Forster—"His greater pains and elaboration of writing became first very obvious in the later parts of *Martin Chuzzlewit.*"

The manuscripts of the earliest works of the Author, *Sketches by Boz*, *Pickwick*, *Nicholas Nickleby*, &c., were evidently not considered at the time worth preserving. The manuscript of *Our Mutual Friend*, given by Dickens to Mr. E. S. Dallas—in grateful acknowledgment of an appreciative review which (according to an article in *Scribner*, entitled "Our Mutual Friend in Manuscript") Mr. Dallas wrote of the novel for *The Times*, which largely increased the sale of the book, and fully established its success,—is in the library of Mr. G. W. Childs of Philadelphia; and that of *A Christmas Carol*—given by Dickens to his old friend and school-fellow, Tom Mitton—was for sale in Birmingham a few years ago, and might have been purchased for two hundred and fifty guineas! It is now owned by Mr. Stuart M. Samuel, and has since been beautifully reproduced in fac-simile, with an

Introduction by my friend and fellow-tramp, Mr. F. G. Kitton. Mr. Wright, of Paris, is the fortunate possessor of *The Battle of Life*. The proof-sheets of *Great Expectations* are in the Museum at Wisbech. Messrs. Jarvis and Son, of King William Street, Strand, sold some time since four of the MSS. of minor articles contributed by Dickens to *Household Words* in 1855-6, viz. *The Friend of the Lions*, *Demeanour of Murderers*, *That other Public*, and *Our Commission*, for £10 each.

At the sale of the late Mr. Wilkie Collins's manuscripts and library by Messrs. Sotheby, Wilkinson, and Hodge, 18th June, 1890, the manuscript of *The Frozen Deep*, by Wilkie Collins and Charles Dickens, 1856 (first performed at Tavistock House, 6th January, 1857), together with the narrative written for *Temple Bar*, 1874, and Prompt Book of the same play, was sold for £300. A poem written by Charles Dickens, as a Prologue to the same play, and *The Song of the Wreck*, also written by Charles Dickens, were sold for £11 11*s.* each. *The Perils of Certain English Prisoners*, a joint production of Wilkie Collins and Charles Dickens, for the Christmas number of *Household Words*, 1857, realized £200; and the drama of *No Thoroughfare* (imperfect), also a joint production, fetched £22.

The manuscripts now belonging to the Nation at South Kensington are placed in a glazed cabinet, standing in the middle of the room, on the right of which looks down the life-like portrait of the great novelist, painted by W. P. Frith, R.A., in 1859. The manuscript volumes are laid open in an appropriate manner, so that we have an opportunity of examining and comparing them with one another, and of observing how the precious thoughts which flowed from the fertile brain took shape and became realities.

Where corrections have been made, the original ideas are so obscured that it is scarcely possible to decipher them. This is effected, not by the simple method of an obliteration of the words, as is common with some authors, by means of a line or two run through them at one stroke of the pen, but by a series of connected circles, or scroll-work flourishes, thus,  which must have caused greater muscular labour in execution. Let any one try the two methods for himself. Dickens was fond of flourishes, as witness his first published autograph, under the portrait which was issued with *Nicholas Nickleby* (1839). Some evidence of "writer's cramp," as it is termed, appears where the C in Charles becomes almost a G, and where the line-like flourishes to the signature thirty years later, under the portrait forming the frontispiece to *Edwin Drood*, are much shorter and less elaborate. All the earlier manuscripts are in black ink—the characteristic *blue* ink, which he was so fond of using in later years, not appearing until *Hard Times* was written (1854), and this continued to be (with one exception, *Little Dorrit*) his favourite writing medium, for the reason, it is said, that it was fluent to write with and dried quickly.

From a valuable collection of letters (more than a dozen—recently in the possession of Messrs. Noel Conway and Co., of Martineau Street, Birmingham, and kindly shown to me by Mr. Charles Fendelow), written by the novelist between 1832 and 1833 to a friend of his earlier years—Mr. W. H. Kolle—and not hitherto published, it appears that he had not then acquired that precise habit of inscribing the place, day of the week, month, and the year which marked his later correspondence (as has been pointed out by Miss Hogarth and Miss Dickens in the preface to the *Letters of Charles Dickens*), very few of the letters to Mr. Kolle bearing any record whatever except the day of the week, occasionally preceded by Fitzroy Street or Bentinck Street, where he resided at the time. It would be extremely interesting to ascertain the reason which subsequently led him to adopt the extraordinarily precise method which almost invariably marked his correspondence from the year 1840 until the close of his life. Possibly arrangements with publishers and others may have given him the exact habit which afterwards became automatic.

In addition to the manuscripts in the Forster Collection in the Museum there are corrected proofs of a portion of the *Pickwick Papers*, *Dombey and Son*, *David Copperfield*, *Bleak House*, and *Little Dorrit*. Some of the corrections in *Dombey and Son* are said to be in the handwriting of Mr. Forster. All these proofs show marvellous attention to detail—one of the most conspicuous of Dickens's characteristics. Nothing with him was worth doing unless it was done well. As an illustration of work in this direction, it may be mentioned that a proof copy of the speech delivered at the meeting of the Administrative Reform Association at Drury Lane Theatre on Wednesday, June 27th, 1855, in the possession of the writer of these lines, has over a hundred corrections on the nine pages of which it consists, and many of these occur in punctuation. On careful examination, the alterations show that the correction in every case is a decided improvement on the original. The following *fac-similes* from the *Hand-Book* to the *Dyce and Forster Collection*, and from Forster's *Life*, illustrate the earlier, later, and latest handwritings of Charles Dickens as shown in the MSS. of *Oliver Twist*, 1837, *Hard Times*, 1854, and *Edwin Drood*, 1870.

the old lady [illegible] very
gently placed Oliver's head upon the
pillow; and smoothing back his hair
from his forehead, looked so kindly
and lovingly in his face, that he
could not help placing his little
withered hand upon hers, and drawing
it round his neck. [illegible]
[illegible]
[illegible]

"OLIVER TWIST," 1837, vol. i. ch. xii.

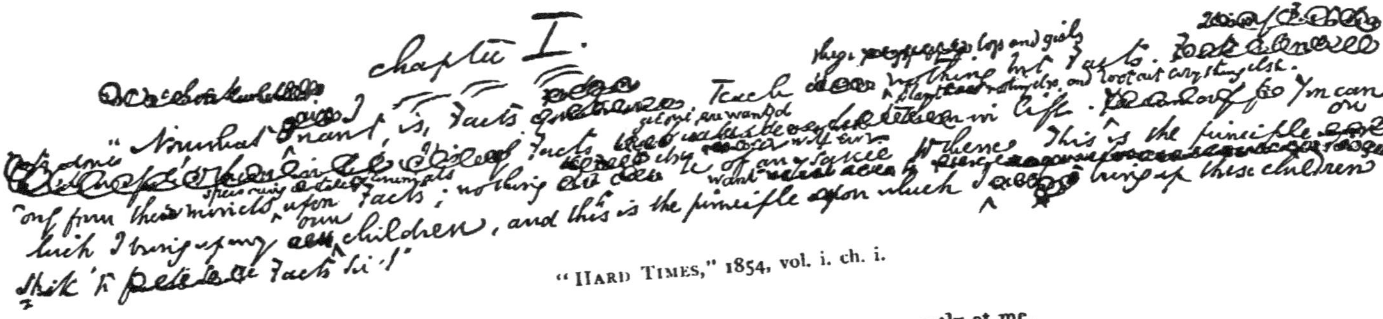

Chapter I.
"Now what I want, is, Facts. Teach these boys and girls nothing but Facts. Facts alone are wanted in life. Plant nothing else, and root out everything else. You can only form the minds of reasoning animals upon Facts; nothing else will ever be of any service to them. This is the principle on which I bring up my own children, and this is the principle on which I bring up these children. Stick to Facts, sir!"

"HARD TIMES," 1854, vol. i. ch. i.

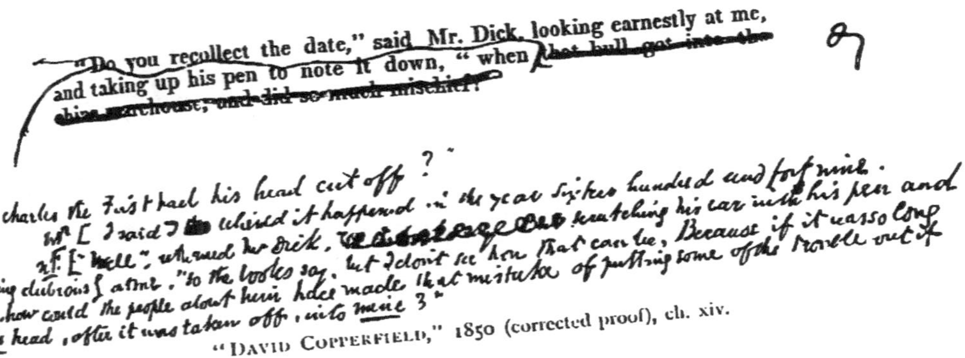

"Do you recollect the date," said Mr. Dick, looking earnestly at me, and taking up his pen to note it down, "when
King Charles the First had his head cut off?"
I said I believed it happened in the year sixteen hundred and forty nine.
"Well," returned Mr. Dick, scratching his ear with his pen and looking dubious at me. "So the books say, but I don't see how that can be. Because if it was so long ago, how could the people about him have made that mistake of putting some of the trouble out of his head, after it was taken off, into mine?"

"DAVID COPPERFIELD," 1850 (corrected proof), ch. xiv.

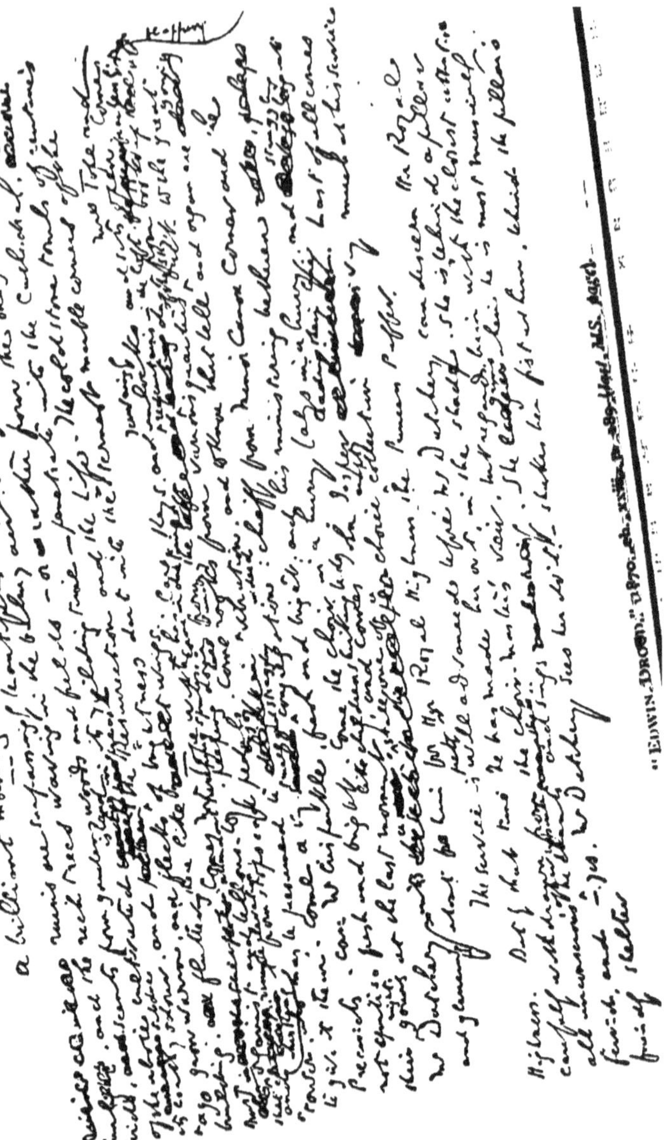

"EDWIN DROOD," 1870 (last MS. page)

A proof of the fourteenth Chapter of *David Copperfield*, 1850, shows that the allusion to "King Charles the First's head"—about which Mr. Dick was so much troubled—was *not* contained in the first draft of the story, for the passage originally had reference to "the date when that bull got into the china warehouse and did so much mischief." The subsequent reference to King Charles's head was a happy thought of Dickens, and furthered Mr. Dick's idea of the mistake "of putting some of the trouble out of King Charles's head" into his own.

Mr. R. F. Sketchley, the able and courteous custodian of the collection, allows us to see some of the other rarities in the museum not displayed in the cabinet—prefaces, dedications, and memoranda relating to the novels; letters addressed by Dickens to Forster, Maclise, and others; rare play-bills; and the originals of invitations to the public dinner and ball at New York, which Dickens received on the occasion of his first visit to America in 1842. After turning these over with reverential care, we regretfully leave behind us one of the most interesting and important literary collections ever presented to the Nation.

We next visit the Prerogative Registry of the United Kingdom at Somerset House, wherein is filed the original Will of Charles Dickens. The search for this interesting document pursued by a stranger under pressure of time, strongly reminds one of the "Circumlocution Office" so graphically described in *Bleak House*. But we are enthusiastic, and at length obtain a clue to it in a folio volume (Letter D), containing the names of testators who died in the year 1870, where the Will is briefly recorded (at number 468) as that of "Dickens, Charles, otherwise Charles John Huffham, Esquire." We pay our fees, and take our seats in the reading-room, when the original is presently placed in our hands. It is one of a series of three documents fastened together by a bit of green silk cord, and secured by the seal of the office, as is customary when there are two or more papers filed. The first document is the Will itself, dated 12th May, 1869, written throughout by the novelist very plainly and closely in the characteristic blue ink on a medium sheet of faint blue quarto letter paper, having the usual legal folded margin, and exactly covering the four pages. It is free from corrections, and is signed, "Charles Dickens," under which is the never-to-be-mistaken flourish. The testatum is signed by G. Holsworth, 26 Wellington Street, Strand, and Henry Walker, 26 Wellington Street, Strand, which points to the fact that the Will was written and executed at the office of *All the Year Round.* He appoints "Georgina Hogarth and John Forster executrix and executor, and guardians of the persons of my children during their respective minorities."

The second document is the Oath of John Forster, testifying that Charles Dickens, otherwise Charles John Huffham Dickens, is one and the same person. The third document is a Codicil dated 2nd June, 1870 (only a week before his death), in which the novelist bequeaths "to my son Charles Dickens, the younger, all my share and interest in the weekly journal called *All the Year Round.*" The Codicil is witnessed by the same persons. The Will and Codicil are both given in extenso in vol. iii. of Forster's *Life*—the gross amount of the real and personal estate being calculated at £93,000.[1]

* * * * * *

[1] Mr. Dolby, in his *Charles Dickens as I knew him*, estimates that £45,000 was realized by Dickens's Readings.

A very short tramp from Somerset House brings us to the last object of our pilgrimage—the grave of Charles Dickens in Westminster Abbey. Surely no admirer of his genius can omit this final mark of honour to the memory of the mighty dead. Many years have rolled by since "the good, the gentle, highly gifted, ever friendly, noble Dickens" passed away; and we stand by the grave in the calm September evening, with "jewels cast upon the pavement of the nave from stained glass by the declining sun," and look down at the dark flat stone lying at our feet, on which is inscribed "in plain English letters," the simple record:—

CHARLES DICKENS,

BORN FEBRUARY THE SEVENTH, 1812.

DIED JUNE THE NINTH, 1870.

We recall with profoundly sympathetic interest that quietly impressive ceremony as recorded by Forster in the final pages of his able biography. "Before mid-day on Tuesday, the 14th June, 1870, with knowledge of those only who took part in the burial, all was done. The solemnity had not lost by the simplicity. Nothing so grand or so touching could have accompanied it, as the stillness and the silence of the vast Cathedral." And he further describes the wonderful gathering subsequently:—"Then later in the day, and all the following day, came unbidden mourners in such crowds that the Dean had to request permission to keep open the grave until Thursday; but after it was closed they did not cease to come, and all day long." Dean Stanley wrote:—"On the 17th there was a constant pressure to the spot, and many flowers were strewn upon it by unknown hands, many tears shed from unknown eyes."

What poet, what philosopher, what monarch even, might not envy this loving tribute to the influence of the great writer, to the personal respect for the man, and to the affection for the friend who, by the sterling nature of his work for nearly thirty-five years, had the power to create and sustain such sympathy?

Forster thus admiringly concludes the memoir of his hero:

"The highest associations of both the arts he loved surround him where he lies. Next to him is Richard Cumberland. Mrs. Pritchard's monument looks down upon him, and immediately behind is David Garrick's. Nor is the actor's delightful art more worthily represented than the nobler genius of the author. Facing the grave, and on its left and right, are the monuments of Chaucer, Shakespeare, and Dryden, the three immortals who did most to create and settle the language to which Charles Dickens has given another undying name."

"Of making many books there is no end," said the wise man of old; and certainly, if we may estimate the popularity of Charles Dickens by the works of all kinds relating to him, written since his death, the number may be counted by hundreds. It may also be said that probably no other English writer save Shakespeare has been the cause of so much posthumous literature. The sayings of his characters permeate our everyday life, and they continue to be as fresh as when they were first recorded. The original editions of his writings in some cases realize high prices which are simply amazing, and—judging by statistics—his readers are as numerous as ever they were. Higher testimony to the worth "of the most popular novelist of the century, and one of the greatest humourists that England has produced," and to the continued interest which the reading public still evince in the minutest detail relating to him and to his books, can scarcely be uttered; but what is better still—"his sympathies were generally on the right side;"—he has left an example that all may follow;—he did his utmost to leave the world a little better than he found it;—as he said by one of his characters, "the best of men can do no more"—and now he peacefully rests as one

> "Of those immortal dead who live again
> In minds made better by their presence."

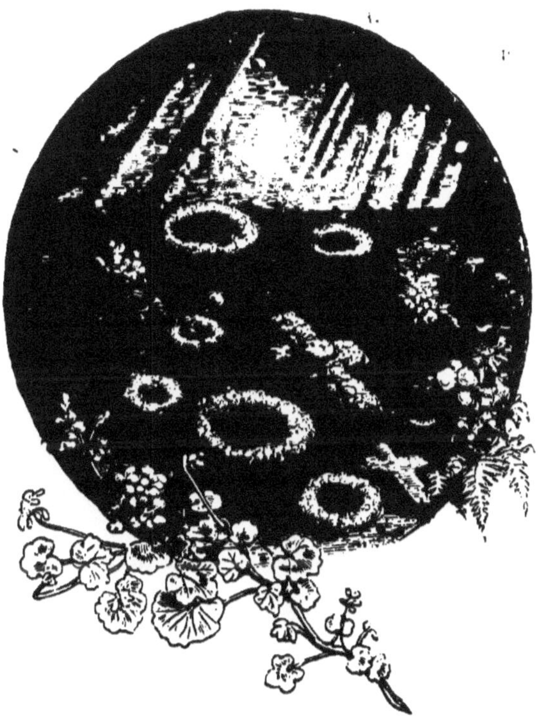

L'ENVOI.

WE—my fellow-tramp and I—naturally feel a pang of regret now that our pleasant visit to "Dickens-Land" is terminated. With a parting grasp of the hand I express to the companion of my travels a cordial wish that ere long we may, "PLEASE GOD," renew our delightful experience, and again go over the ground hallowed by Dickens associations; to which my friend, as cordially assenting, replies "SURELY, SURELY!"

With these two favourite expressions of Charles Dickens (quoted above) I conclude the book, trusting that it will prove worthy of some kindly appreciation at the hands of my readers.

INDEX.

CHIEFLY OF NAMES.

THE END.

Richard Clay & Sons, Limited, London & Bungay.

CATALOGUE

OF THE

Complete Works

OF

CHARLES DICKENS

THOMAS CARLYLE

GEORGE MEREDITH

ETC.

LONDON: CHAPMAN AND HALL, LIMITED,
HENRIETTA STREET, COVENT GARDEN.

August, 1891.

"'LET US BE MERRY.' HERE HE TOOK A CAPTAIN'S BISCUIT."

SPECIMEN.

The eleven boots is to be called at half-past eight and the shoe at nine. Who's number twenty-two, that's to put all the others out? No, no; reg'lar rotation, as Jack Ketch said, wen he tied the men up. Sorry to keep you a waitin', sir, but I'll attend to you directly."

Saying which, the man in the white hat set to work upon a top-boot with increased assiduity.

There was another loud ring; and the bustling old landlady of the White Hart made her appearance in the opposite gallery.

"Sam," cried the landlady, "where's that lazy, idle—why, Sam—oh, there you are; why don't you answer?"

"Wouldn't be gen-teel to answer, 'till you'd done talking," replied Sam, gruffly.

"Here, clean them shoes for number seventeen directly, and take 'em to private sitting-room, number five, first floor."

The landlady flung a pair of lady's shoes into the yard, and bustled away.

"Number 5," said Sam, as he picked up the shoes, and taking a piece of chalk from his pocket, made a memorandum of their destination on the soles—"Lady's shoes and private sittin' room! I suppose *she* didn't come in the waggin."

"She came in early this morning," cried the girl, who was still leaning over the railing of the gallery, "with a gentleman in a hackney-coach, and it's him as wants his boots, and you'd better do 'em, that's all about it."

"Vy didn't you say so before," said Sam, with great indignation, singling out the boots in question from the heap before him. "For all I know'd he vas one o' the regular three-pennies. Private room! and a lady too! If he's anything of a gen'lm'n, he's vorth a shillin' a day, let alone the arrands."

Stimulated by this inspiring reflection, Mr. Samuel brushed away with such hearty good-will, that in a few minutes the boots and shoes, with a polish which would have struck envy to the soul of the amiable Mr. Warren (for they used Day and Martin at the White Hart), had arrived at the door of number five.

"Come in," said a man's voice, in reply to Sam's rap at the door.

Sam made his best bow, and stepped into the presence of a lady and gentleman seated at breakfast. Having officiously deposited the gentleman's boots right and left at his feet, and the lady's shoes right and left at hers, he backed towards the door.

"Boots," said the gentleman.

"Sir," said Sam, closing the door, and keeping his hand on the knob of the lock.

"Do you know—what's-a-name—Doctors' Commons?"

"Yes, sir."

"Where is it?"

"Paul's Church-yard, sir; low archway on the carriage-side, book-

a young gentleman and a young lady on stilts, and Mr. Grinder himself, who used his natural legs for pedestrian purposes, and carried at his back a drum. The public costume of the young people was of the Highland kind, but the night being damp and cold, the young gentleman wore over his kilt a man's pea-

jacket reaching to his ankles, and a glazed hat; the young lady too was muffled in an old cloth pelisse, and had a handkerchief tied about her head. Their Scotch bonnets ornamented with plumes of jet-black feathers Mr. Grinder carried on his instrument.

"Bound for the races, I see," said Mr. Grinder, coming up

Better! a rare strong, hearty, healthy walk—four statute miles an hour—preferable to that rumbling, tumbling, jolting, shaking, scraping, creaking, villanous old gig? Why, the two things will not admit of comparison. It is an insult to the walk, to set them side by side. Where is an instance of a gig having ever circulated a man's blood, unless when, putting him in danger of his neck, it awakened in his veins and in his ears, and all along his spine, a tingling heat, much more peculiar than agreeable? When did a gig ever sharpen anybody's wits and energies, unless it was when the horse bolted, and, crashing madly down a steep hill with a stone wall at the bottom, his desperate circumstances suggested to the only gentleman left inside, some novel and unheard-of mode of dropping out behind? Better than the gig!

The air was cold, Tom; so it was, there was no denying it; but would it have been more genial in the gig? The blacksmith's fire burned very bright, and leaped up high, as though it wanted men to warm; but would it have been less tempting, looked at from the clammy cushions of a gig? The wind blew keenly, nipping the features of the hardy wight who fought his way along; blinding him with his own hair if he had enough of it, and wintry dust if he hadn't; stopping his breath as though he had been soused in a cold bath; tearing aside his wrappings-up, and whistling in the very marrow of his bones; but it would have done all this a hundred times more fiercely to a man in a gig, wouldn't it? A fig for gigs!

Better than the gig! When were travellers by wheels and hoofs seen with such red-hot cheeks as those? when were they so good-humouredly and merrily bloused? when did their laughter ring upon the air, as they turned them round, what time the stronger gusts came sweeping up; and, facing round again as they passed by, dashed on, in such a glow of ruddy health as nothing could keep pace with, but the high spirits it engendered? Better than the gig! Why, here *is* a man in a gig coming the same way now. Look at him as he passes his whip into his left hand, chafes his numbed right fingers on his granite leg, and beats those marble toes of his upon the foot-board. Ha, ha, ha! Who would exchange this rapid hurry of the blood for yonder stagnant misery, though its pace were twenty miles for one?

Better than the gig! No man in a gig could have such

some mangy bird he had caught, and was plucking before eating raw, Jo, the very, very tough subject Mr. Chadband is to improve.

Mrs. Snagsby screws a watchful glance on Jo, as he is brought into the little drawing-room by Guster. He looks at Mr. Snagsby the moment he comes in. Aha! Why does he look at Mr. Snagsby? Mr. Snagsby looks at him. Why should he do that, but that Mrs. Snagsby sees it all? Why else should that look pass between them, why else should Mr. Snagsby be confused, and cough a signal cough behind his hand? It is as clear as crystal that Mr. Snagsby is that boy's father.

"Peace, my friends," says Chadband, rising and wiping the oily exudations from his reverend visage. "Peace be with us! My friends, why with us? Because," with his fat smile, "it cannot be against us, because it must be for us; because it is not hardening, because it is softening; because it does not make war like the hawk, but comes home untoe us like the dove. Therefore, my friends, peace be with us! My human boy, come forward!"

Stretching forth his flabby paw, Mr. Chadband lays the same on Jo's arm, and considers where to station him. Jo, very doubtful of his reverend friend's intentions, and not at all clear but that something practical and painful is going to be done to him, mutters, "You let me alone. I never said nothink to you. You let me alone."

"No, my young friend," says Chadband, smoothly, "I will not let you alone. And why? Because I am a harvest-labourer, because I am a toiler and a moiler, because you are delivered over untoe me, and are become as a precious instrument in my hands. My friends, may I so employ this instrument as to use it toe your advantage, toe your profit, toe your gain, toe your welfare, toe your enrichment! My young friend, sit upon this stool."

Jo, apparently possessed by an impression that the reverend gentleman wants to cut his hair, shields his head with both arms, and is got into the required position with great difficulty, and every possible manifestation of reluctance.

When he is at last adjusted like a lay-figure, Mr. Chadband, retiring behind the table, holds up his bear's-paw, and says, "My friends!" This is the signal for a general settlement of the audience. The 'prentices giggle internally, and nudge each other. Guster falls into a staring and vacant state, compounded of a stunned admiration of Mr. Chadband and pity for the friendless outcast whose condition touches her nearly. Mrs. Snagsby silently lays trains of gunpowder. Mrs. Chadband composes herself grimly by the fire, and warms her knees: finding that sensation favourable to the reception of eloquence.

It happens that Mr. Chadband has a pulpit habit of fixing some member of his congregation with his eye, and fatly arguing his points with that particular person; who is understood to be expected to be moved to an occasional grunt, groan, gasp, or other audible expression of inward working; which expression of inward working, being echoed by some elderly lady in the next pew, and so communicated, like a game of forfeits, through a circle of the more fermentable sinners present, serves the purpose of parliamentary cheering, and gets Mr. Chadband's steam up. From mere force of habit, Mr. Chadband in saying "My friends!" has rested his eye on Mr. Snagsby; and proceeds to make that ill-starred stationer, already sufficiently confused, the immediate recipient of his discourse.

"We have here among us, my friends," says Chadband, "a Gentile and a Heathen, a dweller in the tents of Tom-all-Alone's and a mover-on upon the surface of the earth. We have here among us, my friends," and Mr. Chadband, untwisting the point with his dirty thumb-nail, bestows an oily smile on Mr. Snagsby, signifying that he will throw him an argumentative back-fall presently

"Hurrah!" gasped Mr. Winkle, faintly.

"Hurrah!" echoed Mr. Pickwick, taking off his hat and dashing it on the floor, and insanely casting his spectacles into the middle of the kitchen.—At this humorous feat he laughed outright.

"Let's — have — 'nother — bottle," cried Mr. Winkle, commencing in a very loud key, and ending in a very faint one. His head dropped upon his breast; and, muttering his invincible determination not to go to his bed, and a sanguinary regret that he had not "done for old Tupman" in the morning, he fell fast asleep; in which condition he was borne to his apartment by two young giants under the personal superintendence of the fat boy, to whose protecting care Mr. Snodgrass shortly afterwards confided his own person. Mr. Pickwick accepted the proffered arm of Mr. Tupman and quietly disappeared, smiling more than ever; and Mr. Wardle, after taking as affectionate a leave of the whole family as if he were ordered for immediate execution, consigned to Mr. Trundle the honour of conveying him up-stairs, and retired, with a very futile attempt to look impressively solemn and dignified.

"What a shocking scene!" said the spinster aunt.

"Dis—gusting!" ejaculated both the young ladies.

"Dreadful—dreadful!" said Jingle, looking very grave: he was about a bottle and a half ahead of any of his companions. "Horrid spectacle—very!"

"What a nice man!" whispered the spinster aunt to Mr. Tupman.

"Good-looking, too!" whispered Emily Wardle.

"Oh, decidedly," observed the spinster aunt.

Mr. Tupman thought of the widow at Rochester: and his mind was troubled. The succeeding half-hour's conversation was not of a nature to calm his perturbed spirit. The new visitor was very talkative, and the number of his anecdotes was only to be exceeded by the extent of his politeness. Mr. Tupman felt that as Jingle's popularity increased, he (Tupman) retired further into the shade. His laughter was forced—his merriment feigned; and when at last he laid his aching temples between the sheets, he thought, with horrid delight, on the satisfaction it would afford him to have Jingle's head at that moment between the feather-bed and the mattress.

The indefatigable stranger rose betimes next morning, and,

SPECIMEN PAGE OF CHRISTMAS BOOKS.

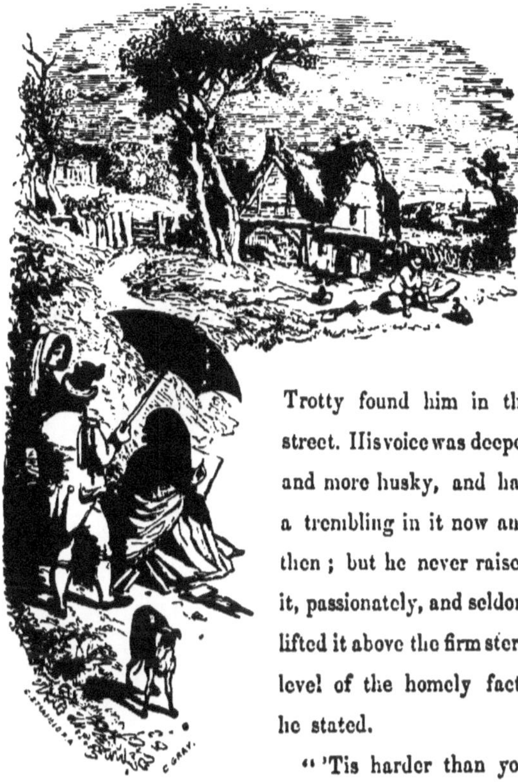

Trotty found him in the street. His voice was deeper and more husky, and had a trembling in it now and then; but he never raised it, passionately, and seldom lifted it above the firm stern level of the homely facts he stated.

"'Tis harder than you think for, gentlefolks, to grow up decent: commonly decent: in such a place. That I growed up a man and

The Editor will here admit that, among all the wondrous provinces of Teufelsdröckh's spiritual world, there is none he walks in with such astonishment, hesitation, and even pain, as in the Political. How, with our English love of Ministry and Opposition, and that generous conflict of Parties, mind warming itself against mind in their mutual wrestle for the Public Good, by which wrestle, indeed, is our invaluable Constitution kept warm and alive; how shall we domesticate ourselves in this spectral Necropolis, or rather City both of the Dead and of the Unborn, where the Present seems little other than an inconsiderable Film dividing the Past and the Future? In those dim longdrawn expanses, all is so immeasurable; much so disastrous, ghastly; your very radiances and straggling light-beams have a supernatural character. And then with such an indifference, such a prophetic peacefulness (accounting the inevitably coming as already here, to him all one whether it be distant by centuries or only by days), does he sit;—and live, you would say, rather in any other age than in his own! It is our painful duty to announce, or repeat, that, looking into this man, we discern a deep, silent, slow-burning, inextinguishable Radicalism, such as fills us with shuddering admiration.

Thus, for example, he appears to make little even of the Elective Franchise; at least so we interpret the following: 'Satisfy your-'selves,' he says, 'by universal, indubitable experiment, even as ye 'are now doing or will do, whether FREEDOM, heavenborn and 'leading heavenward, and so vitally essential for us all, cannot 'peradventure be mechanically hatched and brought to light in 'that same Ballot-Box of yours; or at worst, in some other dis-'coverable or devisable Box, Edifice, or Steam-mechanism. It 'were a mighty convenience; and beyond all feats of manufacture 'witnessed hitherto.' Is Teufelsdröckh acquainted with the British Constitution, even slightly?—He says, under another figure: 'But 'after all, were the problem, as indeed it now everywhere is, To 'rebuild your old House from the top downwards (since you must 'live in it the while), what better, what other, than the Represent-'ative Machine will serve your turn? Meanwhile, however, mock 'me not with the name of Free, "when you have but knit-up my 'chains into ornamental festoons."'—Or what will any member of the Peace Society make of such an assertion as this: 'The lower 'people everywhere desire War. Not so unwisely; there is then a 'demand for lower people—to be shot!'

Gladly, therefore, do we emerge from those soul-confusing

Here was to be hoped the picturesque in scenery, which he much affected; here the new and true in speculation, which he inwardly longed for and wanted greatly more; at all events, here as readily as elsewhere might a temporary household be struck up, under interesting circumstances.—I conclude he went across in the Spring of 1833; perhaps directly after *Arthur Coningsby* had got through the press. This Novel, which, as we have said, was begun two or three years ago, probably on his cessation from the *Athenæum*, and was mainly finished, I think, before the removal to St. Vincent, had by this time fallen as good as obsolete to his own mind; and its destination now, whether to the press or to the fire, was in some sort a matter at once of difficulty and of insignificance to him. At length deciding for the milder alternative, he had thrown in some completing touches here and there,—especially, as I conjecture, a proportion of Colridgean moonshine at the end; and so sent it forth.

It was in the sunny days, perhaps in May or June of this year, that *Arthur Coningsby* reached my own hand, far off amid the heathy wildernesses; sent by John Mill: and I can still recollect the pleasant little episode it made in my solitude there. The general impression it left on me, which has never since been renewed by a second reading in whole or in part, was the certain prefigurement to myself, more or less distinct, of an opulent, genial and sunny mind, but misdirected, disappointed, experienced in misery;—nay crude and hasty; mistaking for a solid outcome from its woes what was only to me a gilded vacuity. The hero an ardent youth, representing Sterling himself, plunges into life such as we now have it in these anarchic times, with the radical, utilitarian, or mutinous heathen theory, which is the readiest for inquiring souls; finds, by various courses of adventure, utter shipwreck in this; lies broken, very wretched: that is the tragic nodus, or apogee of his life-course. In this mood of mind, he clutches desperately towards some new method (recognisable as Coleridge's) of laying hand again on the old Church, which has hitherto been extraneous and as if non-extant to his way of thought; makes out, by some Coleridgean legerdemain, that there actually is still a Church for him; that this extant Church, which he long took for an extinct shadow, is not such, but a substance; upon which he can anchor him-

Captain Weisspriess, saying briefly that he had found Irma in the carriage instead of the little "v," thanked him for the joke, and had brought her back. Pericles was therefore not surprised when Irma, as Michiella, came on, breathless, and looking in an excitement of anger; he knew that he had been tricked.

Between Camillo and Michiella a scene of some vivacity ensued—reproaches, threats of calamity, offers of returning endearment upon her part; a display of courtly scorn upon his. Irma made her voice claw at her quandum lover very finely; it was a voice with claws, that entered the hearing sharp-edged, and left it plucking at its repose. She was applauded relishingly when, after vainly wooing him, she turned aside and said—

"What change is this in one who like a reed
Bent to my twisting hands? Does he recoil?
Is this the hound whom I have used to feed
With sops of vinegar and sops of oil?"

Michiella's further communications to the audience make it known that she has allowed the progress toward the ceremonies of espousal between Camillo and Camilla, in order, at the last moment, to show her power over the youth and to plunge the detested Camilla into shame and wretchedness.

Camillo retires: Count Orso appears. There is a duet between father and daughter: she confesses her passion for Camillo, and entreats her father to stop the ceremony;—and here the justice of the feelings of Italians, even in their heat of blood, was noteworthy. Count Orso says that he would willingly gratify his daughter, as it would gratify himself, but that he must respect the law. "The law is of your own making," says Michiella. "Then, the more must I respect it," Count Orso replies.

The audience gave Austria credit for that much in a short murmur.

Michiella's aside, "Till anger seizes him I wait!" created laughter; it came in contrast with an extraordinary pomposity of self-satisfaction exhibited by Count Orso—the flower-faced, tun-bellied basso, Lebruno. It was irresistible. He stood swollen out like a morning cock. To make it further telling, he took off his yellow bonnet with a black-

O reader, I say not who are Belial's elect. This poor amphibious Pope too gives loaves to the Poor; has in him more good latent than he is himself aware of. His poor Jesuits, in the late Italian Cholera, were, with a few German Doctors, the only creatures whom dastard terror had not driven mad: they descended fearless into all gulfs and bedlams; watched over the pillow of the dying, with help, with counsel and hope; shone as luminous fixed stars, when all else had gone out in chaotic night: honour to them! This poor Pope,—who knows what good is in him? In a Time otherwise too prone to forget, he keeps up the mournfulest ghastly memorial of the Highest, Blessedest, which once was; which, in new fit forms, will again partly have to be. Is he not as a perpetual death's-head and cross-bones, with their *Resurgam*, on the grave of a Universal Heroism,—grave of a Christianity? Such Noblenesses, purchased by the world's best heart's-blood, must not be lost; we cannot afford to lose them, in what confusions soever. To all of us the day will come, to a few of us it has already come, when no mortal, with his heart yearning for a 'Divine Humility,' or other 'Highest form of Valour,' will need to look for it in death's-heads, but will see it round him in here and there a beautiful living head.

Besides, there is in this poor Pope, and his practice of the Scenic Theory of Worship, a frankness which I rather honour. Not half and half, but with undivided heart does *he* set about worshipping by stage-machinery; as if there were now, and could again be, in Nature no other. He will ask you, What other? Under this my Gregorian Chant, and beautiful wax-light Phantasmagory, kindly hidden from you is an Abyss, of Black Doubt, Scepticism, nay Sansculottic Jacobinism; an Orcus that has no bottom. Think of that. 'Groby Pool *is* thatched with pancakes,'—as Jeannie

This excellent Captain was too old a Commander to complain of anything; indeed he struggled visibly the other way, to find in his own mind that all here was best; but I could sufficiently discern that, in his natural instincts, if not mounting up to the region of his thoughts, there was a continual protest going on against much of it; that nature and all his inarticulate persuasion (however much forbidden to articulate itself) taught him the futility and unfeasibility of the system followed here. The Visiting Magistrates, he gently regretted rather than complained, had lately taken his treadwheel from him, men were just now pulling it down; and how he was henceforth to enforce discipline on these bad subjects, was much a difficulty with him. "They cared for "nothing but the treadwheel, and for having their rations cut "short:" of the two sole penalties, hard work and occasional hunger, there remained now only one, and that by no means the better one, as he thought. The 'sympathy' of visitors, too, their 'pity' for his interesting scoundrel-subjects, though he tried to like it, was evidently no joy to this practical mind. Pity, yes:—but pity for the scoundrel-species? For those who will not have pity on themselves, and will force the Universe and the Laws of Nature to have no 'pity' on them? Meseems I could discover fitter objects of pity!

In fact it was too clear, this excellent man had got a field for his faculties which, in several respects, was by no means the suitable one. To drill Twelve-hundred scoundrels by 'the method of kindness,' and of abolishing your very treadwheel,—how could any commander rejoice to have such a work cut out for him? You had but to look in the faces of these Twelve-hundred, and despair, for most part, of ever 'commanding' them at all. Miserable distorted blockheads, the generality: ape-faces, imp-faces, angry dog-faces, heavy sullen ox-faces; degraded underfoot perverse creatures, sons of *in*docility, greedy mutinous darkness, and in one word, of STUPIDITY, which is the general mother of such. Stupidity intellectual and stupidity moral (for the one always means the other, as you will, with surprise or not, discover if you look) had born this progeny: base-natured beings, on whom in the course of a maleficent subterranean life of London Scoundrelism, the Genius of Darkness (called Satan, Devil, and other names) had now visibly impressed his seal, and had marked them out as soldiers of Chaos and of him,—appointed to serve in *his* Regiments, First of the line, Second ditto, and so on in their order. Him, you could perceive, they would serve; but not easily another than him. These were the subjects whom our brave Captain and Prison-Governor was appointed to command, and re-

CHARLES DICKENS AND EVANS,
CRYSTAL PALACE PRESS.

www.ingramcontent.com/pod-product-compliance
Lightning Source LLC
Chambersburg PA
CBHW051233300426
44114CB00011B/715